The Adventures of Jonathan Dennis

For Jay

**Jonathan was a friend of Le Giornate del Cinema Muto.
The festival has contributed to the publication of this book
in his memory.**

The Adventures of Jonathan Dennis

Bicultural film archiving practice in Aotearoa New Zealand

Emma Jean Kelly

British Library Cataloguing in Publication Data

The Adventures of Jonathan Dennis
Bicultural film archiving practice in Aotearoa New Zealand

A catalogue entry for this book is available from the British Library

ISBN: 9780 86196 722 3 (Paperback edition)

Cover photograph: Gareth Watkins

The author has asserted her rights to be identified as the author of this work in accordance with the Copyright, Designs and Patents Act 1988

Published by
John Libbey Publishing Ltd, 3 Leicester Road, New Barnet, Herts EN5 5EW,
United Kingdom
e-mail: john.libbey@orange.fr; web site: www.johnlibbey.com

Distributed worldwide by **Indiana University Press**,
Herman B Wells Library – 350, 1320 E. 10th St., Bloomington, IN 47405, USA.
www.iupress.indiana.edu

Printed and bound in China by 1010 Printing International Ltd.

Contents

Acknowledgements

This book emerged from my PhD thesis and has involved the support of many people including University of Auckland staff Laurence Simmons and Annie Goldson who started me on my way in 2009, and Sue Abel who then stepped in to provide advice on the bicultural aspects of the research. While at University of Auckland I received a grant for archival research. I also received a Ministry of Foreign Affairs and Trade Archive Grant to access the Archives NZ film materials not available through the NZFA. The Jonathan Dennis Trust Fund granted me travel funds for a research trip. When I moved to Auckland University of Technology in 2010 for my employment, Sue Abel was kind enough to continue her support for my thesis. Sue has been a superb secondary supervisor: Kia ora Sue. Lorna Piatti-Farnell has been my equally superb primary supervisor. Others to thank are the interviewees who were so generous with their time. Special thanks to Simon Dennis who introduced me to many of my interviewees and with her daughter Kirsten helped me negotiate access to NZFA materials. Roger Horrocks is often cited as an important mentor to film studies students for very good reason – he generously corresponded with me over the life of the project, providing information and ideas throughout. Helen Martin's histories of NZ film and TV have been hugely useful and she has also discussed ideas with me for the duration of the project. Bill Gosden and Malcolm McKinnon were extremely helpful. Ferry Hendriks was such a kind host and interviewee, as were Fergus MacGillivray and his husband during my visit to London. Sef Townsend and Elaine Burrows were delightful interviewees to meet so far from home. Annie Collins hosted me and is the wisest of women; Elizabeth Alley is perhaps her only equal. Annie, your questions at a particularly important moment have been taken to heart and will always be remembered. Peter Wells was an excellent source of information and thoughtful ideas, along with Bridget Ikin, John Maynard and Gareth Watkins. Genevieve Morris and Mary Righton were my cheerleaders along with Sam Jones, Liana de Jong and Alison Kirkness.

Susan Potter's intelligent work is an inspiration and her friendship a delight. The NZFA staff who helped me through years of visits were Owen Mann, Tania Strauss, Kiri Griffin, Siobhan Garrett, Sarah Davy, Diane Pivac and Jane Paul. Thank you for your generous help and intelligent support – your work is not easy. Geraldene Peters, Tui O'Sullivan and Ella Henry have provided support along the way. The Harris family have also been helpful to me, and reminded me to be always cautious and humble. The JWT (*Just Women Talk*) breakfast club has been wonderful. Lynne Giddings and Kate Prebble have been vital feminist intellectual companions and mentors. The posse of the Foucault discussion group led by Joanna Fadyl has been very important. Engaging with academics outside my own discipline to try and understand Foucault has been enlightening. Thanks to the AUT Research Office who have kept us solvent through my employment there, and particularly to Richard Bedford and Filomena Davies for supporting me through a month long residency at the National Film and Sound Archive Australia (NFSA) at Canberra which was instrumental to my data collection. NFSA Staff were great – Graham Shirley has continued to help me since I first met him there in 2011, as has Jenni Gall. Meg Labrum allowed me to interview her, and Christine Guster ensured that interview is archived at the NFSA. Ray and Sue Edmondson have also been generous with their time, knowledge and contacts. Thanks also to David Parker and Suzanne Hardy for their work. My Kelly and Hollows family have always encouraged me in my studies even when they have been bemused by them. I particularly thank my father John who is my hero, finding interest in the everyday and inspiring creativity and love in all who meet him. My other hero is my partner Jay Hollows who dug me out of intellectual and emotional ditches, made me coffee and inspired me with his tenacity, endless creativity and intelligence throughout his own studies as well as mine. Thank you to Professor Judith Pringle who provided 'a room of one's own' for me and also reminded me that academics are humans too. Thanks to Jeremy Sherlock (Tainui, Ngāti Apa) for final macron checking – any further errors are my own. Finally, thank you to the family and friends of Jonathan Spencer Dennis who have been hugely generous in allowing a stranger to poke and prod into the life of your loved one. There were many tears, some of which were mine as well as yours.

This is dedicated to Jonathan Mane-Wheoki and Paul Bushnell, and to Sam Prebble and Emily Cater.

Glossary of terms

Unless otherwise stated all definitions by P.M. Ryan, The Reed Dictionary of Māori Language, *1995, Auckland, New Zealand, Reed Publishing.*

Aotearoa New Zealand – since the 1980s the typical nomenclature for the country (Pollock, 2005 p.550) generally shortened to "NZ" throughout the book for the sake of brevity. "Aotearoa" is often translated to "Land of the Long White Cloud" by association with various legends.[1] "New Zealand" is the name given the land by Dutch explorer Abel Tasman in 1642.

Hapū –sub-tribe, clan

Iwi – tribe

Kaumātua – old man, elder

Kaupapa – strategy, theme, philosophy

Kaitiaki – guardian

Kuia – old lady, (e kui, form of address), matron

Mana – integrity, charisma, prestige

Māori – ordinary, native people, (the indigenous peoples of Aotearoa New Zealand).

Marae – meeting area of whānau or iwi, focal point of settlement, central area of village and its buildings

Mihi – greet, admire, respect, congratulate

NZFA – *New Zealand Film Archive Ngā Kaitiaki o ngā Taonga Whitiāhua* (Guardians of the Treasured Images of Light). Since August 2014 the institution is called *Ngā Taonga Sound & Vision* to acknowledge the acquisition into the collection of the Television NZ Archive and Sound Archives from Radio NZ.

Paepae – orator's bench

Pākehā – non-Māori, (usually applied to European, Caucasian)

Taonga – property, treasure

Whakapapa – genealogy, cultural identity, Book of Chronicles, family tree, recite genealogy

Whānau – extended family

Whare-nui – whare = house nui = large (often used as the name of the main meeting house)

---

1   Retrieved 25/05/14 http://www.teara.govt.nz/en/1966/aotearoa.

In te reo Māori, the vowels are pronounced differently than in English. A macron creates a longer sound.

A = pronounced as in the English "far"

E = pronounced like the ea in "leather"

I = pronounced like the English "e" as in "me" or "he"

O = pronounced as the English word "awe"

U = pronounced like the double o in "moon" (Ryan, 1995 p.7).

Note: I have used macrons on Māori words throughout the book, except where the original text quoted did not include them.

Archival sources and key:

New Zealand Film Archive Personal Papers Jonathan Dennis (uncatalogued). Referencing an uncatalogued collection is challenging. I have provided as much information as available. Sometimes papers were loose in a box, and sometimes they were in folders. This is always specified. The collection is referred to throughout as = **NZFA PP JD Box #**

Annie Collins Personal Papers (uncatalogued) = **AC PP**

Alexander Turnbull Library Manuscript collection of Personal Papers Jonathan Dennis (catalogued) = **ATL PP JD MS #**

National Film & Sound Archive Australia (catalogued) = **NFSA NZFA collection**

Interviews:

There are three main interviews with Jonathan Dennis which form the basis of the biographical research. These are:

(1) Diane Pivac and Jonathan Dennis recorded on 28 January 2000 and referred to throughout as: **(Pivac & Dennis 2000)**. New Zealand Film Archive ACCN AUD 0672.

(2) Elizabeth Alley & Jonathan Dennis – this interview exists in multiple edits which are discussed in Chapter Six – it was recorded by Gareth Watkins and the interviewer was Elizabeth Alley. Referred to in its broadcast version edited by Paul Bushnell and broadcast after Dennis' death as: **(Alley & Dennis 2002)** and in its unedited form as: **(Dennis in Alley et al. 2001)**. New Zealand Film Archive AUD 1129, AUD 1130.

(3) Judith Fyfe interviewed Dennis not long before he died with Annie Collins as camera/audio person. This is referred to as: **(Fyfe & Dennis 2001)**. New Zealand Film Archive 2002.0974.

Authors note: In August 2014 *The New Zealand Film Archive Ngā Kaitiaki o ngā Taonga Whitiāhua* changed its name to Ngā Taonga Sound and Vision, *Ngā Kaitiaki o Ngā Taonga Whitiāhua me Ngā Taonga Kōrero* to acknowledge the incorporation of the sound and television acquisitions from state institutions. However this book uses the term NZFA as a shorthand to refer to the institution. The name is discussed within this book as names and the changes that are made to them always have significance beyond the superficial (Giddings, L. Personal correspondence 22/04/15).

Chapter 1

Introduction

This work explores the philosophy and nature of film archiving in Aotearoa New Zealand (NZ) through an analysis of the role played by Jonathan Dennis, firstly at the New Zealand Film Archive, Ngā Kaitiaki o ngā Taonga Whitiāhua (NZFA), from 1981 until 1990 and thereafter as a freelance film curator until his death in 2002. The construction of a film archive in the early 1980s offers a valuable moment in which to analyse the wider purpose and the more specific process for the formation of a film archive. As a national institution presenting materials from the past, an archive quickly becomes a focus point for debates about the national past, present and future. How materials from the archive are cared for and presented offers opportunities both in their presence and absence from which to critique the notion that the archive may be a biography of the nation. This exploration of Dennis, film archiving and national identity is driven by a set of questions. Firstly, what is an archive and what should it do? Secondly, what relationship does an archive have to changing concepts of the nation as expressed by social and political movements? Finally, how might a film archive and its archivists respond to the materials within and the movements outside its walls?

In order to address these questions Jonathan Dennis, founding director of the NZFA has been used as a conduit for an examination of the tensions and debates prevalent at a particular period of time in a specific country. This examination engages with indigenous and non-indigenous values in relation to audiovisual materials from the past. It considers a specific colonised country as a place in which competing perspectives are at play, and analyses how the New Zealand Film Archive and its materials became part of that competition.

During the years 1981–2002 Dennis worked to present and preserve indigenous and non-indigenous film archival materials with an awareness of the social and political changes occurring in the country. This resulted in a film archive and

1

curatorship practice which differed significantly from that of the North American and European archives he originally sought to emulate. As a Pākehā with a strong sense of social justice, he argued for an awareness of geographical location and cultural context in his work. As a gay man he had an understanding of being an outsider and this motivated him to see things differently.[2] He supported a philosophical shift in archival practice by engaging indigenous peoples in developing creative and innovative exhibitions and programmes.

Jonathan Dennis' life did not fit the hegemonic discourse represented by the stereotypical "kiwi bloke" as Pākehā, fit, ruggedly handsome and able to drink and play rugby (Bannister, 2005; Campbell, 2000; Phillips, 1996 2nd ed.). At the time in which he was growing up "the consequences of being exposed as a homosexual were frightening: newspapers carried accounts of homosexuals on trial in New Zealand courts; homosexuals were targeted in America by McCarthy …" and local writer Frank Sargeson had been entrapped as a young man by laws criminalising homosexuals (Millar, 2010 p.vii). It was illegal to perform male to male sexual acts in New Zealand until 1986 (Brickell, 2008).[3] In Jock Phillips' seminal cultural history of the New Zealand Pākehā male, he describes how the understanding of a successful normative identity formation was closely linked to the stereotype of the pioneer, the soldier, and the rugby player whose heterosexuality was defined against indigenous identities (Phillips, 1987 first ed.). Dennis, as a homosexual man in a society which favoured heterosexual males as "defined against" the indigenous other, could easily relate to those categorised with him as unacceptable during the time when he was forced to become "transparent" during boarding school in order to survive the bullying that occurred there (Dennis in Alley, Watkins, & Dennis, 2001).

Anita Brady has recently argued specifically in the context of the NZ South Island area where Dennis grew up, that the nostalgia for "the way New Zealand 'used to be'" in the High Country and the rural South, makes it "a complex and privileged place in the narratives of authenticity on which notions of pakeha masculinity depend … the South Island is often positioned in New Zealand media as a destination 'back beyond the effete suburbanization of New Zealand manhood'" (Brady, 2012 p.359). Dennis was never "boysy" (Dennis in Fyfe &

---

2   This is in no way to suggest that homosexual and indigenous perspectives are the same.

3   In a separate study I interviewed an older gay man who had lived all his life in NZ and asked him about the fears he had in the 1950s–1980s period in relation to "coming out". He remembered his father speaking with "disgust for queers" and in particular of Oscar Wilde's trial at the end of the 19th century. The interviewee knew of Frank Sargeson's arrest and he also cited the treatment of Alan Turing who was forced to take hormones after being accused of homosexual acts and eventually committed suicide in England as reasons to be frightened of declaring his sexuality (Personal Correspondence for *Queer Stories Our Fathers Never Told Us* project, Kelly, J. 2012).

Dennis, 2001) and at his South Island boarding school populated with the sons of wealthy farmers, his gender identity would have been considered "effete". There is a tension between a populist nostalgia for a "simpler" time in New Zealand which is at odds with the memory of many marginalised peoples who know that nostalgia is false, at least in their experience. In fact nostalgia is bound with power relations and used to "maintain, resist, construct and reconstruct identities in times of difficulty and change" (Matykiewicz, L. & McMurray, R. 2013 p.323).

This is not only the case for NZ. In a transnational gender identity study R. Connell discusses a similar pattern in colonised countries such as Australia, which led her work to the notion of hegemonic masculinity (Connell, 1995) which, like the concept of heteronormativity is constantly in flux but underlines the hierarchy of masculinities (Connell & Messerschmidt, 2005 p.831). Connell illustrates how, as Phillips also shows in this context, physical performance is used to ascribe gender to bodies (Connell, 1995 p.50).[4] Connell goes further than Phillips in that she illustrates the synergies between the notion of hegemonic masculinities, heteronormativity and queer theory. She argues that queer theory is a useful development in relation to hegemonic masculinities, as it "celebrates the symbolic disruptions of gender categories" (Connell, 1995 p.59) and in turn homosexuality itself is a disruption of hegemonic masculinity (Connell, 1995 p.58). When young men and women in NZ were not able to express their non-heteronormative sexuality, they often silently sought representations of themselves in popular culture, to find their identity through others who may share their desires. A popular culture vehicle for doing so was the watching of films. This has been identified in queer theory as one of the ways in which young people sought to find an expression of difference. For example, in Eve Kosofsky Sedgwick's text, *Tendencies* (Sedgwick, 1993), she includes a consideration of gay youth alienation survived through identifying cultural objects which have some hint of homosexuality about them. "I think that for many of us in childhood the ability to attach intently to a few cultural objects ... whose meaning seemed mysterious, excessive or oblique in relation to the codes most readily available to us, became a prime resource of survival" (Sedgwick, 1993 p.3). Sedgwick's work in cultural studies has been fundamental in re-reading key texts as queer works, or at least, works which could be identified as having queer elements which were anchors for non-normative readers/viewers who did not identify with heterosexuality. Her *Epistemology of the Closet* (1990) is useful in understanding the elaborate codes

---

4   Connell acknowledges the influence of Judith Butler's *Gender Trouble* (1990).

through which people understood themselves and the cultural world around them at a particular moment in history.

Author and filmmaker Peter Wells supported Sedgwick's notion of the cultural objects which create anchors for survival in relation to his and Jonathan Dennis' experience of attending the movies as children and young men when he commented that "Cinema allows a kind of ambidextrous sexual reality" (Personal correspondence P.Wells, 30/06/2009). This "ambidextrous sexual reality" is something akin to hybridity and queerness, an in between space of otherness, an interstitial perspective or marginalised position from which the possibility of desiring and engaging imaginatively is possible beyond heteronormative assumptions.[5] Cinema was Dennis and Wells' delight and escape, and eventually their working lives would allow them to create and support narratives which explored non heteronormative identities in a more open manner as times changed, as censorship laws loosened and more diverse sexualities were able to be represented on screen. In other words, gay men and women's stories would be able to be represented on screen.

In his work and personal life, Jonathan Dennis like other people who did not identify as heterosexual, appeared to construct his own cultural codes in his public and private lives and develop his own "schema of relations" (Foucault in discussion with Barbedette, 1982 pp.38, 39). Most of this was expressed silently – at least in his younger years. As he became an adult, aesthetically speaking, Dennis began to wear bright clothing and was described in terms of his dress and manner as "blatant rather than latent" (Personal correspondence, P.Wells op.cit.). He used elements of kitsch as well as bright colours and unusual clothing combinations incorporating materials from the South Pacific. For example, he referenced non-"kiwi bloke" cultures by often wearing items which in his time were unusual, such as colourful Italian scarves, while carrying kete (Māori woven bags). He also wore unusual spectacles in bright colours including turquoise, and some of these even glowed in the dark of the cinema (Personal correspondence S.Bartel 03/12/09; S.Dennis 06/02/09; M.Leonard 01/04/10).

Dennis' choice of clothing was a non-verbal signifier of "otherness" which may seem inconsequential, but at that time men in NZ were not encouraged to stand out from the crowd (Phillips, 1987 1st ed.). Every interviewee for this study commented on the effect of Dennis' sartorial style. Fellow cinéaste Professor

---

5   Cinephilia is an entire body of work which could be used to analyse Dennis' life and work. However I would argue that Dennis' passion for film also crossed into an engagement with all forms of art: painting, writing and crafts, and therefore "cinephilia" would be limiting if it was the only lens used to consider Dennis' practice.

Emeritus of Film Studies Roger Horrocks suggested Dennis had a camp aesthetic, if the meaning of "camp" is that of Susan Sontag's *Notes on Camp* (Personal correspondence, R.Horrocks 25/10/11). Foucauldian scholar David Halperin's definition of camp is similar to Sontag's and suggests something akin to Dennis' approach to his appearance as it was described by interviewees and observed in photographic evidence. Dennis was camp in the sense of "parody, exaggeration, amplification, theatricalization, and literalization of normally tacit codes of conduct" (Halperin, 1995 p.29). Dennis played with codes of masculinity using clothes as performance and declaration of self.

These tacit codes, these silent signals of difference, these unsaid devices for asserting ones' agency in the world seem to have been important for Dennis. They were unspoken strategies by which he performed his sense of self in the wider world of life and work. They were the silences in the discourse, disrupting the "kiwi bloke" stereotype, creating a signal of difference. Dennis' ability to live in Lauren Berlant's "counterconventional" fold within the normative world is one of the in between spaces, the unspoken interstitial moments where a new or different perspective was possible for him (Berlant, L. 2011). Interviewees certainly felt this to be true and some explicitly referred to Dennis' approach as "queer" (Personal correspondence, C. O'Leary 10/12/09).

David Halperin's conception of camp and his work in general is part of what he refers to as "queer studies", which for him emerged from the activist movement in the United States. The word *queer* is an attempt to consider a non-heteronormative sexuality without being reduced to essentialism through identity politics or binaries. In the sense that the word *queer* avoids an essentialist view, queer theory is a poststructuralist term denoting the provisional and contingent nature of identity (Jagose, 1996 p.7). It seeks to assert the potential for new and different relational possibilities (Halperin cited in Howe, 2004 p.35). However, unlike other subjects who are often marginalised, Dennis as a Pākehā from a middle class family always had the option to not reveal his "otherness". Marginalised peoples do not often have this luxury. In NZ, the option of blending into the hegemonic majority (or "passing") is generally only available to Pākehā. This leads to tension, even if Pākehā are sympathetic to the sensitivities of multiple perspectives. Indeed, it is the space between the essentialist and non-essentialist nature of identity politics and queer theory which creates the most difficulty, but is the most productive position from which to analyse Dennis and the NZFA in the geographical location of the South Pacific. "Postcolonial" and certainly the "postcolonial queer" are contested concepts which this work does not seek to resolve.

However, being aware of the discourse is helpful in examining the life of a gay man who engaged with indigenous peoples. He demonstrated a strong identification with those who were marginalised in some way by a society which viewed the heterosexual Pākehā male as the mainstream norm in his lifetime.

Judith Binney suggests that any historian engaging with "a society that evolved from a divided past [which] attempts to become bicultural in its later reconstruction … must also become consciously 'bihistorical'" in order to accept "alternative cultural codes" (Binney, 2009 p.xiii). Although Binney's work refers to the state (governmental) perspective on the "bicultural" in relation to the Treaty of Waitangi, she, like the poststructuralist and postcolonial thinkers, advocates for a multiplicity of perspectives. The current moment in NZ is perhaps best described as a time of "cultural colonialism" which acknowledges ongoing psychological, educational and sociological assumptions regarding who "we" are as a "nation".[6] Stephen Turner suggests there is a "settler culture" of Pākehā in NZ who generally control state decisions and dominate normative values without explicitly acknowledging their role (S. Turner, 1999) just as Halperin argues the "tacit codes" of masculinity which camp resists are unspoken (Howe, 2004).

There are challenges in using European theory when speaking of indigenous experience, and indeed this study does not try to identify with or explain indigenous perspectives. Yet the balance is a fine one. An alternative to postcoloniality is the discourse of decolonisation which has become common in NZ in recent times. For example, Jo Smith and Sue Abel argue that Māori television is a tool of decolonisation for both Māori and Pākehā (J. Smith & Abel, 2008). Linda Tuhiwai Smith used Foucault in her seminal text, *Decolonizing Methodologies: Research and Indigenous Peoples* (Tuhiwai Smith, 1999/2012) in order to critique Western discourse in relation to indigeneity. Māori activists and scholars since the 1970s have campaigned vigorously to ensure an indigenous voice is heard in NZ, quite literally in the case of the legal status of the Māori language (Ratima, 2008). This has led to a peculiar situation where the term "bicultural", referred to by Binney and celebrated in the 1980s as a partnership model between the two peoples of the Treaty of Waitangi, has become a theoretically and politically tired proposition. Consequently postcolonial works are sometimes

---

6   Many artistic and curatorial projects have challenged the assumed inclusivity of the term "we" in recent years. For example a 2012 exhibition of art at Te Tuhi Centre for the Arts at Pakuranga in Auckland was entitled "What do you mean, *we*?" It was an example of a curated exhibition which sought to "examine prejudice in its various forms" (Publicity Poster, 3 March – 6 May 2012). The original question "What do you mean, we white man?" was spoken by Tonto, North American "Indian" (indigenous American) sidekick to the white cowboy *The Lone Ranger* in response to the cowboy's statement "we're surrounded by Indians" in the long running US book, radio, television and film series.

useful but do not necessarily define the historical specificity and cultural context of NZ today (O'Sullivan, 2007).

NZ is a country whose national boundaries have not changed since 1840 when the Treaty of Waitangi was signed and has only ever had one independent film archive.[7] The NZFA became the sole independent national repository for the film materials of a nation with stable borders.[8] The founding director of that Archive, Jonathan Dennis, left rich personal materials from which to attempt to understand the development of the institution and his motivations. Dennis continued after his Directorship to engage with archives and evolve his philosophy. The most compelling reason to focus on Dennis when exploring questions of film archiving practice in NZ is that his name is repeated by many scholars, archivists and filmmakers as one which represented an emerging practice in the 1980s which was different from that of archives, museums and art galleries before that period. For example an Emeritus Professor of Film TV and Media Studies at University of Auckland remarked that Jonathan Dennis was an "... unsung hero of the film culture" (Personal correspondence, Horrocks, R. 21/10/08).

"With a strong sense of place" is the way in which authors Sarah Davy and Diane Pivac described the development of the NZFA in its founding years, in a chapter they contributed to a book on NZ film culture (Davy & Pivac, 2008). The phrase "a sense of place" was made popular by a 1984 photography book by Robin Morrison, a Pākehā New Zealander who specialised in images of the everyday in New Zealand (Morrison, 1984). Dennis, like Morrison and others had become increasingly aware that the unique aspects of NZ were its geographical location and cultural diversity.[9] They consequently sought strategies through which to work regionally, nationally and internationally with a "sense of place" (Dennis in Fyfe & Dennis, 2001). Beyond this point of difference they also began to understand the history of their own country, largely because Māori insisted on

---

7   "The Treaty of Waitangi of 1840 is New Zealand's founding document, establishing the relationship between Māori and the Crown. In ensuing years the terms of the Treaty were consistently violated by the Crown, resulting in the alienation of Māori from the land and their impoverishment. In 1975 the Waitangi Tribunal was established, with the goal of redressing grievances resulting from the contravention of the Treaty. By 2010 the Tribunal had received over 2000 claims, and had paid out around $950 million in settlements" (Morris, 2013). This process has been useful (though extremely painful for many) because hapū, whānau and iwi have collected oral and written accounts of their history and shared them as part of the panel hearing process, allowing for a greater understanding by all New Zealanders of the history which had not been previously shared in the dominant cultural institutions of school, museum, and state sanctioned historical discourse (Binney, 2009).

8   Having said NZ is a "stable nation", some iwi did not sign the Treaty and one in particular Ngāi Tūhoe was and is an independent nation, though various governments have chosen not to accept this view and Tūhoe are often represented as troublemakers in the mainstream media (Binney, 2009).

9   Though cultural nationalism had been in existence for many years (Jensen, K. 1996), I would argue Dennis' version was a less masculinist one.

remembering, rather than forgetting the colonial roots of the nation (S. Turner, 1999).

Jonathan Dennis began his work from the perspective of a European man, rich in knowledge and experience of the western world, but "ignorant" of Te Ao Māori [The Māori world] (Dennis in Alley & Dennis, 2002). By the end of his life he had shifted his view, incorporating ways of being and doing he had learned from Māori with whom he had worked for over two decades. As he learned to listen harder he became something other than European in the continental sense. This is not to claim an indigeneity for him, but to state a distinction based upon his awareness of his geographical location and personal sense of marginalisation. "Being Pākehā", as historian Michael King discovered, is not to be embraced as indigenous, but it is to be something other than those of European descent born and living elsewhere (King, 1985). Nor does being Pākehā automatically make one sensitive to indigenous concerns. Filmmaker Barry Barclay (iwi affiliation Ngāti Apa) who worked with Dennis and critiqued the NZFA, argued that Pākehā and Māori quite literally talk past each other. He suggested that in the Pākehā world there is often a tendency to speak and debate in a linear fashion, whilst in the Māori world listening is highly valued and discussion can often be cyclic (Barclay, 1990 p.14). Barclay's work in film and film archiving, his position as both Māori and Pākehā (of Scottish and French descent) (Martin, 1994 p.103) and his writing on his ideas is useful to this present study because he was interested in the tension between two cultures and the creative possibilities which emerged from that space.[10] This book is also interested in the creative possibilities inherent in the in between space.

In 2009 a review of the New Zealand Film Archive described an institution which seemed to have reached some sense of equilibrium between indigenous and non-indigenous perspectives – "the [New Zealand Film] Archive has devoted much time and energy to ensuring that indigenous rights are fully respected ... [and] ... has achieved international recognition for its innovative work in this area" (Horrocks, Labrum, & Hopkins, 2009 p.27). How the NZFA developed from a European institution in 1981 to one internationally recognised for its honouring of indigenous rights has not been previously described in detail in either the academic literature or by the archive and museum movement. Beyond Dennis' own interviews with media in the 1980s and 1990s (for one of many examples, see Crosbie, 1990, March 11) and papers he wrote for industry related

---

10 Barclay always acknowledged his Pākehā as well as Māori genealogies. For example see biographical note to *Mana Tūturu* (Barclay, 2005).

journals, such as that of the Art Galleries & Museums Association of Australia & New Zealand (Dennis, 1989), there has been no study made of more than a chapter in a wider book in which an author sets out to methodically investigate Dennis' practice. Dennis' work led to an archive, which he felt by the time of his resignation in 1990, was a "living archive" engaging with "biculturalism" (Dennis, Report to FIAF Congress 1990). Nor has any single work examined the years from 1990 until 2002 when Dennis was free of his directorial responsibilities and able to create new works with archival materials in many different media. This deepened his engagement with a "sense of place" through an evolving philosophy which was influenced by wider socio-political movements.

Over a decade since his death, why should we care about the work of a film archivist from the South Pacific? More specifically, why did I embark on this study? The work of filmmaker and author Barry Barclay on the subject of film archiving and indigenous perspectives led me to the work of Jonathan Dennis (Barclay, 2005). In the 2000s period I worked as an image archivist and I had struggled as a Pākehā (of English, Irish Republican and Scottish Highlander descent) to incorporate the methodologies of a western based practice with the indigenous materials of the archive in which I worked at the NZ Herald, a national newspaper. In seeking examples of good practice I read Barclay's texts which investigate appropriate indigenous processes in both filmmaking and film archiving. Included in one publication was a section devoted to Jonathan Dennis and the work of the NZFA (Barclay, 2005 pp. 93–136). That chapter and Peter Wells' film about Dennis and his friend and colleague Witarina Harris, *Friendship is the Harbour of Joy* (2004) piqued my curiosity. In undertaking a study which seeks to explore questions of practice and philosophy in the film archive, I hope to enrich and inform my own practice and that of others working in the field of image and film archiving and also museum and art gallery practices in postcolonial territories, where handling and engaging with indigenous materials and working with the peoples related to them is common.[11]

Because Dennis was an archivist he left rich evidence of his life in the form of correspondence and photographs held at the NZFA. There are also sound

---

11 "Postcolonial" is a problematic concept. Scholars interested in the "differing responses to ... incursions" and the "contemporary colonial legacy" in communities such as NZ, challenge the use of the term *postcolonial* itself, asking – "If we're postcolonial does that mean the colonists all went home?" (Meredith, 1998 p.3). David Pearson argues that although "Outdated 'master narratives' about nation and state building, modernisation and national identity have seemingly given way to a new relativism in which national and ethnic boundaries are viewed as discourses in flux and cultural identities are multiple imaginings" in what is often viewed as postcolonial times "heralding the end of the nation-state however is somewhat premature" (Pearson, 2001 pp.2, 3). Furthermore, Meredith contends that the "the 'post' in post-colonial requires some thought" (Meredith, 1998 p.3).

recordings from his radio shows, television programmes and publications which he co-edited and co-wrote with his many collaborators. These materials were a useful platform from which to consider and analyse Dennis' work, but there were many gaps in the information available. Therefore I began to interview his friends, colleagues, family and industry peers. These conversations recorded as oral history interviews and themselves destined to become materials deposited in the NZFA, offered information unavailable through the previous written or recorded evidence of Dennis' life. They introduced ideas and discussions about Dennis' practice and the wider context in which he lived and worked and suggested the importance of his personality to the project. The seeming contradiction between the charismatic individual leader and the committed collaborator they described became increasingly intriguing.

Michel Foucault is instrumental to this work because his writings on the "history of ideas" are an appropriate approach for a study which seeks to examine how particular concepts have been understood in a specific time and place. Linda Tuhiwai Smith (iwi affiliations Ngāti Awa, Ngāti Porou) is a scholar who like Foucault underpins this work in that she provides tools for "decolonising" theories and practices for indigenous researchers which can be useful for those working in postcolonial territories. Her texts absorb and re-understand the works of various local and international thinkers such as Foucault and offer a resulting method and methodology through which to re/contextualize research by and with indigenous peoples in the geographical space of NZ. This is done in such a way that European intellectual thinking is not rejected but instead reappraised in the light of indigenous epistemology. Both Tuhiwai Smith and Foucault consider the philosophical concept of "archive" in their work in relation to the regulation of knowledge. In addition my work is influenced by critical discourse analysis which acknowledges the contribution of feminist inquiry seeking to address sites of oppression (Grant & Giddings, 2002). This brings it into tension with many scholarly readings of Michel Foucault's work which argue he does not acknowledge hierarchies of power. This tension then becomes yet another space from which to explore varying perspectives and perhaps arrive at a new understanding of the power/knowledge nexus of the film archive and scholarship related to it. And if that sounds too academic, I mean to say that disagreement, anger, despair and rage are all part of healthy conflict which can help people and institutions evolve in their thinking, if they are able to do so in an environment of trust and collegiality.

Beyond the academic scholarship, film archivists and filmmakers themselves often provide philosophical perspectives which emerge from their own practice. Barry Barclay is one such writer and filmmaker, as is Merata Mita who spoke and wrote in various fora about the NZFA and Jonathan Dennis in particular; for example Mita & Dennis, (1991). Italian born film archivist Paolo Cherchi-Usai is also helpful in this regard. Being someone who worked alongside Dennis to support presentations of silent film, Cherchi-Usai, like Mita and Barclay, offers personal insights into the character of Dennis, but more importantly into the philosophy and practice of film preservation, presentation and the politics of the field. Curatorship, something Cherchi-Usai argues Dennis practiced, was (and perhaps still is) regarded as the antithesis of film archiving practice when the preservation of materials is prioritised.

Archives, like museums and art galleries are often expected to present exhibitions which reflect the history or identity of the nation they are based in. There are many competing approaches to concepts of national identity in NZ. Biculturalism itself is often regarded as a tired term; kaupapa Māori (Māori centred philosophy and practice) has developed but does not replace the idea of partnership intrinsic to the bicultural process. Appropriately, where Pākehā sit in relation to kaupapa Māori or any Māori centred philosophy, is problematic for Pākehā practitioners in any field. Dennis, like many curators, museum workers and archivists struggled to understand where he was positioned in relation to the work he did with indigenous peoples.

Kaupapa Māori principles emerge from the work of a number of Māori in both the academic and regional communities and are dynamic. Below are the set of principles recorded by Linda Tuhiwai Smith who cites Ngahuia Te Awekotuku as her source:

- Aroha ki te tāngata – respect for people

- Kanohi kitea – the seen face, that is, present yourself to people face to face

- Titiro, whakarongo ... kōrero – look, listen, then speak

- Manaaki ki te tāngata – share and host people, be generous

- Kia tūpato – be cautious

- Kaua e takahia te mana o te tāngata – do not trample over the mana of the people

- Kaua e māhaki – don't flaunt your knowledge

(Te Awekotuku in Tuhiwai Smith, 1999/2012 p.124).

Kaupapa Māori research methodology is a "nascent" method and methodology (Ratima, 2008). It seeks to address some of the indigenous concerns about research in the past which tended to be *done to* rather than *with* indigenous peoples.

Professor of Museum Studies Paul Tapsell's (iwi affiliation to Te Arawa) work on Gilbert Mair's collection and the exhibition which was produced from that work (Tapsell, 2006), has been fundamental to my Pākehā understanding of *ngā taonga*. This term is now ubiquitous in NZ archival and museum circles as it is used to describe the material objects of the archive, acknowledging their spiritual aspects and the living relationship to descendants of the iwi they originated from. Tapsell articulates key concepts in the discussion of biculturalism which are analysed in this study. The history of the use of the term biculturalism and its practice before the NZFA began, with a particular focus on the previous two generations from whom many ideas and skills were developed which were incorporated into the eventual kaupapa/constitution of the Archive is central to this work. Once this definition of taonga is established, it is possible to understand how Dennis embraced the term and engaged with it in his life and work.

This work is a cultural and social history, and the work of historian Judith Binney has been influential – she relied on both written documentation and also the active collection of new oral histories of (largely) Ngāi Tūhoe tribal elders to create her historical works such as *Stories Without End* (Binney, 2010). She and fellow Pākehā scholar from University of Auckland, Professor Anne Salmond, acknowledged where their own Pākehā centred experience and knowledge failed in the writing of cross-cultural history. In their work they do not presume to understand the whakapapa (genealogy) and iwi knowledge of others, but work effectively with Māori people – not as the holder of power, but as the listener and the learner in the process (Shepard, 2009 p.161). Binney and Salmond's work lies in their respective fields of history and anthropology, but it also emerges from a feminist perspective where these women became aware of their own position *as women* experiencing forms of oppression whilst undertaking their scholarship (Shepard, 2009 p.128). This impacted upon their individual practices, encouraging sensitivity to the oppression of others – this was the experience of many intellectuals in Aotearoa New Zealand in the 1970s/1980s period including Dennis. Salmond and Binney consciously began to incorporate practices of reciprocity and an awareness of their own lack of knowledge of anothers' culture into their work (Shepard, 2009 p.137). Jonathan Dennis was a contemporary of these two scholars and met and discussed his practice with Anne Salmond. He was influenced by her and other feminist friends and colleagues of the time (Personal correspondence E. Alley 11/06/10).

Jonathan Dennis' upbringing in grand hotels and his boarding school days were experiences which he and every interviewee for this study raised as influential in his life.[12] Dennis saw these experiences as shaping his thinking, and that in itself is significant. Dennis had many opportunities to explore his own narrative and sense of self as he was interviewed for various purposes. His own experience of oppression through being a gay man at a particular time was certainly part of his sensitivity to the diverse experience of being part of the nation. This narrative co-construction (McHugh, 2012) is explored explicitly in this work where his own stories and those told by others are analysed in Chapter Six.

This book seeks to open out the archive of Jonathan Dennis. It is by no means an exhaustive study, but simply offers some signposts towards materials available inside and outside the archive walls through which many different studies might be continued – using Dennis' physical archive material in the New Zealand Film Archive for example to consider filmmakers and critics such as Kenneth Anger and Peter Wells' correspondence. Further engagement with Dennis' extensive *Film Show* review recordings and raw materials is possible, or further discussion of the *Amamus* theatre group through the Alexander Turnbull collection materials, or the oral histories recorded with Irihapeti Ramsden and Patricia Grace – all these materials lie in wait for interested listeners to activate them.

---

12 People would talk to me about this even when I had not asked them directly about Dennis' life. For example I was lucky enough to meet Professor Jonathan Mane-Wheoki while he was Head of Elam School of Fine Arts at the University of Auckland who told me Jonathan Dennis' story of unhappiness at boarding school in Christchurch (Personal discussion, J.Mane-Wheoki Auckland 2012). Vale Professor Mane-Wheoki.

Chapter 2

The practice of the archive

The cultural practice of archiving physical materials in dedicated institutions emerges from European museums and libraries and is adapted by film archives, which over time have developed their own styles most appropriate to the media which they house. In examining the literature on the physical archive it becomes quickly apparent that at times the pragmatic everyday aspects of archiving can seem very far removed from the more philosophical discussion, and that archivists may be under-resourced and overworked to the point where they take for granted the perspectives which ingrain their practice. The divide between the everyday work and the philosophical and academic concerns of the archive can cause tensions and challenges understood in terms of the debate "Preservation Versus Presentation" or "Archiving Versus Curatorship" (Cherchi Usai, Francis, Horwath, & Loebenstein, 2008). This tension stems from dual questions which can be interpreted as philosophical or pragmatic – "What is an archive?" and, "What is its function?"

It is the work of the archivist to ensure the safety of the objects they preserve. In the traditional Western, North American (settler) or Continental European context, "safety" is defined as the maintenance of the integrity of the physical object. But the archivist generally emerges from the majority culture of their community and will be imbued with its values. Therefore even what is deemed "safe" (for the objects as well as the people who care/have guardianship over them) will depend on their personal, cultural and philosophical understandings (Maere, 2004). From an indigenous perspective, preservation of the integrity of an object would include the cultural and spiritual safety of both the physical object and the guardians of that object who may be the descendants of those in the archival image or descended from those who made an object or used it. These differing views of the concept of "safety" can create a cultural clash for those caring for archival materials (Cherchi Usai, 2000; Mita, 1992). Cultural and spiritual perspectives regarding archiving practice question the assumptions of the archivist and the source of their mandate to care for the material objects of a community (Barclay, 2005).

The day to day processes and practices of the archivist from the majority culture are driven by guidelines encapsulated in publications such as *Keeping Archives* (Ellis, 1993) or *Managing Records; a handbook of principles and practice* (Shepherd & Yeo, 2003) in which procedures regarding management of different formats, systems, and organisational structures are discussed. However, the philosophical, cultural and spiritual concerns of archive users and the communities who have gifted objects to the archive are rarely mentioned in these textbooks. Terry Cook describes the risk of this approach from the perspective of the archivist – "We are deciding what is remembered and what is forgotten, who in society is visible and who remains invisible, who has a voice and who does not" (Cook, 1999). It is argued by some that in colonial societies, archives are by-products of power relationships where the colonists tend to be keepers of the public memory through archives and museums (Jimerson, 2010). Through their practice, archivists are able to interpret the archives, frame (curate) archival materials and present the story of the nation as they understand it through the objects within the collection. This story is a version of a biography of a nation, if the archive's purpose is to reflect the culture and history of the nation, or national identity. This responsibility to present a cohesive view of the nation is enormous and under-theorised by archivists themselves (McCarthy, 2011). The NZFA was developed out of the legislation of the New Zealand Film Commission which was understood to be part of a strategy to "forge a national identity" in the late 1970s (Waller, 2008) and therefore was required to engage with these concerns, particularly in relation to the concept of biculturalism.

Biculturalism in the archive

Issues regarding power and control of the national story are played out in museums and archives but also universities and other institutions of learning. Pākehā scholar Danny Butt for example suggests that in NZ there is a vast gulf between Māori and Pākehā ways of undertaking research and that this is a "meta-truth" to be taken into account, particularly in relation to discourses of biculturalism. He says "there is a crisis in our own subjectivity that must be staged within our own practices" (Butt, 2005). Pākehā scholar Conal McCarthy uses both Butt's concept of this crisis as well as Pierre Bourdieu in his research work on museums and Māori. McCarthy's work is helpful in considering the discourse of biculturalism in the time Jonathan Dennis worked with archival materials.

Unfortunately, McCarthy's analysis does not include the work of any moving image archives specifically beyond a cursory nod to Dennis' contribution (McCarthy, 2011). Barry Barclay does however, and as a writer and a filmmaker offers a view from an indigenous perspective working in the same era as Dennis. Barclay worked with the NZFA during and after the time Dennis was Director and considered the need for indigenous peoples to take control of the image in regards to production, presentation and preservation in order to tell an alternate story (Barclay, 2003).[13] Barclay's work offers a response to Butt's "crisis in our own subjectivity". Barclay's texts, written and audiovisual, question the assumptions of the film archive in the wider sense of the possibilities of the enunciable subject. For example Barclay turned the tables on the normative subject as early as the film *Autumn Fires* (1977) in which Pākehā were studied as a curious subject presented in ethnographic terms (Prod. Keating., Dir. Tuckett, 2009).

Barclay later made a documentary called *The Neglected Miracle* (1985) which addressed a topic considered then "obscure"; plant genetics and the rights of indigenous peoples in relation to them (Barclay in Dennis & Bieringa, 1992/1996 p.117). Although it was a transnational film he took a "marae approach" to the topic which was highly unusual at the time. Barclay challenged assumptions of subjectivity and objectivity by his filmmaking process which he likened to a traditional Māori hui (meeting often held on a marae), where "there is opportunity for all to speak … Mana is recognized, of course, but over the days of a hui, the little person, the 'nobody', is given room too … It matters little whether you happen to be a city lawyer or a breaker of horses. All have a voice" (Barclay, 1996 p.119).

Barclay's work questions the discourse of the subject, the archive, the Pākehā and the Māori. He asks "who has the right to speak?" and responds that Māori can and must speak for themselves (following a kaupapa Māori mode). By changing the practice of filmmaking itself, a new kind of discourse was created which in turn created the possibility for further and new works and ways of being and doing. When his film on genetic engineering was screened, he described how some audience members hissed "communist" and left the theatre. These audience members were "eminent men, famous amongst peers … from the developed world …" (Barclay quoted in Dennis & Bieringa, 1992/1996 p.118). These "eminent men" tried to silence Barclay's discourse, which offered an alternate

---

13   Barclay posited the "camera on the shore" to encapsulate the notion of a "fourth cinema" – filmmaking from an indigenous perspective. What if, he asked, Māori had a camera, filming events as colonisers first arrived in NZ? (*Camera on the Shore,* Prod. Keating, A., Dir.Tuckett, 2009).

view from the perspective of indigenous peoples who he felt needed to have "power over the plants you use for food, for dyes, for fibre, for medicines and so on [in order] to have the dignity of sovereignty" (Barclay, 1992/1996 ibid).

Barclay was creating a new and different discourse which was not considered valid for those "first world" audience members. He was speaking as an indigenous filmmaker trying to create a new conversation amongst "third world" peoples who were usually the "nobody" without a voice, the "breaker of horses". Their voices were just as important to the discursive practice of the film as the views of the "city lawyer". Barclay was responding to the question "who are *we*"? Who is represented or excluded by the documentaries, films, and materials of the archive? Barclay asked who was considered a valid subject for public discourse – who was allowed to "have a life?" He insisted that Māori people needed to be present on screen and in the production and preservation process in order for their stories to be represented appropriately.

Barclay and the other prominent Māori filmmaker of the period in which Dennis was alive, Merata Mita, offered through their films and writings an alternate perspective and also a way of being which had not previously been articulated by those in a position to decide what is and is not enunciable. Barclay and Mita acknowledged Butt's "crisis in our own subjectivity" and suggested possible ways of enacting that crisis within their own practice. They worked both within NZ and also outside the nation's boundaries. They took a transnational view and engaged with indigenous peoples across the world (Barclay, 1990; Mita, 1992). Barclay and Mita both worked with and challenged NZFA practice over the course of their careers. Their practice (and that of many others) which attempted to regain control of the process of making and doing has become known as "kaupapa Māori" over time, but in the 1980s period when Jonathan Dennis was still at the NZFA it was much more common to use the term "biculturalism". Kaupapa Māori developed in response to a feeling that biculturalism had failed as a philosophy and a practice (McCarthy, 2011). The feeling that biculturalism had failed was evident through the data collection phase of this study, as stories and evidence emerged of the sometimes ferocious disagreements between Māori and Pākehā, in relation to film archiving and calls for social justice. These disagreements at times led to new and productive pathways, and sometimes led to silence.

Significantly, Michel Foucault does not think that silence leaves no trace. For him, silence is the archive beyond enunciation – "There is not one but many silences, and they are an integral part of the strategies that underlie and permeate discourses" (Foucault, 1976 p.27). Silence still carries meaning – it is not *stumm* (as Jacques Derrida has claimed) but something else (Derrida, J. 1996). Foucault recognises that in the naming of things there is risk. The confessional is an example of the naming of behaviours which can then be judged and regulated as sin. Foucault suggests that in *not naming*, silence may in some regards become Lauren Berlant's "fold within the normative world" (Berlant & Prosser, 2011 p.182) where one may be oneself without censure – "the agency of domination does not reside in the one who speaks (for it is he who is constrained), but in the one who listens and says nothing; not in the one who knows and answers, but in the one who questions and is not supposed to know" (Foucault, 1976 op.cit.). Silence may be a way to protect oneself from exploitation, from misinterpretation, from untruth. In this regard, silence is productive and powerful, not *stumm* or mute and the archive beyond enunciability therefore becomes a place of possibility.

Paula Amad has noted that neither Jacques Derrida nor Foucault, the great philosophers of the archive directly addressed *film* archives themselves: "As much as Foucault and Derrida deconstructed the concept of the archive, for the most part their work neglected the material example responsible for unwittingly reinventing that concept in the early twentieth century, the *film archive*" (Amad, 2010 p.21 Amad's emphasis). Film archiving is a subset of archiving practice, and often takes as a model the practices of other institutions which house different media (such as paper manuscripts). And yet, as Amad argues, the film medium is quintessentially different to the material found in other archives, thus she argues the archive she analyses is a "counterarchive" (Amad, 2010).[14]

Archive as biography of the nation

Judith Butler also supports the productive nature of silence when she says – "The categories by which social life are ordered produce a certain incoherence or entire realms of unspeakability" (Butler, 2001 p.3). If this is the case, then how is an archive supposed to present a coherent narrative of the nation? The NZFA, like many other national repositories including the National Library, Te Papa o Tongarewa (National Museum) and the Alexander Turnbull Library have specific duties and responsibilities to collect the cultural heritage of "the nation". The

---

14   In the late 1970s Dennis worked with ARANZ, the national archiving association as a partner to develop the policy which would influence the NZFA. Later the NZFA joined FIAF, the international film archiving association which was regarded as a better fit for film archive specific practice and discussion.

policy document for Te Papa states in part – "The unified collections of the Museum are managed as a total resource and drawn upon in new and varied ways to present insights into our national identity" (Te Papa Policy document 2013).[15]

By drawing materials from the collection for exhibition to "present insights into our national identity", these institutions create a version of the biography of the nation. As truth itself "is never value-neutral and absolute but rather necessarily interpretive and perspectival" (Clare & Hamilton, 2003 p.105), the archive is not a true representation of an objective history, but an imperfect, contingent representation of the nation's past at a particular moment in time which is created by curators and interpreted by its audience. As the Te Papa Policy document states, it has a "narrative approach" to the collection (Te Papa Policy document 2013). This interpretation, the narrative, may well be the most significant and telling aspect of the exhibition, revealing much more about the policy makers and museum workers than about the nation itself at a particular moment in time.

At the time the NZFA was being developed, the idea of promoting "national identity" was popular in many government departments (Sinclair, 1959/1991). A growing awareness of the need to redress in practical ways the Pākehā perception that their history was the only history of the nation was catalysed through various indigenous protest movements. In conjunction with protests by indigenous groups there were calls by feminist and gay advocates to redress the balance of power. This was reflected in the context of filmmaking. Lawrence McDonald describes a moment in New Zealand, later than the counter-culture movements of other Western countries, where "the Māori renaissance and the rise of feminism, fostered a period in which filmmakers tackled such topics as sexuality, childbirth, mental health, racial discrimination and biculturalism, existential meaning and national identity in innovative and provocative ways" (McDonald, 2011 p.156). During the 1980s, archives, museums and libraries were increasingly expected to reflect these sometimes violent and certainly passionate changes in social, political and cultural practices to support growing and developing perceptions of what it meant to be a "New Zealander".[16] If this is the case then

---

15 The policy is drawn from the National Museums Act. Retrieved 18/11/13 http://tepapa.govt.nz/ResearchAtTePapa/CollectionCareAndAccess/Pages/Te%20Papa%20Policy.aspx. Because the NZFA is a charitable trust, it does not have exactly the same responsibilities as a crown entity, and yet as an archive follows general protocol, particularly as it houses materials of national significance.

16 In a New Zealand government report on the use of the term "New Zealander" in the national census it was stated that "The development of national identity within a colonial context is intricately connected with the construction of social groups and with social relations between settlers, ... (and) ... the Native Other ..."(Cormack & Robson, 2010 p.2). Cormack and Robson demonstrate how in the early days of colonisation "New Zealanders" were Māori as colonisers chose to define themselves as British. Later as Māori populations were reduced by disease, poverty and war "New Zealanders" became the new majority, the British. They argue the term "indicated those who had become

the archive or museum expected to reflect insights into the nation is arguably a biography of the collective identity of New Zealanders – the question is, who is a New Zealander, and who is not?

The archive as both a physical institution and as a philosophical concept, contains its own silence. Although they appear to be the repositories of "authentic truth" and evidence of past activity, in the same way a biography can be assumed to provide evidence of a life, the archive (as concept) and the Archive (as physical repository of materials) are not simple manifestations. Materials for a biographical study reside in the physical archive, as well as in the memory of those who knew the subject. The concept of "memory" itself is attached in the popular imagination to "the archive" as an institution which is often assumed to be an unproblematic source of authentic truth in relation to the past and in turn allows for the idea that an archive or museum represents the "national identity". Memory itself is a discursive formation through which to consider the archive (Byatt & Harvey Wood, 2009). "Memory" is indeed an important concept to the archive, but actually "memories" do not exist in the archive, and viewing objects deposited in it does not engender memory in an audience where no prior experience of a depicted event or object had occurred. The archive as described in a manual of archiving is paralleled in the philosophical discourse (via Michel Foucault) with the interpretation of the archive as one of the social institutions in which power is discursive and norms are internalised (Corber & Valocchi, 2003 p.10). There are "silences in the telling of the story" of the archive as well as the multiple silences within the materials of the archive where memory is absent. Out of these silences and narratives, stories will inevitably be told, and this is one such story, of Jonathan Dennis.

---

the 'normal' or 'usual' inhabitants of the country.... This new national identity might have embraced some Māori symbols and markers, such as a few words or artistic motifs to distinguish it as unique, but it was primarily defined by descent from Britain, and to that extent was exclusionary of Māori" (Cormack & Robson, 2010 p.3).

Chapter 3

Jonathan Spencer Dennis and the early years

B arry Barclay described Jonathan Dennis' work and his "stumbling pre-science back in the first years ..." which "... showed, at least in film archive circles, certainly in this country and perhaps internationally too, how he was much ahead of his time" (Barclay, 2005 p.107). Conal McCarthy's text, *Museums and Māori: Heritage Professionals Indigenous Collections Current Practice* (2011) also briefly commented on Dennis' work during the early 1980s which he said "demonstrated through an active public programme and community outreach how a small cultural organisation such as the archive could begin to take on board Māori values and practices" (McCarthy, 2011 p.42). Both authors specifically name Jonathan Dennis as the person who developed an "active public programme" in relation to film archiving and indigenous communities, but their words raise more questions than they answer. Most immediately, how did Dennis come to his practice? What were his influences and who guided him? Why did this Pākehā have such passion for Māori process? How had the social, cultural and political issues of his day affected his work? How did *film* archiving itself relate to these issues? Could Dennis' practice be used as an example for others? But first of all, where did Dennis come from and why did he choose his particular path in life and work?

Jonathan Spencer Dennis was born on the 27th September 1953 at Taumarunui, a town in the North Island of NZ.[17] At the time of his birth the Dennis family lived at The Chateau, a large hotel built in the 1920s at the base of Mt Ruapehu

---

17 "Spencer" was the family name of his godparents (Fyfe & Dennis, 2001).

on the Central Plateau. Dennis later described the hotel as having a "sense of splendour" with "an extraordinarily spacious, beautiful lounge, with dripping chandeliers and the great picture window looking over the mountain" (Dennis in Alley & Dennis, 2002). The hotel was a base for tourists who explored the walks in the area and for ski parties who spent their days on nearby Mt Ruapehu. Prior to her arrival at The Chateau, Dennis' mother Patricia (Pat) had lived in Dunedin, in the South Island where she had been born in 1916 to the O'Reilly family. The O'Reillys later moved to New Plymouth where she grew up with two brothers and two sisters. Pat's first job after completing her schooling was as a receptionist in the office at The Chateau where she met Laurence (Lawrie) Dennis (born 1915), who was at that time most likely the Manager of Stores at the Hotel.[18] They married in 1940, and their first child and only daughter Simon was born in 1942, followed by Michael in 1944, Timothy in 1951 and finally Jonathan.[19] Although the hotel itself was cosmopolitan and there were many international visitors, the family lived in a couple of rooms at the end of a corridor. Simon remembered that Pat worked very hard in the early years with limited resources to raise the children. Once Timothy was born, their two bedrooms were made into a self-contained flat by putting a door across a corridor, "but they were literally two bedrooms on one side of the corridor joined by a bathroom ... The deluxe bedroom became the lounge and the bathroom, the toilet was boarded over and Mum had a little stove there" (Personal correspondence, S. Dennis 13/07/10).

In later life many people understood Dennis to have had a grand and privileged upbringing (for example Personal correspondence, S. Townsend 05/07/10). In terms of personal material possessions this does not appear to have been the case, as they lived in a grand hotel while their own accommodation was basic. However in 1958 when Jonathan was 5 years old, Lawrie was offered the job of Manager of The Hermitage. Like The Chateau, it was one of the government-owned chain of hotels organised under the Tourism Hotel Corporation. At the Hermitage at the base of Mt Cook (also known as Mt Aoraki) in the South Island the family had a separate house behind the hotel which meant for the first time they had their own home. The Hermitage at the time was "the height of modern, the new flash hotel ... I didn't know any different – what I didn't realize was that other

---

18 Simon Dennis, keeper of the Dennis family archive is unsure what her father's specific role was at that time (Personal correspondence, S.Dennis 29/04/09).

19 Simon does not know why she was given this particular name which is traditionally used for males. It is not one traditional to the family, and when she asked her mother Pat she was not given an explanation (Personal correspondence, S. Dennis ibid.).

people didn't live in those kinds of places" (Dennis in Alley & Dennis, 2002). Dennis' childhood from that time was privileged and insulated from the outside world until he went to boarding school.

Dennis' brother Timothy said that growing up in such an environment with parents who were open-minded and interested in the world meant that he and his siblings felt that anything was possible, and this gave them confidence. They met people from a wide variety of backgrounds and interacted with everyone from maids and cleaning staff to royal guests. Timothy says his father treated them all with equal respect and interest, even if he could not always remember everyone's names (Personal correspondence, T. Dennis 05/08/09).[20] Tim's experience may have been quite different from Jonathan's. Their niece Kirsten remembers her mother Simon describing picnics when Jonathan was a child where he would insist that no one but immediate family was present. He would panic if there were others in the vicinity and ask that the family go somewhere more isolated (Personal correspondence, E. Burrows & K. Dennis 08/07/10).[21] Dennis himself said he was never "boysy" or outgoing (J. Dennis in Alley & Dennis, 2002) and in later life was extremely selective regarding who he chose to spend time with. He was often rude to those he did not wish to be part of his social circle (Personal correspondence, S. Townsend 05/07/10). It may be that Dennis' early life spent sharing his home with strangers led him to feel protective of his personal space.

Reinforcing the idea that they had very different experiences, Jonathan's brother Timothy remembered The Hermitage as an "extended outdoors adventure" where he would shoot rabbits outside the picture windows while the guests were dining, help his "mentor" Bob Simpson with building work around the property, and go on hiking trips. In contrast, he said Jonathan was not interested in the outdoors – "Jonathan always had dolls in his room. The women at the hotel gravitated to him, idolized him, looked after him" (Personal correspondence, T. Dennis 05/08/09). For the rest of his life Dennis' friendships tended to revolve around female figures (Personal correspondence, E. Alley 11/06/10).

Simon Dennis remembers Jonathan as being a "collector of small things", with pockets full of little stones, toys and other items he picked up during the day (Personal correspondence, S. Dennis 29/04/09). In later life one of the comments

---

20 Timothy and his sister Simon told many entertaining stories of their parents handling a variety of situations, including an outbreak of sexually transmitted diseases among the staff and of a cook who was dismissed and in response tried to poison the flour before leaving (Personal correspondence, S. Dennis; T. Dennis op.cit.).

21 Kirsten Dennis was insistent on the point that the Dennis family were mostly introverts. Jonathan and Kirsten got along very well and he was more open with her than many people in his life. Most of his friends felt he had a very extroverted personality, but Kirsten explained this was not the case.

often made about his house that it was full of small collections of items – toys, pictures, playful objects (Personal correspondence, N. Brand 13/07/10; B. Gosden 08/12/09).[22] The boys had a series of governesses to help them with correspondence school work because at the time there was no formal school in the area, so a group of children would gather for lessons. They once picked up one of the governesses who threatened to tell their parents about their behavior and put her on top of the cupboard "until she came to her senses" (Personal correspondence, T. Dennis op.cit.). Clearly, although the boys were quite different, there were some things they were able to agree upon. Around this time their parents felt there were enough children in the area to start a more formal school system. Their father Lawrie sent hotel staff to pick up an unused schoolhouse from Tekapo. They put it on the back of a truck and brought it up to The Hermitage. Eventually, someone at Tekapo noticed the schoolhouse was missing and wrote to Lawrie, who invited them up for a weekend at the hotel and the matter was never mentioned again (Personal correspondence, T. Dennis op.cit.). Lawrie's decision to take the unused building without seeking appropriate permission was told by various family members as an amusing anecdote. It does suggest (like the story of the boys putting their governess on the cupboard) that some family members did take an unusual amount of initiative. This was interpreted by others at times as an overdeveloped sense of privilege or entitlement on the part of the Dennis family. Jonathan Dennis in later years was sometimes perceived as presumptuous, and did describe himself as selfish and blinkered at various times (Dennis in Alley & Dennis, 2002; Dennis in Fyfe & Dennis, 2001). His sister Simon commented that from her perspective it seemed that "he expected something to be done and it was" (Personal correspondence, S. Dennis 13/07/10).

The family certainly enjoyed a degree of privilege; the boys owned ponies and attended Pony Club, they had a lamb each year from Glen Tanner Station, cats and a border collie and even a red eared turtle. This childhood experience reflects Dennis' later comment that he took for granted the fact that everyone had the things he grew up with and that it was a surprise to find that they did not. Simon Dennis said while Jonathan was still quite young "skiing on the glacier became tour du jour" and the DC3 flights introduced from Christchurch to Mt Cook made it much easier to access The Hermitage. This also meant it was easier to travel away from the hotel, and when Tim and Jonathan were still at primary

---

22 Jonathan Dennis told the story of opening every breakfast cereal packet in the hotel stores to get the free toy once as a child (Dennis in Alley & Dennis 2002).

school the family went to Fiji for the first time, as Lawrie and Pat were offered the opportunity to temporarily manage a hotel at Sigatoka. They were to continue to travel after this time, with Pat in particular being very active in this regard (Personal correspondence, S. Dennis 13/07/10).[23]

As suggested by the overseas trips, as Lawrie Dennis was promoted into management positions the prospects of the family had improved. Jonathan Dennis remembered The Hermitage as a place where people did things "properly" – one dressed for dinner, formal table arrangements were followed and etiquette observed (Dennis in Fyfe & Dennis, 2001). Dennis appreciated these practices and would follow them throughout his life. Sharon Dell as an Alexander Turnbull librarian in the 1980s, remembered Dennis hosting film screenings with a vase of flowers, decoration and arrangements which she felt lent the screening a sense of occasion. She had not seen any other archivist or museum curator include such practices in their exhibitions (Personal correspondence, S. Dell 10/09/10). It was both a personal touch and a gesture which formalised the event and gave it a sense of prestige.

In interviews Dennis described his attraction as a young boy to the converted games room at The Hermitage which had been transformed into a 16mm film theatre for guests. He started his film education watching the local tourism newsreels of the National Film Unit or NFU (government funded filmmakers) there. The hotel also played a 16mm feature each week (either American or British), and these were enthralling for the young boy who felt his dreams were "going at 24 frames per second, and they were big, big on the screen. And I suppose I used to imagine myself being part of those dramas, part of those imaginings that were taking place in front of me there in the dark" (J. Dennis in Alley & Dennis, 2002).

Perhaps it was easy to imagine himself in films, because many of those he viewed were local and he and his family even had a cameo in one – "they were mostly [National] Film Unit films so I watched most of the NFU scenic films that were

---

23　The Dennis family continued to have a relationship with Fiji for many years, as eldest son Michael bought a resort hotel island called Toberua. Lawrie and Pat would help run it while Michael was away and all the siblings would visit at various times. Pat particularly spent much time with the locals and helped raise funds for new schools and water supplies. When Pat and then Lawrie died, Fijians asked for the family to visit so local funerary customs could be followed, and this was an important part of the grieving process and something the Dennis family were very proud to be involved in (Personal correspondence, S. Dennis 05/08/09) (Dennis in Fyfe & Dennis 2001). Dennis was also involved with Sharon Dell and Susan Bartel of the National Library in curating an exhibition entitled *The Heart of Fiji* (1993). This was a presentation of photographer Arthur Hocart's work and was undertaken as a reciprocal project with the local Fijian community of Wellington. A particular highlight of the cross-cultural exercise was that the cleaner at the Library turned out to be a Fijiaan man of high birth and therefore became involved in hosting the exhibition (Personal correspondence, S.Bartel 06/02/09).

1950s and 1960s and I'm in one of them – *SkyHigh in New Zealand*' (1961).[24] Dennis also remembered *Journey for Three* (Prod. Andrews, S., Dir. Furlong, M. 1950) and *The Snows of Aorangi* (Prods. Scott, G. & Morton, C. Dir. Brake, B. 1955) from this time (Dennis in Pivac & Dennis, 2000).[25] Watching locally made films as well as British and American features must have given Dennis the impression that films were made in New Zealand at a time when many people assumed they were exclusively produced overseas.[26] Yet the manner in which Dennis watched the films was sometimes curious. Elizabeth Alley interviewed him shortly before he died. She remembered one of the things that struck her as significant in their discussion was Dennis' description of hiding under the table in the dark watching films at the hotel – "I thought that was really interesting … partly hiding from his parents so they didn't know he was watching movies, but he also liked hiding in the dark. He liked that feeling of invisibility at that stage" (Personal correspondence, E. Alley 11/06/10).

"Invisibility" and "escape" became important for Dennis when his family sent him to school at the age of 10. First Tim left for Cathedral Grammar in Christchurch for the last year of primary school, moving on to St Andrews College for secondary school. Jonathan was to follow two years later. Tim knew few boys of his own age and did not find it easy to fit in when he arrived, even though he was an outdoors and sporty type. In retrospect he saw that Jonathan had "an absolutely awful time" and realised as an adult that Jonathan was "always gay" (Personal correspondence, T. Dennis op.cit.). By this time Simon, their oldest sibling, had completed her nursing training and was living in Christchurch. Jonathan would sign out of school by saying he was visiting her but would often go to the movies both because he enjoyed them and to escape from school (Personal correspondence, S. Dennis 13/07/10).

Many people interviewed for this study commented on Jonathan's stories of being bullied at school and how he was made to feel that he had to be "transparent" or "invisible". Interviewees often suggested that his bright and unusual sartorial display as an adult was at least in part a response to the miserable time he experienced (Personal correspondence, S. Dennis 13/07/10; E. Alley 11/06/10).

---

24   NZFA catalogue description of *Skyhigh in NZ* does not provide details of Director or Producer: "Mount Cook and the Hermitage are reached via the Mckenzie country. It promotes the unique scenic wonderland and local recreational activities: skiing, climbing and hunting. Painter Duncan Darrick (sic), has lived in and painted the area for 35 years. Includes brief footage of the Dennis family who ran the Hermitage" (retrieved 01/07/13 NZFA Online Catalogue Ref F3067 National Film Unit Travelogue 1961).

25   *Snows of Aorangi* was nominated for an Academy Award (Dennis & Bieringa, 1992/1996 p.223).

26   Only three feature films were made in NZ during the 1940s to early 1970s period (Pivac et al. 2011).

Dennis himself said he "Practised invisibility at boarding school – the horrors – later I could reverse being invisible – I could be visible in a slightly different dimension – that person in public was me but also I could be helping him along from the sidelines" (Alley & Dennis, 2002). This understanding of self from both within and without as a "public" and "private" persona continued throughout his life.

Michael Armstrong was a contemporary of Dennis' at St Andrews College but unlike the boarders was a "day boy" because his parents lived in Christchurch. Armstrong was friends with Dennis because they were both "arty". He remembered the school having a strong academic atmosphere. It was conservative and focused on sports such as cricket and rugby; even soccer was not allowed – "The place itself was at that time very old and run down, with worn out and cold wooden rooms, full of chalk and borer dust. The door to the boarders' dining area and the kitchens always stank of boiled cabbage and cheap meat; it must have put the poor bastards off their food … Cultural and artistic affairs were never mentioned in assembly … The rules were very strict ..." (Personal correspondence, M. Armstrong, 13/02/13).

Dennis had lived in a grand hotel where he and his brother had been free to do what they liked, so the experience described by Armstrong must have been difficult as Armstrong suggests. The "boiled cabbage and cheap meat" after the food of a grand hotel, the strict rules after having a teacher whom they could tease, and the focus on sports for a young man who previously stayed indoors and played with dolls must have been alienating. The assumption of a particular style of masculinity as normal would not have suited Dennis. Armstrong remembered clearly his own dislike of the headmaster who was an ex-military man and a well-known cricket commentator, thus fitting into the stereotype of masculinities popular during this period (Phillips, 1987 1st ed.). The descriptions echo Anita Brady's remarks on the South Island High Country as an example of the "blokey egalitarianism" and the "kiwi bloke" ideology that was key in the cultural imaginary of the NZ national identity (Brady, 2012 p.359).[27] When Armstrong was asked what Dennis may have thought of the school, he replied that it was hierarchical and there was terrible bullying. He thought that "Jonathan maintained a distance around himself that kept them away; words and maybe sarcasm but something effective, because I can never remember him being on the receiving

---

27   Matthew Bannister also writes on this issue (Bannister, 2005).

end, nor did I ever see him bullying younger boys" (Personal correspondence, M. Armstrong, 2013, op.cit.).

In contrast to Dennis' memory of his own "invisibility", Armstrong remembered a forthright boy who seemed quite confident in challenging the bullying – he thought he managed to "maintain a distance" and was "outspoken". Perhaps Dennis' efforts to hide his own vulnerabilities led to feelings of "transparency" which were not obvious to others, or this "distance" was another form of transparency. Perhaps Dennis' feeling that he could be "visible in a slightly different dimension" started earlier than he imagined (Dennis in Alley & Dennis 2001). It is clear from both Armstrong and Dennis' accounts that it was not easy being at St Andrews for some boys.

During this time Dennis was watching as many films as he could, sometimes going to multiple sessions on the weekend at the local cinema (Crosbie, 1990, March 11). He kept diary entries for each film he saw and included the length of the film in his records. He felt he "escaped" into the films he watched to remove himself from boarding school "horrors". His family had a "strategic plan" to keep him at boarding school (Dennis in Alley & Dennis, 2002) and certainly at this time his letters to his parents are full of questions about when he will see them next.[28] As he matured, Dennis was sometimes bad tempered with his parents, writing to them with venom when they annoyed him.[29] He described this to Elizabeth Alley in an interview as a "delayed reaction" to his boarding school days in which he was angry with his parents for sending him away. He acknowledged however that in retrospect his behavior was unfair and they were very tolerant of him (J. Dennis in Alley et al., 2001). Dennis' anger at his parents was something only his immediate family generally witnessed (Personal correspondence, T. Dennis op.cit.). Most people felt he had a positive relationship with his parents. However, intimates knew that he did not censor himself with them when angry, and that he resented for many years their decision to send him away to boarding school, even though they had done the same to his three older siblings (Dennis in Fyfe & Dennis, 2001).

Many people interviewed for this research had contradictory views of Dennis which are perhaps explained by his passionate and difficult relationship with his parents and his sense of having both a "public" and "private" persona due to the

---

28 Examples found in NZFA PP JD Box 11.

29 16 April 1979 JD to his parents from Amsterdam – letter opens "Dear Dad and Mum Alright lets get this clear right off – you do not sent out my letters to all and sundry. You can tell them butcha don't show them. OK? It better be" (ATL MS Papers JD 9114–08).

difficulties of his school days. Those who were fond of him often referred to him as "my best friend" and described his loyalty, generosity and love (Personal correspondence, S. Bartel 03/12/09; S. Dell 10/09/10; D. Young, 03/08/11). Others witnessed or experienced snubbing from him, public "cutting down and coldness" (Personal correspondence, S. Townsend 05/07/10; S. Rainbow 29/01/09). These strongly contrasting perspectives perhaps related to a childhood which on one hand had been loving, warm, and privileged, while boarding school was full of "horrors". Dennis, like many other young people of that time, endured this with no counselling or other opportunity to reconcile his experiences. Particularly for young New Zealand men, who at this time were expected to conform to a post-war ideal masculinity where outdoor pursuits and sporting prowess were considered important, Jonathan Dennis' penchant for dolls, his failure to be "boysy" and his interest in films would have made him feel alone and isolated at a boarding school inhabited by the sons of Canterbury farmers.[30]

Those afternoons at the picture theatre were a consolation and would provide Dennis with an excellent film education. Armstrong remembers the cinemas at that time around Christchurch as "rundown and uncomfortable … obviously with low patronage, and some of the suburban theatres like the Papanui corner one which showed westerns and silent movies closed around then" (Personal correspondence, M. Armstrong 13/02/13). The westerns and silent movies were films of an earlier period, and silent movies were to be become Dennis' favourite films for the rest of his life (Alley & Dennis, 2002).

Author and filmmaker Peter Wells, Dennis' contemporary, has written about his relationship with cinema as a young gay man, and he discussed this with Dennis after Wells' autobiography *Long Loop Home* was published (Wells, 2001). Wells remembered that Dennis particularly remarked on a similar experience of identification with non-traditional gender roles in the films they watched. Wells described in detail their mutual relationship to images on the screen which offered each a silent opportunity to fantasise about the male characters kissing them, even

---

30 I do not pretend a knowledge of psychology and this study is not psychoanalytical. This view is offered because so many interviewees raised the "boarding school horrors" and the need for "invisibility" themselves. Other reasons for Dennis' sometime rude behavior could be, as suggested by some, the influence of his maternal grandmother Nanna Nell (Nellie Blanche May Plummer). Dennis "adored" Nell and loved her rude behavior. She was judgmental of perceived defects in personalities and appearances and would loudly state her views in public. Denise Young described being invited to Christmas with Jonathan and his partner Ferry Hendriks at Queenstown when Denise was heavily pregnant. Nanna Nell was horrified and muttered about a pregnant woman who clearly had no husband. Nell made it obvious she was unhappy to have a "fallen woman" at the dinner table, which Dennis found hilarious (Personal correspondence, D. Young 03/08/11). Supporting the view that she was an influence, before he died Dennis was determined to go to Australia and walk around Ayers Rock (Uluru) because Nanna Nell had been born in Australia and Dennis wanted to honour the connection. He was able to do so with the help of his friend and ex-partner Fergus MacGillivray (Personal correspondence, F. MacGillivray 05/07/10).

though one would never have discussed it with one's friends at the time (Personal correspondence, P. Wells 30/06/09). This theme of searching for signs of homosexuality in cinematic representations has been investigated in popular culture in the 1995 documentary film *The Celluloid Closet* in which diffuse clues and hints were interpreted as moments of homosexuality by audiences (Dirs. Epstein, Rob & Friedman, Jeffrey).

When not at the cinema or at school, Dennis' other artistic stimulation came from an uncle, his mother Pat's older brother. Ron O'Reilly was the Chief Librarian of Canterbury Public Library in Christchurch and a member of the Film Society. He was interested in both overseas and local artistic expression. O'Reilly collected local art and organised exhibitions as well as writing influential art reviews. O'Reilly made an impression on Dennis during family visits to Christchurch, and later when Dennis was on his own while at boarding school (Fyfe & Dennis, 2001).

Born in 1914, O'Reilly was a friend of modernist artists such as Colin McCahon and Toss Woollaston and an early champion of their work, having met McCahon through the theatre scene in Dunedin.[31] As Chief Librarian of the Canterbury Public Library (from 1951–1968) he introduced a free book loan system and a scheme by which the public could pay a small charge to borrow from a lending library of New Zealand art. He slowly persuaded the City Council that funds should be used to purchase New Zealand art for the lending library collection (Drent & Sutherland, 1989). O'Reilly arranged an early joint exhibition of Woollaston and McCahon paintings in Wellington at the Helen Hitchings gallery in 1949 (Hall, 2010).

O'Reilly's daughter Rachel Watson (Jonathan Dennis' cousin) remembered the Dennis family visiting the two-storey Victorian brick and stone librarian's house at 109 Cambridge Terrace, next to the old neo-Gothic Canterbury Public Library. She recalled Jonathan's mother Pat (Ron's sister) arguing with Ron over the "obscene" paintings he had hanging in the house (Personal correspondence, R. Watson 03/10/10).[32] Jonathan Dennis remembered his mother saying that O'Reilly's paintings "were not proper". They were strange art works which frightened him but left a "deep impression". They were "unsettling and scary",

---

31 Colin McCahon is one of the best known modernist painters in NZ. Jonathan Dennis purchased his McCahon painting *Paul to Hebrews*. After his death the painting was sold and the resultant money divided between a number of benefactors of his will who considered the amount "generous" (Personal correspondence, M. McKinnon 23/11/09).

32 Unlike the contemporary art gallery space with pristine white walls, the librarian's house had densely patterned old fashioned wallpaper upon which the modernist paintings were hung (Personal correspondence, R. Watson 03/10/10).

and indeed some were "floor to ceiling" works. They had a "sense of landscape formed differently" (Dennis in Fyfe & Dennis, 2001). O'Reilly himself was a "disconcerting man" who liked to take wild drives in the country. On one occasion he drove Dennis into the Canterbury Plains in his usual erratic fashion while describing Antonioni's *Blow Up* (1966) in such a way as to make a serious impression on Dennis who had never heard anyone critique a film before (Dennis in Fyfe & Dennis op.cit.).[33] In contrast to O'Reilly's taste, the artworks on display at the hotels where the Dennis family lived were classic representational landscapes of the area by local artists such as Aston Greathead and Duncan Darroch hung for the guests to purchase (Personal correspondence, S. Dennis 13/07/10).

The world of Ron O'Reilly was a great contrast to both Dennis' boarding school and his life at The Hermitage. The Film Society of which Ron was a member (Personal correspondence, M. O'Reilly 12/06/10) was part of the modernist art movement of the time, considered to be home to radical intellectuals, largely due to the fact that they were able to watch films banned by the censor for public viewing in NZ. As a result they were treated with suspicion and were sometimes assumed to be "perverts and radicals" (Sigley, 2003 p.91) by "doggedly practical New Zealanders" disinterested in "the mind and the spirit" (King, 2000 p.131).[34,35] Bill Gosden, later to become the Secretary of the Federation of Film Societies, said prior to censorship legislation changes, the film societies "exploited to the hilt" their access to movies unavailable to general audiences in order to increase their membership (Personal correspondence, B. Gosden 08/12/09).[36] O'Reilly and his friends were part of the younger generation challenging not just their elders but also their peers, working out a new and local understanding of art and identity through a form of "cultural nationalism", gaining their ideas through both local and international artistic practices including film (Jensen, 1996). As Roger Horrocks later described it, the "public disliked their links with

---

33 In his thesis on film reception, Sigley says that by the 1960s some New Zealanders were interested in "art films", by Bergman and others and specifically mentions Antonioni's *Blow Up* (1966) and *Zabriski Point* (1970) (Sigley, 2003 p.305).

34 Michael King's description of New Zealand in the 1950s when author Frank Sargeson was encouraging writer Janet Frame, who had just completed her first novel, to go overseas and experience Europe where the "life of the mind", creativity and intellectual freedom were assumed to be in abundance.

35 O'Reilly was an unconventional thinker for his time and place. In his book *Mates and Lovers*, Chris Brickell (2008) comments that poet "Rex Fairburn's friend Ron O'Reilly, the Christchurch City Librarian, espoused the opposite view (to those who felt that homosexuality was a very small minority), suggesting that all men had a homosexual element. 'Don't you think' he wrote to Fairburn, 'it as well for us to accept that there is a latent homosexuality about us all rather than dissipate our energie (sic) in trying to repudiate this whole phase of life?'" (Brickell, C. 2008 p.196). There is no evidence that Dennis and O'Reilly discussed sexuality.

36 The Cinematograph Films Amendment Act 1934 allowed Film Society to pay a nominal fee to the Film Censor who was able to grant them license to screen films. The Minister of the day had to be agreeable to the issuing of the special license (Sigley, 2003 p.120).

modern art and their critical attitude towards New Zealand. The artists were creating a local culture that the country did not yet know it needed" (Horrocks in Pivac et al, 2011 p.8).

For a young man who loathed his schooling which reflected a dogmatic and conservative aspect of New Zealand, O'Reilly's world, like that of the cinema he championed, must have seemed beguiling. The arguments between Pat and Ron about the paintings in the librarian's house surely intrigued a young man angry with his parents for sending him away to boarding school. As an adult Dennis became a collector of some significant McCahon paintings including *Paul to Hebrews* and he remembered his uncle's McCahon collection touring the country in the late 1970s.[37] Although a teenager at the time, Dennis was to say that O'Reilly's art made a definite impression on him, as did the conversations about the films O'Reilly was seeing and describing (Dennis in Alley & Dennis, 2002).

In 1968 significant changes occurred in the Dennis/O'Reilly clan. O'Reilly left the Christchurch Library, the Dennis family left The Hermitage for Wellington and Michael, the oldest Dennis child, competed as a skier in the Olympic Games at Grenoble in France (Dennis in Alley et al., 2001). Because Jonathan "loathed and detested" school he insisted on completing his education at Wellington College (which meant he could live with his parents) rather than finishing at St Andrews in Christchurch (Personal correspondence, S. Dennis op.cit.). He then went on to study for a Bachelor of Arts in English Literature at Victoria University which he completed in 1976 (NZFA PP JD Box 11). Dennis recalled his university days as being "just an excuse" to be involved in theatrical work and that the film studies course of the time was "unbelievably pathetic".[38] He continued to watch as many films as he could, recalling in his interview with Di Pivac the wild programming of the smaller picture theatres in the 1970s such as the Roxy and the Princess. The small cinemas did not have access to the latest films so they held "crazy repertory screenings" and at theatres such as the *Lido* there were double bills on Sundays which included "Bergman films or what have you. So it was possible to catch up with a huge range of '50s and '60s films and foreign films from the '40s, '50s, '60s, within a strange nutty repertory" (Dennis in Pivac & Dennis, 2000).

---

37 In 1969 Peter McLeavey, Wellington art dealer held an exhibition of O'Reilly's personal collection of McCahon paintings (Hall, 2010). This was the first year Dennis lived in Wellington and he may have meant the late 1960s rather than "1970s" as he said in the interview.

38 It seems that in New Zealand, film was not "taken seriously" as either an art form nor considered worthy of scholarly analysis for many years. According to Simon Sigley it was Adult Education Classes organised by the Workers Educational Association (WEA) which were influential in the promotion of the study of film during the 1930s–1960s. Film studies were much slower to be incorporated into university teaching (Sigley, 2003 p.79).

Dennis was seeing a wide range of films which informed his largely autodidact film education. The "fledging film course" at the University was not completely "pathetic", as the lecturer did invite New Zealand's earliest feature filmmaker Rudall Hayward to speak. He came with his second wife Ramai, and Dennis remembered Hayward as a "consummate gentleman", friendly, knowledgeable and full of stories. He recalled the experience of viewing Hayward's films for the first time – "Seeing Bush Cinderella … being mesmerised by it, loving various sequences, the dance in the ploughed field … it was sort of thrilling, it was personal. It was like my discovery at the same time of feeling a connection to McCahon paintings, of things I was looking at as a different landscape, and in the early '70s it was a different landscape because there really wasn't anything else of NZ stuff to see" (Dennis in Pivac & Dennis, 2000). Hayward as a local director making feature films excited Dennis' curiosity and it was "personal". He felt it was "thrilling" and he was "mesmerized" by it. He felt excited that, like his favourite modernist painter, there was a local filmmaker trying to see differently. Related to this was his concern that in general there "wasn't anything of NZ … to see". This concern was shared by Dennis' elders who were at this time campaigning for governmental support for locally made artistic productions.

The drive to represent a "national identity"

In 1970 while Dennis was finishing his schooling at Wellington College, the "Arts Conference 70" was held at Victoria University of Wellington. It included discussion on "The role of film and television in establishing a nation's identity" (Conrich, 2008 p.2). One significant session was chaired by Bill Sheat[39] and speakers included Dr Roger Manvell, a "seminal writer about film as a serious art form"; Lord Goodman, the Chairman of the Arts Council of Great Britain and John O'Shea, New Zealand filmmaker and film reviewer (also a historian by training) (Programme Arts Conference 70, O'Shea, 1970).[40] Also involved were Peter Munz, Professor of History at Victoria University, Christopher Thompson, TV Director, Anthony Williams, Film Director, Douglas McIntosh, the Film Censor, and "Miss Catherine de la Roche", an "international writer on film" (O'Shea, 1970). At the conference it was recorded in Resolution 117 and 118 that a Television and Film Archive was needed in NZ (Personal correspondence,

---

39 Bill Sheat "is a lawyer by training and has had a long involvement with the creative disciplines, restoration projects and arts governance. He was Chair of the Queen Elizabeth II Arts Council, now known as Creative New Zealand, founding Chair of the New Zealand Film Commission and Chair of the Royal New Zealand Ballet" (Retrieved 21/08/13 from http://gg.govt.nz/node/4406).

40 For a brief history of John O'Shea's work and life see *Don't Let It Get You*, a memoir edited by Jonathan Dennis and Jan Bieringa and named for one of O'Shea's feature films from 1966 (O'Shea, 1999).

B. Sheat 31/01/11). Bill Sheat was then Chair of the Queen Elizabeth II Arts Council of New Zealand and remembered that time with enthusiasm – "we actually commissioned John Reid to write us a position paper" on the need for a Film Commission and Film and TV Archive following the 1970 conference (Personal correspondence, B. Sheat op.cit.).[41]

It was at this time in the early 1970s that Jonathan Dennis' personal history and the growing interest in a New Zealand film and television industry coalesced, as reflected by the resolution of the Arts 1970 Conference. His experience at this time sheds light on his later work driving a publicity campaign to recognise the importance of local historic film culture in the late 1970s and then through the 1980s as Director of the Film Archive. His passion for the local was developed by his experiences. He was to say of the 1970s period that "we were not seeing local content, and so we created it" (Dennis in Alley et al., 2001). Denise Young (then Maunder) was the co-founder of local theatre troupe *Amamus* at the time with her husband Paul who was also working at the National Film Unit (the source of the films Dennis watched in the hotels as a child). They were both important points of contact for Dennis as he developed his sense of NZ culture.

Amamus was formed in 1971 and Jonathan joined as a "17 or 18 year old … by far he was the youngest in the group". He was not a great actor, but a "wonderful physical presence … and because so much of what we did was physically oriented his boundless energy and his sheer size was great – he was tall and young and vigorous and he was willing to do absolutely anything" (Personal correspondence, D. Young 03/08/11). The cast fluctuated depending on projects and availability, but in 1973 it included Denise Maunder, Gael Anderson, John Anderson, Sam Neill, Jonathan Dennis, Michael Bajko, Jane McKechnie, Pat Birdling, Olwyn Taylor, Anne England and Paul Maunder (Unknown author Wanganui Chronicle, 1973). Anna Campion, sister of Jane Campion was also involved at various times. Many in this group were active in the film scene; some through Paul Maunder's productions (Personal correspondence, D. Young 03/08/11). Dennis' experience with *Amamus* taught him performance skills and the importance of telling local stories, as well as something of the resistance audiences might have for local content when they were more familiar with foreign productions.

The group followed Polish theatre director Jerzy Grotowski's "poor theatre" model using few props and exploiting their own experiences through sharing their

---

41   John Reid was himself a filmmaker and actor who was to be involved in some Paul Maunder film productions (Pivac et al., 2011 p.158).

memories and feelings. Prompted by Paul Maunder they shared their diary entries to develop plays about the "New Zealand condition" (Personal correspondence, S. Townsend 05/07/10).[42] However, like Horrocks' description of the public who did not yet know that they wanted to see local productions, *Amamus* was not always popular with audiences – "it became so abstract that in many cases audiences couldn't accept it, didn't want to see it … it was very intense and sometimes our audiences were less than the cast members, you know, eleven people" (Personal correspondence, D. Young op.cit.).

Englishman Sef Townsend was at that time involved in another group called *Theatre Action*. The two companies met in the Manawatu for joint workshops. Townsend recalled that the *Amamus* style was "so cerebral … precisely what theatre audiences don't need" but upon reflection in later years he considered that "there were some good performances … and it was quite good at dealing with the New Zealand condition, with the whole Gallipoli thing and what it meant to a small nation like New Zealand" (Personal correspondence, S. Townsend 05/07/10). By "the whole Gallipoli thing" Townsend is referring to the growing notion that New Zealand identity (Pākehā and male) was forged during its involvement in WWI.

When they first met, Townsend was the partner of Ferry (Ferdinand) Hendriks. Hendriks explained – "I had seen him [Jonathan] before at films, at the Film Society. Being so tall, he stood out, and I remembered him … I was still living with Sef [Townsend], and it was a novelty in 1975 to have a, what do you call it, a threesome, a ménage à trois, but it all worked out really well, it seemed to suit everybody" (Personal correspondence, F. Hendriks 28/11/09). Sef Townsend and Jonathan Dennis "got together" the first weekend they met at the Manawatu, and Townsend then "brought Jonathan home" to meet Hendriks, and the three became involved. At one point they moved in with Dennis' parents who would often entertain diplomats and the like. Sef described with amusement the memory of Pat and Lawrie at the dinner table introducing their son Jonathan "and his friend Sef, and his other friend Ferry" and watching peoples reactions. At that time Jonathan had a large waterbed, which was quite unusual in New Zealand, and all three slept in this, with father Lawrie bringing cups of tea in the morning for whomever was staying at the time (Personal correspondence, S. Townsend op.cit.).

---

42 Jerzy Grotowski was a Polish experimental theatre director who wrote texts about and taught his "poor theatre" style. He was influential in the West during the 1970s (Wolford & Schechner, 1997).

In the year Townsend, Hendricks and Dennis met, a review of the *Amamus* theatre production *Gallipoli* featured a picture of Jonathan Dennis holding a (fake) gun. The article described the eschewing of "visual means" such as lighting and props, "But much more radical than the simplicity of these elements in *Gallipoli* was the use made of language. Words were not the primary means of communication, but more a sort of accompaniment to the movements of the actors" (Unknown author *Critic Magazine*, 1975 p.19). A reviewer in the University of Auckland student publication *Craccum* was impressed and explained that the influence of the Polish "poor theatre" tradition was very effective. "Their material, their workshop and their system can only be described as mind boggling. No wonder they've received grant money from the Arts Council. New Zealand needs them" (McGill, 1975).

Maunder and the *Amamus* cast's film and television broadcasts received equally mixed reviews ranging from bemusement to enthusiasm. *Gone Up North For a While* (1972) was *Amamus'* first television production produced through the National Film Unit where Paul Maunder worked. This was the tale of a young woman who became pregnant and the subsequent choices she made – at that time there was no Domestic Purposes Benefit to support her and often women were sent away to an unmarried mother's nursing home in Auckland (the euphemism being "gone up north") until the baby had been born and the young woman could adopt it out. Dennis features in one shot in a scene from the film but is not credited.[43] He is sitting in a "milk bar" holding a cigarette near the main characters played by Denise Maunder and a young Paul Holmes (later to become a television personality and radio host). Paul Maunder also made an experimental film called *One of Those People Who Live in the Real World* (1973) about patients in a mental hospital which featured actual patients in the film. A further film *Landfall – A Film About Ourselves* (1975) won first prize at the Abu-Shiraz Young Filmmakers Festival in Iran but no television channel in New Zealand (there were only two at the time) was willing to screen it initially. In an article entitled *Now is the time for all good Kiwis to submit to punishment* a reviewer states – "An ambitious film, *Landfall* is typical of the style we have come to expect from its director, with bleak and often obscure imagery [with an] undercurrent [of] serious moral issues". It was to play at the Wellington Film Festival and "Auckland film critic Roger Horrock" [sic] is quoted as saying that it was "utterly disgraceful" that the film

---

43 I have verified with Simon Dennis that it is her brother and Denise Young also confirmed he was in the film (Personal correspondence, D. Young; S. Dennis op.cit.).

should not have shown on NZ screens earlier (Unknown author, ATL JD MS folder 1 4418 Amamus).

Simon Sigley's description of the place of the arts in the 1930s is similar to the 1970s situation for the *Amamus* theatre group whose productions were sometimes lauded, but often misunderstood or dismissed. The "heroic days for the arts in NZ, when an interest in 'modern' ideas had something of the feeling of a shared crusade or conspiracy" (Sigley, 2003 p.111) seems true for the reception of the theatre/film group. The varying reviews of the *Amamus* productions (stage, television and film) reflected the competing conservative and liberal opinions of the 1970s in New Zealand at a moment where the younger generation were challenging their elders. Roger Horrocks was later to describe this time when "the young took revenge upon the staid values of their parents' generation, challenging conservative New Zealand in films such as *Gone Up North for a While* [Prod. Bowie, R., Dir. Maunder 1975], *The God Boy* [Prod. & Dir. Reece, M. 1976], *Landfall* [Prod. Fowler, D., Dir. Maunder, P. 1975] and *Sons for the Return Home*" [Prod. Blakeney, D., Dir. Maunder, 1979] (Horrocks in Pivac et.al. 2011 p.11). Three of the films Horrocks referred to were directed by Paul Maunder and involved *Amamus* cast members. Maunder and the cast's work in television and film broadcasts as well as through the plays they were writing and performing, set them on a course to develop various projects with a distinctly (Pākehā) "New Zealand" flavour through the 1970s and 1980s. Some, like actor Sam Neill, later gained international recognition for their work. The friendships and networks Dennis made during his time with *Amamus* would continue to be active throughout his life, though as Young described it, his close friendships were all with the women in the group (Personal correspondence, D. Young op.cit.).

In 1975 *Amamus* travelled to Poland for a student theatre festival celebrating Grotowski. Ferry Hendriks recalled the props they took across Europe in the trains with amusement given they were supposedly under the influence of the "poor theatre" – a large wooden cross and a fake gun which looked real (Personal correspondence, F. Hendriks 28/11/09). The cast of *Amamus* began to change after this tour as Denise and Paul separated (Personal correspondence, D. Young, 03/08/11). However, Ferry and Jonathan had enjoyed travelling together and attended the Cannes Film Festival for the first time (Personal correspondence, F. Hendriks op.cit.). Dennis left the company in 1978 as his involvement in the Film Society and local annual film festival began to outweigh his interest in theatre. He had realised after seeing himself on film that he was never going to be a great actor and recalled with laughter that he never thought Sam Neill would be either because of his "nasal" voice (Dennis in Fyfe & Dennis, 2001). However, this grounding in theatre and the development of local productions which were not always popular with mainstream audiences taught Dennis many things. He had a determination to express his ideas and those of his peers even if their message was unpopular; he was aware of the importance of performance in various settings; he knew that local stories needed to be told, and he had made many connections with others in the cultural industry.

By the mid 1970s Dennis was starting to deliver the occasional live film review on Sunday mornings on radio channel 2ZB and also became involved in programming for the Film Society. The two experiences became quickly intertwined. His involvement started "more or less with my complaining on the radio about the choice of some of the films that Lindsay [Shelton] was getting for the Film Festival" (Dennis in Pivac & Dennis, 2000).[44] Lindsay Shelton, committee member of the Wellington Film Society since 1969, was elected President in 1970 and in the same year became the programmer for the NZ Federation of Film Societies. The Wellington Film Festival was founded in 1972 (Conrich, 2008 xiv). Dennis joined the Film Society in that year, having seen the 1971 season which included films Shelton had bought in London such as Kenneth Anger's *Scorpio Rising* (1964), *Eaux d'artifice* (1953) and *Invocation of My Demon Brother* (1969) (Sigley, 2003 p.335). Dennis was impressed by these films and was to cultivate a correspondence with Kenneth Anger which lasted the rest of his life.[45] Anger's work had always been controversial due to its homerotic content. There had been issues for many years with film censorship laws in New Zealand which restricted accessibility, but the film societies had special dispensation to screen some works as they were deemed a private society. In 1976, with a sympathetic Minister for the Arts (Allan Highet), legislation was finally enacted which allowed changes to censorship laws (Sigley, 2003 p.328).[46] When Dennis complained that

---

44 Shelton's response to Dennis' complaint is testimony to the mentoring that occurred between older and younger generations – Shelton chose to involve Dennis in the Film Festival programming rather than be offended by his very public complaint. Shelton continued to generously champion Dennis throughout his life and after his death (Shelton, 2002, 2005).

45 In 1993 Dennis invited Anger to New Zealand for a retrospective screening of the *Magick Lantern Cycle* works. Included in Dennis' personal papers is an advertisement for a screening on Thursday 15 April 1993 – "The Paramount Theatre and the Wellington City Art Gallery present Kenneth Anger Hollywood Babylon featuring The Magick Lantern Cycle and Kenneth Anger in person. Screening two cycles of Magick Lantern – Session 1 *Fireworks* 1947, *Puce, Moment* 1949, *Rabbit's Moon* 1950, *Eaux D'Artifice* 1953, *Inauguration of the Pleasure Dome* 1954. Screening 2 *Scorpio Rising* 1963, *Kustom Kar Kommandos* 1965, *Invocation of My Demon Brother* 1969, *Lucifer Rising* 1970–1980. With Kenneth Anger presenting and signing his book 'Hollywood Babylon'" (Jonathan Dennis Personal Papers NZFA Box 11 Folder 'Kenneth Anger'). The Dennis/Anger correspondence in the NZFA is worthy of further analysis as a separate project, as is the Peter Wells/Dennis correspondence.

46 (David) Allan Highet (b.1913 d.1992) was an MP from 1966–1984 with the National Party. In 1975 he became Minister of Internal Affairs, Minister of Local Government, New Zealand's first Minister for the Arts, and Minister for Sport (Retrieved 26/11/13 http://en.wikipedia.org/wiki/Allan_Highet).

there were few films which reflected personal experiences for New Zealanders, gay experiences were some of those which were missing, and in fact many of the organisers of the Film Society and Film Festival were or were to come out as gay men, interested in films which reflected more than the representations of the "kiwi bloke" they were beginning to see in the late 1970s and early 1980s as New Zealand developed a film culture of its own (Farnell & Green, 2011).

During the 1970s, interest in both foreign and local films was increasing, and with a Minister of Arts engaged by film culture it was becoming possible to imagine a film industry emerging with government support (Personal correspondence, L. Shelton 07/12/09). As we have seen, groups such as *Amamus* were developing New Zealand content for stage and screen. Others who would later play important roles in that developing culture were beginning to meet and form alliances and friendships. Through the film societies and festivals they were bringing films into the country which represented different ways of being and doing in the world. Bill Gosden, current Director of the New Zealand International Film Festival was working at New Zealand Film Services in Kent Terrace in the late 1970s. It was "an independent film company with a very strong back collection of European films, a very strong contemporary collection of mildly erotic European films" and the Film Society had space hired in the Film Service offices (Dennis in Pivac & Dennis, 2000). Dennis was a frequent visitor to the office and Gosden remembered meeting him – "I was immediately curious about who he was because he was always larger than life. An enormously colorful character swanning in and out … he dressed like people were dressing in San Francisco [at the time]" (Personal correspondence, B. Gosden 08/12/09). Lindsay Shelton also remembered Dennis because at early Film Festival screenings "he would sweep into the Paramount and sit right at the front, and in winter of course, he'd be wearing a scarf, a long brightly coloured scarf so you noticed his arrival" (Personal correspondence, L. Shelton op.cit.). Dennis sat in the front and centre of the theatre to watch films all his life and this was remarked upon by many interviewees (For example, Personal correspondence, E. Burrows 08/07/10). This was the classic seat for the cinéaste, the connoisseur of film (Sontag, 1996).

Because of his connections to the Film Society and the work he undertook cataloguing their collection, Dennis began to bring films home for private screenings which were also conducted in the tradition of the European cinéaste. Gosden remembered attending screenings of films at Dennis and Ferry Hendrick's house including "*L'Atalante* which was a revelation to me, a wonderful film". He also saw the D.W Griffith Screenings at the Wellington Public Library

– "I can't remember exactly how many films were involved, but he [Dennis] had cued up music, he and Ferry were playing DJs [laughs] before DJs were DJs and that was quite wonderful. I was bowled over by those films, of course one had always read about the Griffith movies but to see them presented so carefully was exciting" (Personal correspondence, B. Gosden op.cit.). Gosden was impressed by the careful presentation, and the novelty of Dennis and his partner providing the soundtrack. These screenings were a "revelation" but they were also fun – it was an exciting time to be sharing films with each other in a small country isolated from the major film centres of the world. Dennis mentioned these events in various interviews too, saying that they screened *Intolerance* (1916) because – "I'd met Lillian Gish briefly, she'd been my favourite, hence we got into the Griffiths". He also remembered how strict he was on the audience when he screened films at home – "People weren't allowed to talk, even in the reel changes they had to just sit and watch" (Dennis in Pivac & Dennis, 2000). At this point in time Dennis' presentation of films was very much in the formal European tradition, but it was also a wonderful experience for the people who attended these screenings, as Gosden described. Dennis had at this time a very European aesthetic in Pierre Bourdieu's (1984) sense of the term, considering himself an elite cinema-goer interested in modern film from the Northern Hemisphere, and Gosden's reference to his look being that of people from San Francisco at this time suggests he held a certain exotic, gay and cosmopolitan cache.

Lindsay Shelton remembered this time as cooperative and exciting. "Everybody … shared the joy and the pleasure of making films available to audiences" (Personal correspondence, L. Shelton, op.cit.). Jonathan Dennis, Bill Gosden and Lindsay Shelton were to remain stalwarts of "the joy and the pleasure" of films for many years to come as paid employment became possible in the new film industry, with Gosden becoming Director of the NZ International Film Festival and Lindsay Shelton a key player at the New Zealand Film Commission.

The New Zealand Film Commission is established

In 1973 Jonathan Dennis was twenty years old and the United Kingdom joined the European Union Community. This ended the close relationship NZ had enjoyed as the "dairy" of the United Kingdom, with trade between the nations no longer protected or guaranteed. Partly spurred by this change, some New Zealanders became interested in asking (or re-asking) questions about national identity – was NZ still an English colony? What did it mean to live in New Zealand? (Conrich, 2008 p.2). The 1970 Arts Conference had explored "establishing a national identity" through art, and the developing film industry was part of this exploration. In the late 1970s, Michael (Mike) Nicolaides was commissioned by the Arts Council to write a further report to that of J. Reid (1970) on the importance of government support for a film industry, "and by this stage the thing is starting to gather momentum and in 1977 we set up as the Interim Film Commission. We didn't have any legislation … One of our tasks was to write our own … Now you actually cannot ask for more than that … Allan Highet [Minister for the Arts] obviously had … faith in us" (Personal correspondence, B. Sheat op.cit.). Although the events of this time are often portrayed as being male dominated, Sheat pointed out that, "One of the people who was really pushing it and to whom I pay considerable tribute was Allan's wife, Shona McFarlane … Shona had been on the Arts Council during my time … But you see there were all sorts of other things going on; a whole range of influences … Roger Donaldson made [feature film] *Sleeping Dogs* [Prod. & Dir. R. Donaldson, 1977] and Tony Williams made [feature film] *Solo* [Prod. Hannay, D., Dir. T. Williams, 1977], on which I was Executive Producer". Hamish Keith was the Queen Elizabeth II Arts Council Chair at the time and "was very supportive of the whole film thing" (Personal correspondence, B. Sheat op.cit). The legislation, which was written by Sheat et al., stated in part –

> The Film Commission Act 1978 has in its Functions and Powers: 17 (c) To encourage and promote the proper maintenance of films in archives (d) To encourage and promote, for the benefit of the New Zealand film industry, the study and appreciation of films and film making 19 (2) (c) With the consent of the Minister of Finance (may) establish endowments or create trusts … and appoint trustees in respect of such trusts (NFSA collection NZFA FD9/4/71 Dennis, 1985).

Dennis was disappointed that the Act did not directly charge the Film Commission with responsibility to *establish* a film archive, but only to "encourage and promote" proper maintenance of films (Dennis in Pivac & Dennis, 2000). Since 1977 Dennis had been involved with Clive Sowry (at that time the National Film Unit archivist) and others in a senior working group examining the need for a Film Archive. This group included Judy Holbrook (then Chief Archivist of the National Archive), Frank Mahoney, Education Department (senior to George Peart, Head of the National Film Library) and representatives from the Interim Film Commission (Dennis in Pivac & Dennis, 2000). Furthermore, in anticipation of the NZFC establishment, the newly founded "Archives and Records Association Film Archives Committee [ARANZ] recommended that the New Zealand Film Commission when it was established, have the creation of the NZFA as one of its statutory responsibilities" (NFSA collection NZFA FD9/4/71

Dennis, 1985). Dennis and Sowry were also involved with the ARANZ committee. ARANZ's more strongly worded proposal would have ensured ongoing and guaranteed funding was available to a stand alone film archive. Instead, it has been vulnerable to the whims of various chairs and government officials who at times have waxed and waned in their enthusiasm for "the proper maintenance of films in archives" (Horrocks et al., 2009).[47]

Ostensibly, there was already a repository for New Zealand film; the National Library's Film Library (NFL). This made it problematic to suggest a completely separate and new archive be created even though the NFL was apparently doing very little at this stage (Dennis in Pivac & Dennis, 2000). Dennis and Sowry sought to publicise the moribund state of the National Film Library. By 1979 they had an intimate knowledge of the collection of nitrate film which was stored in munitions bunkers at the Army Barracks outside Wellington at Shelly Bay (Davy & Pivac, 2008 p.87).[48] Dennis and Sowry were able to contribute to a public campaign which included filmmakers and scholars who recognised the need for a proactive film archive, such as those in other countries, to develop concurrently with the Film Commission.

In a repeat of his earlier screenings of films, as described previously by Bill Gosden, Dennis and Clive Sowry presented a slide show and talk for anyone interested in listening to the story of the plight of the country's historic films. For example, Roger Horrocks reviewed the 33rd Annual Conference of the New Zealand Federation of Films Societies held in Napier in April 1979, where Federation President David Gascoigne lamented the loss of so many films by NZ filmmaker Rudall Hayward from the time of his "community comedies" such as *Natalie of Napier* or *Patsy of Palmerston*. He also discussed the loss of the "Colossal Historical Film Classic *The Birth of New Zealand* shot in 1922 by Harrington Reynolds" (Horrocks, 1979). Horrocks quoted Dennis & Sowry – "We have lost, probably irrevocably, between 12 and 15 of our New Zealand feature films, which is more than have been produced here in the last 20 years" (Horrocks 1979a). The article described how the work of earlier film librarians, Walter Harris and Ray Hayes, had been resumed by Dennis, who had been "hired by the NFL under the Government's temporary employment programme". He was joined by Sowry, a

---

47   Having said this, even government funding is not guaranteed. For a review of the ongoing funding challenges for the NZFA see this report accessible online at: www.parliament.nz/resource/0000147599.

48   Cellulose nitrate film was the earliest film stock and was highly flammable. It was often burned by studios or sold as waste and made into combs or belts by other companies (Smither & Catherine, 2002) but in New Zealand government film that was saved was kept in bunkers in case of fire. There were also local collectors of commercial films on nitrate stock who gradually began to deposit these in the NZFA during the 1980s (Dennis in Alley & Dennis, 2002).

"member of the [Film Society] federations' working committee".[49] They had "been sorting out a million metres of old nitrate film owned by the NFU and held in an ammunition store at Shelly Bay in Wellington. That done, they began working on Hayward's epic 1925 production *Rewi's Last Stand* which they showed the conference, along with NZ's oldest film, 1901 Salvation Army footage of the Duke and Duchess of Cornwall and York visiting Rotorua" (Horrocks 1979a).

Dennis said later that *The Birth of New Zealand* was their "showcase" for publicising the loss of NZ film culture as it was by then nearly completely destroyed. The title had useful overt nationalist or at least patriotic connotations with which to argue the terrible loss of NZ film culture. Its rotting nitrate was photographed and these images were shared widely (Dennis in Pivac & Dennis, 2000). Gascoigne, Horrocks, Dennis and Sowry were quite deliberately emphasising the link to a loss of "national culture" which these films represented. By doing so they hoped to encourage both public and governmental support for a NZ film archive. Dennis' background in theatre had made him acutely aware of the performance element to what he was doing and his interest in the "personal" NZ films and stories that motivated him (Dennis in Pivac & Dennis, 2000).

The struggle to establish the Film Archive

Dennis and Sowry's publicity campaign to establish a national film archive was not appreciated by the head of the National Film Library, George Peart who, unlike previous librarians Walter Harris and Ray Hayes did not have a strong relationship with the Federation of Film Societies, nor did he seem to have an appreciation of the film culture developing in New Zealand. Dennis said George Peart "was a pig really … He was boastful, and pompous, and he was very pleased with himself about the archive that they had at the National Film Library, which was in those days in Kent Terrace in Kent House" (Pivac & Dennis, 2000). Bill Gosden, though more diplomatic in his description, agreed George Peart's style was less collegial. Gosden remembered – "The National Film Library serviced our [Federation of Film Society] bookings and attended to the physical distribu-

---

49   In 1942 Walter Harris, a teacher who had used photo stills and films to teach geography with great effectiveness became head of the National Film Library under the auspices of the Education Department (Sigley, 2003 p.206). He began actively collecting films (funding permitting). Concurrently the National Film Unit (founded in 1941) at Miramar had begun producing weekly 35 and 16mm films of New Zealand wartime activity, all of which required an archive space in which to store them (Sigley, 2003 p.207). Harris hired Ray Hayes who had worked in the New Zealand Army Film Unit (Sigley, 2003, pp.208, 209).

tion of the films. I can't remember what the financial arrangement was but you know, it was a tacit governmental condoning of the activities of the Film Society in a way. Before George Peart [became Director of the National Film Library] I think Walter Harris had a foot in both the Film Society and Education side of things. George Peart's approach was, um, not quite as holistic shall we say" (Personal correspondence, B. Gosden op.cit.). In later years, part of Dennis' frustration with George Peart was due to his close relationship with early New Zealand filmmakers Rudall and Ramai Hayward. Peart assured the Haywards he was working assiduously to look after their films, but apparently this was not the case. Dennis regretted the fact that he never succeeded in his aim during his directorship to have the Hayward films rehoused at the NZFA (Dennis in Pivac & Dennis, 2000).

As described in the 1979 Horrocks article, Dennis and Sowry had quickly "developed really a spectacularly good public campaign of drawing people into what a Film Archive was and … the dramas and tragedies of what we were confronted with. It wasn't especially carefully designed to begin with, it was just wide open to promote the fact that we had a cultural disaster on our hands, and that initially the only thing that would prevent that disaster … was getting some money" (Dennis in Pivac & Dennis, 2000). As previously noted Dennis and Sowry began to invite film and television crews to view the rotting and damaged nitrate film at Shelly Bay in an effort to spur public opinion into supporting the creation of a Film Archive. Although this did work, it caused resentment from some government officials (Dennis in Pivac & Dennis, 2000). Dennis' initiative echoed his father's earlier decision to take a schoolhouse and move it to The Hermitage so that his children and those of the surrounding areas could have a space in which to learn. The sentiment was a good one, but by not seeking permission he potentially created an issue. In Lawrie's case it was dealt with by offering a free weekend at the hotel to the complainant. Issues for Dennis were not always so easily rectified. He said later that the Archive had become "too successful" causing jealousy (Dennis in Alley & Dennis, 2002).

Dennis felt it was important for NZ that an Archive should be formed, and to that end spent a year and a half in Europe and North America largely self-funded, learning the art of film archiving. This experience was hugely influential and through it he not only learned the skills of film archiving unknown to anyone else in the country apart from Clive Sowry, but made networks, friends and contacts which he would enjoy for the rest of his life (Dennis in Pivac & Dennis, 2000).[50] Like his mother Pat, who sent and received hundreds of Christmas cards a year, (Personal correspondence, D. Young op.cit.) Dennis was to send postcards whenever he travelled, to a huge number of friends and acquaintances which were remembered during interviews for this research (For example; Personal correspondence, M. McKinnon 23/11/09; S. Bartel 03/12/09).[51] Lindsay Shelton notably recalled the postcards Dennis sent while on his 1979/1980 archive tour which simply said, "Where is the Film Archive?" Shelton was bemused at the time, but said it was an effective reminder that Dennis had high expectations that while he was gone there were developments occurring which would result in a film archive being established (Shelton, 2002). Annie Collins remarked that the postcards, often with only one or two words on them reminded the recipient of how much they were loved by Dennis (Personal correspondence, A. Collins op.cit.)

Dennis' study trip is worth considering in some detail for the connections he made and his experiences which he discussed for the rest of his life. The fact that he undertook such an extensive study trip with no guarantee of a job at the end of it is characteristic of his passionate and determined style. Europe and the United States were both important destinations for him as they were associated with some of his favourite films, but also because the first film archives in the world were established there (FIAF, 2002). He ensured he attended the Cannes and Berlin Film Festivals as well as visiting film archives, film directors and film exhibition spaces (ATL PP JD 9114–08 Dennis). Dennis was guided in his choice of destinations by a report written by Ray Edmondson, a film archivist at the National Library in Australia at Canberra. Edmondson's report of a trip to North America and Europe and the learnings he had gleaned were taken to heart by Clive Sowry and shared with Dennis (Dennis in Pivac & Dennis, 2000).

Although Dennis did receive a Queen Elizabeth II Arts Council grant it was for a sum which did not cover all his expenses, and therefore much of the trip was funded by Dennis' parents who helped him during a financially difficult period where he had little income. He did receive small amounts from the New Zealand Film Commission while he was away to support his travel and training (Dennis in Pivac & Dennis, 2000). There was no guarantee of a job when he returned to

---

50   The National Film Unit paid for Sowry to work at the British Film Institute for a short period in 1979 to become trained in film repair, and Dennis soon followed, using a small Queen Elizabeth II Arts Council grant (Dennis in Pivac & Dennis, 2000). Within the personal papers collected at the NZFA are notebooks with meticulous notes taken during his training. Jane Paul, a film repairer for the NZFA, confirmed that Dennis' technical film archiving knowledge was sophisticated (Personal correspondence, J. Paul 03/02/11).

51   Simon Dennis and Susan Bartel both have large collections of Dennis' postcards at their homes (Personal correspondence, S.Dennis., Bartel, S. op.cit).

New Zealand, as his six months on a government work scheme had ended.[52] Ferry Hendriks travelled with Dennis throughout this time, and remembered Dennis weighing up the decision to either attend a movie or eat lunch because he could not afford both. The decision to attend the film was characteristic of Dennis for the rest of his life – films were his priority. Hendriks laughed when he recalled he would have preferred a wiener schnitzel (Personal correspondence, F. Hendriks 28/11/09).

Elaine Burrows, a staff member from the British Film Institute also remembered Dennis' poverty when she reflected on his choice of lunches, which were often rhubarb and custard "and you suddenly think, hang on, I should have offered to buy lunch … it never struck me that someone who's sent on an official mission wasn't properly paid" (Personal correspondence, E. Burrows 08/07/10). It was not an "official mission", although it would have been understandable if Dennis presented it as such. Having received Queen Elizabeth II Arts Council funding he could say he had government support to pursue training in film archives. At this time the British Film Institute staff arranged for Dennis to work at the National Film Theatre next door to earn money (Dennis in Pivac & Dennis, 2000). Dennis remembered the poverty of the time with humour, and described living on "banana, cream cheese and honey sandwiches … I remember before Lindsay [Shelton] left just emptying him of every bit of spare British currency he had, to keep me going a bit longer" (Dennis in Pivac & Dennis, 2000).

Although without much ready money, Dennis was excellent at seeking out well-known people associated with films and archives and he was most fortunate that Mary Meerson, partner of Henri Langlois, the flamboyant founder of the first Film Archive in the world, the Paris Cinémathèque (Cinémathèque Française) met with him while on his study tour.[53,54] She was an eccentric woman but had contacts all over the world and would introduce him via phone calls to

---

52   In a letter to his parents Dennis says "I've been workin and workin, I'm very good at it all but must say I'm getting a bit pissed off not knowing (sorry Mum wash my mouth) just what to expect from NZ – 're getting an archive they could actually let me know, tell me what is in it for me and say if they need me home sooner or later" [all me's are circled] (ATL PP JD 9114–08 Combined Ferry and JD letter, Ferry writing on one side and JD on the other dated 15/1/80).

53   Film aficianadoes were always very impressed that Dennis had met Mary Meerson, Kenneth Anger, and also silent movie star Lillian Gish. As Ferry Hendriks described it: "He had a knack for finding out famous people, where they were …" Lillian Gish was one of his favourite silent film stars, and in the mid 1970s she was travelling on a cruise ship in Wellington: "He knew she was on the cruise ship, and … [she] would not leave the ship, so he organized to meet her and I thought that showed a level of initiative that a lot of people do not have. He was determined, she was an old star from the past, and in a lot of movies he was very fond of" (Personal correspondence, F. Hendriks 28/11/09).

54   Langlois had recently died.

people he wanted to visit.[55] Dennis was to say that Mary Meerson was an inspiration because she taught him that films were "living objects" and needed to be in front of an audience to be "alive" (Dennis in Alley & Dennis, 2002). This alludes to the competing demands of preservation versus presentation of films. The debate has been long running and is well known to film archivists and others involved in the industry. The issue is particularly urgent with film stock which is highly flammable (cellulose nitrate) and subject to degradation when handled and fed through a projector (Cherchi Usai, 2001).

The competing positions were exemplified by the supposed feud between Meerson's partner Henri Langlois and Ernest Lindgren who ran the British Film Institute (Kula, 2002). Lindgren would not screen a film unless he had a preservation copy, but budgets were often tight and it was not always possible to make one. Under Lindgren's directorship a film could not be screened without a preservation copy. Langlois however insisted that films were like "turkish rugs" and improved with wear and therefore always played them, even if he only had a single nitrate copy (Kula, 2002). Part of this discourse were "heroic" stories of the students of the 1968 cultural revolution in Paris calling for Langlois to be reinstated after he had been made to resign from the Cinémathèque (Personal correspondence, E. Burrows op.cit.).[56] Dennis, like all Western trained film archivists knew these stories and the legendary lengths early film archivists had gone to in order to preserve and present early films. In the late 1970s he was confident that he could see how the NZFA could compromise between the two extremes of Langlois and Lindgren. Dennis thought very carefully about his film and archiving heroes and how they could influence the Film Archive he wanted to create.[57] He saw the endeavour as a very personal one because he cared so much

---

55 Dennis wrote to his parents from Cannes Film Festival: "Yes I saw Mary Meerson several times and had totally extraordinary times with her as usual. We went out to some friends of hers for supper one night tho she remained in the van for hers. …" (ATL MS Papers JD Letters to his parents 9114–08 letter dated 15 May 1980).

56 "The firing sparked protests from Parisian film students, from others among Paris' half-million strong student community who frequented the Cinematheque to view the films, and from such French film luminaries as Francois Truffaut and Jean Paul Belmondo. The French nouvelle vague directors had learned about the movies at the Cinematheque, and they vocally supported Langlois. French directors Chabrol, Demy, Godard, and Truffaut proudly proclaimed themselves as 'children of the Cinémathèque.' The turmoil helped trigger the student riots of May 1968. Malraux was forced to back down, and Langlois was reinstated" (Retrieved on 4th October 2013 from http://www.imdb.com/name/nm0486581/bio?ref_=nm_ov_bio_sm.)

57 The Paris Cinémathèque and BFI were founding members of FIAF under Langlois and Lindgren. FIAF's mission statement: "Film archives and film archivists are the guardians of the world's moving image heritage. It is their responsibility to protect that heritage and to pass it on to posterity in the best possible condition and as the truest possible representation of the work of its creators … Film archives recognise that their primary commitment is to preserve the materials in their care, and – provided always that such activity will not compromise this commitment – to make them permanently available for research, study and public screening" (FIAF, 2002). This assertion of the primary responsibility of preservation over presentation was quite deliberately inserted in an effort to protect archivists from the pressure to present films even if there is no preservation print available due to lack of resources which was a common issue (Personal correspondence, E. Burrows 08/07/10).

for the films he loved, and he certainly modelled the Archive after those who he felt had been successful in their work (Dennis in Pivac & Dennis, 2000).

On this late 70s/early 80s study tour Dennis also met with ex-patriate NZ kinetic artist, filmmaker and sculptor, Len Lye. By then Lye had been brought to the attention of New Zealanders interested in the arts as an early artistic "ancestor" and there was discussion about bringing his films and sculptures back to New Zealand to be housed at the Govett Brewster Art Gallery (whose first director was John Maynard with whom Dennis had a good relationship. The second director was Dennis' Uncle Ron O'Reilly). In a 1979 letter to his parents Dennis described meeting Lye – "He is a wonderful old man and Anne his wife equally lovely. He told me he had leukaemia but referred to it as the 'sissy kind' that old people get. The studio had some amazing paintings and new sculptures he showed me through and we all talked for hours" (ATL PP JD 9114–08). Dennis and Lye had corresponded briefly before his trip to New York, and in a letter Dennis was to quote for the rest of his life, Lye asked if the archive would "support creativity". This idea was very important to Dennis and gradually infused his work with the recognition that although the day to day business of an archive could at times be monotonous, it was also a rich source of creativity.

In Dennis' letter about Lye, he went on to say as if incidentally, "Oh – I've been accepted for an archive summer school in East Berlin in August – held every 2 years only 25 people. It's getting a bit serious all this archiving now which is a drag …" (ATL PP JD 9114–08). The FIAF Summer School in 1979 was to be a very important event for Dennis, and although he said the seriousness of the archiving was "a drag" it's clear that he was most enthusiastic about working with film. Dennis' reference to archiving being tiresome is a reminder that at this time he was only 26 years old and was taking on a great responsibility at a very young age. His passion was film, as evidenced by the efforts he took to meet the early film stars and contemporary filmmakers and archivists he admired. In order to work with it he had found a niche – the films of New Zealand needed preserving, and he was going to run the archive which performed that function.

The Film Archive is founded

Dennis and Hendriks returned to Wellington in 1980 and Dennis went back on the "dole" (unemployment benefit) which "was a bit dispiriting" (Dennis in Pivac & Dennis, 2000), but eventually the Trust Deed for the Film Archive was written under the Charitable Trusts Act as it had become clear from the various committee meetings that no single government department was willing to wholly commit to fund, resource and house the Film Archive. This meant that it would stand outside the umbrella of any government department.

> In late 1980, the Film Commission drew up a Trust Deed ... which, subscribed to by representatives of the Commission, National Archives, the Education Department, the Broadcasting Corporation, the Federation of Film Societies and the National Film Unit, enabled in March 1981, The NZFA to be established as an autonomous Charitable Trust. Later the Minister for the Arts appointed a representative to the Board as well. In the Deed, the aims and objectives are detailed as:
>
> 1. To collect, preserve and catalogue film materials;
> 2. To provide premises and facilities for preserving, storing, consulting, viewing and displaying film materials;
> 3. To provide access to material held by the Archive consistent with overriding preservation and copyright requirements
> 4. To issue publications, screen archives films and by similar means encourage and promote public interest and awareness in film materials, film history and culture, preservation matters and film archives generally.
> (NFSA collection NZFA FD9/4/71 Dennis, 1985).

The Trust Deed quite deliberately echoed North American and European Film Archive policy in relation to the importance of preservation. Like all FIAF (International Federation of Film Archives) accredited institutions, it also committed to the promotion of film materials and culture. Film archives, unlike libraries which only collect published materials, collect all paraphernalia published or unpublished which is associated with film including sound tracks, stills, designs, posters, costume, slides and promotional, critical and historical materials and film equipment (NFSA collection NZFA FD9/4/71 op.cit). This means they are extremely resource intensive as they hold multiple formats of materials, all of which have different preservation requirements (and machines which can project each type of format must also be maintained). Film archives are therefore extremely expensive to run, and this is presumably a reason why no government department was willing to take full responsibility for its funding and resourcing.

The 1970s and early 1980s Film Archive working party members were to largely become the first board of the NZFA. They were John O'Shea (representing the Minister for the Arts), "Judith Hornabrook (Chief Archivist)'[58], Doug Eckhoff[59]

---

58 This quote is from Ron Ritchie. He has misremembered the name "Judith Hornabrook" who was Judith (Judy) Holbrook, Acting Chief Archivist of the National Archives. By the time the Trust Deed was signed Ray Grover had taken over the Chief Archivist position (Personal correspondence J. Komik & P. Stuart 02/02/11).

59 Eckhoff would sit on the Board for the next thirty years (Personal correspondence, D. Eckhoff 09/06/10).

(National Film Unit), Frank Mahoney (Education Department), Ken White (Broadcasting Corporation), Ron Ritchie[60], David Fowler[61] and also Lindsay Shelton (New Zealand Film Commission)" (Pivac, 2005 p.4). Fowler was to be the first Chair of the NZFA Board and Dennis said that he was crucial – "There was no question, I couldn't have done it without him and I wouldn't have wanted to ... he was a kind of wonderful, generous person who adored film and loved all range of cinema" (Dennis in Pivac & Dennis, 2000).

David Fowler was indeed enthusiastic about the Archive and loved to look through the National Archive duplicate collection stills Dennis had brought back in a tea chest from London. When an early cache of posters was retrieved from the Majestic Theatre, Fowler was the first to suggest the Archive exhibit them immediately (Dennis in Pivac & Dennis, 2000). Dennis particularly notes that Fowler was "wonderful" and "generous". These are traits he appreciated and the fact that Fowler "adored film" meant that Dennis felt close to him as Fowler too took film "personally". The passion Dennis himself felt always meant that others who also "adored" film would be prioritised in his world over those who did not.

Dennis was initially disappointed that the Archive was not to be organized under the wing of a government department, largely because funding would have been guaranteed through that mechanism. However, in later years he came to believe it was to their advantage to stand independent from government because they were able to be more flexible and responsive than a state institution (Dennis in Pivac & Dennis, 2000). In its first year the Archive shared offices with the Federation of Film Societies in "cramped conditions". In its first twenty months its funding was limited and there was only one full time staff member, Jonathan Dennis. A part time film repairer and assistant were then employed.[62] Dennis

---

60   "b. 15/10/1924 – d.24/10/2007 Ron Ritchie's commitment to film culture began in the 1940s when he was an early committee member of the newly-formed Wellington Film Society and the New Zealand Federation of Film Societies. This began an involvement which continued for more than four decades, in the roles of Treasurer, President and Secretary. Ritchie represented the film society movement at the 1980 planning meetings which established the Film Archive, and followed on as the Film Societies' representative and a founding member of the Archive Board. He continued as a most active and thorough Trustee until 1999 after which time he continued to serve as a Convocation member. Ritchie also served as the Film Archive's first Treasurer" (NZFA Newsreel No 58 Retrieved on 3rd September 2013 http://www.filmarchive.org.nz/projects/newsreel/newsreel-58-summer-2007–08/.)

61   Due to heart trouble David Fowler had stepped down as head of the National Film Unit and was replaced by Doug (Douglas) Eckhoff (Personal correspondence, D. Eckhoff op.cit.).

62   In the early years since the only other trained film archivist in the country was Clive Sowry, Dennis looked for nimble fingered people to work at the Archive. He had hired a cake decorator but she became sick. The next employee was Tony Concannon who was a violinist. When he was playing with the orchestra he would take photos of the cinemas for the Archive. Colin Feldwick, was a "darling of a man" who had worked as a film projectionist. He became the second employee. Dennis described him as "loving and generous". Wendy Osbourne, who had worked at TVNZ and been on a working party in the 1970s regarding the NZFA was employed as "a great film repairer" as was Ann Manchester who had worked as an editor at the Film Unit (Dennis in Pivac & Dennis, 2000). Later employees during the 1980s were Paul Sakey, Bronwyn Taylor and Jane Paul who was hired part time in 1986. She described the early staff as "a network of friends" (Personal correspondence, J. Paul 03/02/11).

explained in a 1985 report that funding had always been a challenge – "despite the involvement at Board level of several State enterprises, the Archive is not a Government body, and has no guaranteed sources of finance …" (NFSA collection NZFA FD9/4/71 Dennis, 1985).

Allan Highet, Minister of the Arts gave the Film Archive a series of "one off, never to be repeated" $100,000 grants. Dennis regarded Hyatt, Peter Tapsell and Michael Basset as three key ministers.[63],[64] He was closest to Peter Tapsell because the NZFA staff would often meet with him at hui (gatherings). "Witarina [Harris, first kaumātua of the NZFA] was very clear that it was useful to sleep with your minister on a marae. Peter Tapsell would have his mattress, and I would have mine, and Witarina would be next to that. So it helps to discuss your funding problems with your minister while you're having a shower … *(laughter)*" (Dennis in Pivac & Dennis, 2000). With Harris' help, Dennis began to understand the importance of "kanohi ki te kanohi" or face to face interactions as Ngahuia Te Awekotuku described them in her argument for kaupapa Māori practice (Te Awekotuku, 1991).

By 1985 the NZFA collection consisted of 6,000 stills from the National Film Archive in London, stills from the Museum of Modern Art in New York, stills for approximately 100 NZ titles, 3,000 film advertising posters including about 40 NZ titles, many of these brought back from Dennis' study tour, and "the beginnings of a major film-book reference library".[65] The Archive had moved to premises in the centre of Wellington where they had been able to open a "Museum of Cinema" space. This "Museum" included NZ and overseas film materials including "photographs, programmes and posters … restored projection and camera equipment." There was also a permanent exhibition related to "pioneer NZ born experimental filmmaker Len Lye". According to Dennis, the purpose of this museum was "to actively encourage the public to take an interest in the

---

63　"Sir Peter Tapsell, the first Maori Speaker of the House … was born and raised in Rotorua. He entered Parliament as a Labour MP in the 1981 election following a career as an orthopaedic surgeon. He remained an MP until 1996, serving as Internal Affairs Minister, Arts Minister, Police Minister and Defence Minister at various stages of his career" (Retrieved 01/06/13 http://tvnz.co.nz/national-news/former-house-speaker-sir-peter-tapsell-passes-away-4820053.)

64　Michael Bassett has a PhD in history and is a historian. Between 1987 and 1990 he was Minister of Internal Affairs, Local Government, Civil Defence and Arts and Culture. He was Chairman of the New Zealand Lottery Grants Board and of the 1990 Commission that commemorated the 150th anniversary of the signing of the Treaty of Waitangi (Retrieved 05/06/12 http://www.michaelbassett.co.nz/biography.htm.)

65　This library was started with Dennis' personal book collection and continued to be added to by him over the time he was at the Archive (NZFA PP Box 11). When he left there was a correspondence with the NZFA Board in which they agreed to purchase the books from him. Eventually this Library was to be named *The Jonathan Dennis Reference Library*. One interview subject claimed with glee and much laughter that Dennis stole many of the early books he collected because he had no money to buy them but felt it was imperative he should own them (Personal correspondence, D. Young op.cit.).

work of the Archive and the collections it holds … Access by the public to their film culture and heritage is the main thrust of the NZFA in the future" (Dennis, 1985).

This modest exhibition space and the collection of film stills, posters, films and paraphernalia was the culmination of the work of many men and women dedicated to the exhibition of film in NZ over a period of nearly a century, including Walter Harris, Ray Hayes, the Arts Conference 1970 delegates, Bill Sheat, John O'Shea, Roger Horrocks, Clive Sowry and many others. However, Diane Pivac, New Zealand film archivist, has stated that "the archive would never have happened at that time without Jonathan" (Personal correspondence, D. Pivac 26/11/09). This remark was echoed by many interviewees for this research who, if intimate with the political landscape at the time knew that the Government was not willing to commit to long term funding for a Film Archive (Personal correspondence, L. Shelton 07/12/09; B. Sheat 31/01/11). It was clear to all interviewees that Dennis' self-proclaimed "missionary zeal" (Fyfe & Dennis, 2001) for film and his enthusiastic engagement with audiences was the driving force behind the Archive in its first ten years (Personal correspondence, R. Horrocks 21/10/08; E. Alley op.cit).

By the time Dennis wrote the 1985 report in which he stated – "Access by the public to their film culture and heritage is the main thrust of the NZFA in the future", he was signalling an emphasis on taking films out to the public wherever they may be; an approach influenced by Witarina Harris, the star of a 1929 film which Dennis and the Archive had recovered, and this approach would dominate the second half of the 1980s at the NZFA. Dennis' passion for films linked to an interest in "national culture" and what that might mean, was to drive the Archive towards a bicultural model through the 1980s and see the Archive exhibit at NZ Film Festivals where Dennis became a guest curator each year. He also screened films at hui [gatherings], on marae [traditional iwi meeting spaces] all over the country, at national and international film exhibitions and, in 1989, at the largest ever exhibition of New Zealand film *Te Ao Marama* in Torino, Italy. During the 1970s and early 1980s period there had been a dearth of representation of indigenous experience through the media of film and certainly a lack of representation by Māori in filmmaking and film archiving. "Biculturalism" was beginning to become a dominant discourse in NZ public life in the 1980s period, and the NZFA which was engaging with Māori people all over the country was inevitably to become part of that lively debate. How this came about, and Witarina Harris' enormous contribution are described in the following chapters.

Jonathan Spencer Dennis
27th September 1953 – 25th January 2002

Left:
Jonathan
Dennis as a
young boy.

Right:
Jonathan
Dennis and
Santa Claus.

Centre right:
Laurence
(Lawrie)
Dennis with
Pat (Patricia)
Dennis
at The
Hermitage
1959

Right: Fergus
MacGillivray
(left),
Jonathan
Dennis,
Ferdinand
(Ferry)
Hendriks
(standing).

Above: *Tim and Jonathan Dennis at Tasman Glacier, South Island, New Zealand.*

Below: *Pat Dennis holding Jonathan Dennis with Timothy (Tim) at her feet, 1954.*

Above: *Jonathan Dennis (left) with Harry Aires' children and others, The Hermitage, Mt Cook, South Island.*

Below: *Jonathan Dennis 1975, during Amamus Theatre troupe visit to the International Student Festival where the play 'Gallipoli' was performed, Poland.*

Above: *Paolo Cherchi-Usai, Jonathan Dennis, Megan Labrum, 1992.*

Below: *Dame Catherine Tizard presents the Queen's Service Medal to Jonathan, 1991, Wellington, New Zealand.*
Bottom left: *Irihapeti Ramsden (left), Patricia Grace and Jonathan Dennis, 2001, book launch, Ngāti Pōneke Young Māori Club (The Silent Migration book launch), Wellington.*
Bottom right: *Susan Bartel and Jonathan Dennis.*

Left:
*Bridget Ikin
and Jonathan
Dennis in
Bridget and
John
Maynard's
backyard –
Surry Hills,
Sydney
Australia
2000.*

Right:
*Elizabeth Alley and Jonathan Dennis on the
occasion of the interview, late 2001,
14 Edge Hill, Mt Victoria, Wellington.*

Lower right:
*Jonathan Dennis, Rāhiri Wharerau
and Witarina Harris, 14 Edge Hill, Wellington.*

Below:
*Jonathan Dennis on the occasion of the award of
his Queens Service Medal, 1991, with Annie
Collins and Witarina Harris.*

Right:
Jonathan and Simon Dennis, Ahipara Beach, Northland New Zealand December 2001.

Below right, centre:
Gareth Watkins (left), Elizabeth Alley, Jonathan Dennis with 'Paul to Hebrews' painting by Colin McCahon

Lower left:
Sharon Dell, Jonathan Dennis weaving.

Lower right:
Jonathan Dennis, Simon Dennis, Tim Dennis and friend, Mt Cook in front of planes, returning to school.

Above: *Jonathan Dennis with fake gun,
Amamus Theatre Company performance 1970s.*
Above top: *Jonathan Dennis New Zealand
Film Archive 1980s.*
Above right lower: *Simon, Pat, Jonathan,
Witarina Harris, Kirsten Dennis and Lawrie,
on the occasion of Jonathan receiving the Queens
Service Medal, 1991*
Below left: *Jonathan Dennis.*
Below right: *Jonathan, Witarina Harris,
Kirsten Dennis at Te Papaiouru Marae,
Ohinemutu, Rotorua.*

Above:
Jonathan Dennis' back garden at 14 Edge Hill, Mt Victoria, Wellington by Lorraine Tarrant.

Left:
John and Cormy O'Shea, Annie Collins and Jonathan Dennis at Wadestown in the 1990s.

Right:
Lawrie and Jonathan in the wild lupins at Mt Cook, South Island, New Zealand.

Chapter 4

Biculturalism and the NZFA

D uring the late 1970s and 1980s period in which Dennis was locating and collecting film materials, social and political shifts were occurring in NZ. Jonathan Dennis was one figure in a wider landscape, and the previous chapter has described his personal experience as well as the development of the Film Commission and Film Archive. We now move to the parallel macro-social movements and cultural shifts which meant indigenous peoples began to speak more openly about their experiences and concerns. This chapter focusses on the origins of material which is held by the NZFA, which includes significant early ethnographic films featuring various iwi and also early feature films. Given the nature of these materials, it was inevitable that the impact of the bicultural discussion would be felt in Dennis' fledgling institution. The Archive had been established with a strong influence from the European and North American archives Dennis had visited during his study trip. But in the mid 1980s, indigenous people suggested the Archive needed to acknowledge its geographical and cultural position in the South Pacific. The understanding of the definition of Māori materials of the archive as taonga became particularly significant during the 1970s and 1980s and is discussed here in some detail.

This chapter situates film archiving in relation to wider museum and art gallery practice. It considers the social and political pressures which resulted in legislative changes which would impact on the heritage sector. Conal McCarthy's definition of "museums" is utilised here. He includes: "museums of history, science, war and transport, art galleries, contemporary art spaces and many organisations with elements of libraries, archives, heritage and tourism" (McCarthy, 2011 p.15). Ideas of Māori and other indigenous academics, philosophers and artists are employed concomitantly with continental philosopher Pierre Bourdieu's analysis of power structures in institutions. Bourdieu's work offers a European philosophical lens through which to consider the NZFA in relation to a contestation between "actors" in a "field" (Pierre Bourdieu, 1986). By this he refers to people working within and outside an institution and their interactions based on their own backgrounds and understandings. Bourdieu's analysis of the negotiation of social, economic, political and cultural capital in institutions is valuable as a perspective to think through relationships at this time (Bennett et al., 2013 p.132) but it has its limitations in the New Zealand context, particularly because indigenous peoples were never part of Bourdieu's perspective. Bennett et al. argue that "Bourdieu's empirical concerns, after his Algerian studies, focused resolutely on French issues and materials" (Bennett et al., 2013 p.130).[66] His conception of the cultural field depicts social actors struggling for power within autonomous spheres of prescribed values and regulative principles (Kloot, 2009 p.471). Bourdieu's notion of the field in which cultural capital dominates is unsettled by the idea that his European sense of cultural capital is redefined by Māori whose doxa (beliefs in the game and its rules) and habitus (upbringing and history) may be radically different to Pākehā, which in turn may be dissimilar to European based peoples.

Avril Bell has argued in the NZ context that museum exhibitions, such as those at the state museum Te Papa o Tongarewa, function to present biculturalism as an "achieved state" where settlers and indigenous peoples are equals who share power (Bell, 2006 p.263). "Biculturalism" as it was understood in the 1980s was an attempt towards Māori and Pākehā partnership by way of the Treaty of Waitangi, which arguably set out the conditions under which power would be shared equally.[67] The term "biculturalism" is considered specifically as a concept in this chapter because during the 1980s when Dennis founded the NZFA it was, as McCarthy describes it, one of the three interweaving "prevailing discourses of the time – national identity, heritage and biculturalism" (McCarthy, 2011 p.53). What has been called State sponsored biculturalism (government legislative changes and movements within government departments) has functioned as a tool through which government has attempted to negotiate redress for historical wrongs enacted since colonisation. Redress was prompted by Māori calls for recognition and demands for a degree of autonomy (Bell, 2006).

In the 1970s various Māori rights activists were challenging institutional engagement with the materials of the museum, archive, library and art gallery. These

---

66 There are some examples of Bourdieu's work being employed within the context of Australia but less in New Zealand in the *Journal of Sociology* special edition entitled *Antipodean fields: Working with Bourdieu* (Bennett et al., 2013).

67 This is not to say this state was ever achieved. Much of the debate since that time has been related to interpretations of the Māori and Pākehā versions of the Treaty (Orange, 1987).

materials were seen as examples of how Pākehā re/constructed or erased indige-nous presence and forgot colonial oppression (Barclay, 2005; Tuhiwai Smith, 1999/2012). Those materials were insistent reminders of Māori presence and absence, with the *Te Maori* exhibition of the 1984–1987 period encouraging awareness among young urban Māori in particular about their heritage, what it was and where it was housed. The *Te Maori* exhibition of Māori carvings was opened at the Metropolitan Museum in New York in 1984 (McCarthy, C. 2011 p.50). *Te Maori: Te Hokinga Mai* (the return home) opened on 16 August 1986 at the National Museum in Wellington (McCarthy, C. 2011 p.53). The exhibi-tion was groundbreaking for presenting various iwi carvings as art rather than ethnographic object. It was popular in its tour of the United States, but drew blockbuster crowds in NZ upon its return. It changed the museum and art gallery approach to Māori materials (Simmons, D.R, 1994). This burgeoning awareness brought new challenges to the cultural heritage sector because Māori began to question Pākehā rights to manage their materials housed in institutions (McCarthy, 2011 p.78).

The cultural heritage sector of any country is entangled with issues of sovereignty, power and control. It is difficult to understand contemporary or past museum, archive, library or art gallery practice as "natural" and "ahistorical", or "free from the effects of power" (McCarthy, 2011 p.19). Following Bourdieu, Conal McCarthy explains – "Culture comprises social fields made up of values, beliefs, schemes and techniques. 'Cultural practices' are the ways in which things are done – the ways that individual social agents construct their worlds" (McCarthy, 2011 ibid).[68] When those "individual social agents" are brought together within an institution there may be competing values at play.

At the same time there were creative responses to social and cultural issues outside the institutions; new painting and sculpture, film and television broadcasts and also theatre works. These are included in this chapter in a discussion of the cultural heritage sector to signal a wider conversation with not only McCarthy's list of "museums, libraries, archives, art galleries" (McCarthy, 2011 p.15), but also works and people outside those fields. Many of these works, as we shall see, have become associated with Jonathan Dennis and the NZFA. For example Witarina Harris' film work would be presented by Dennis, and he would work with writers Patricia Grace (iwi affiliations Ngāti Toa, Te Āti Awa, and Ngāti Raukawa) and Irihapeti Ramsden (iwi affiliations Te Awe Awe o Rangitāne, Tikao o Ngāi Tahu)

---

68   McCarthy ends this paragraph with a footnote referring to Pierre Bourdieu's *Outline of a Theory of Practice*. Translated by Richard Nice. Cambridge: Cambridge University Press, 1977.

to collect Harris' oral history as part of the project to record the stories of the Ngāti Pōneke Young Māori Club which was eventually published as a book (Grace et al., 2001).

As the first kaumātua of the NZFA, Witarina Harris influenced and shaped Dennis and the progress of the NZFA in relation to Māori works housed and exhibited by the Archive. Witarina (Te Miriarangi Parewahaika) Harris nee Mitchell (b.1906 d.2007 iwi affiliation Ngāti Whakaue) officially became the kaumātua of the NZFA in the mid 1980s (Dennis, 1987) but she and Dennis met in 1982 (NZFA PP JD Box 19). As a young Māori woman she had been part of the "silent migration" of Māori to the cities from rural areas in the 1930s and 1940s (Grace et al., 2001). In her twenties she was selected by politician Āpirana Ngata to become his secretary in the capital city. She described that experience – "Coming from Rotorua, we were used to mixing with the Pākehā people. So when I came to Wellington and felt so lonely it was a surprise to me. This thing sort of built up within me – I thought, 'I want to see a Māori face!'" (Grace et al., 2001 p.32). This led her to become involved in the Ngāti Pōneke Young Māori Club, a group of Māori cultural performers.[69] In her later years she often spoke of her dedication to her Māori and Pākehā worlds (Harris in Alley & Dennis, 2002; Harris in Wells, 2004). She understood these worlds as separate, but they were both hers to enjoy and belong to. She was negotiating her own experience and understanding of biculturalism in her everyday life.

Harris' employer Āpirana (Turupa) Ngata (iwi affiliation Ngāti Porou) and his colleague Dr Peter (Henry Te Rangihiroa) Buck (iwi affiliation Ngāti Mutunga), both members of the Young Māori Party, were working to ensure Māori voices were heard nationally in the early part of the century within the national parliament.[70] Āpirana Ngata was using the term *biculturalism* by the 1940s to

---

69   Āpirana Ngata was patron to the Ngāti Pōneke Young Māori Club. Both the club and the man himself are today criticised in some circles as Ngata's general stance was seen as one which pushed Māori to be part of the Pākehā world (and therefore is understood by some as "assimilationist"). For example, he did not encourage the speaking of te reo Māori within the Young Māori Club except when performing songs, and although the language of the songs was te reo Māori, the tunes tended to be popular Pākehā numbers of the day (Paul Potiki quoted in Grace et al., 2001 p.95). Some also argue that his iwi background impacted on the manner in which he treated other iwi (Binney, 2009 p.7). But many people did feel the Club was important for bringing different iwi together and creating a sense of identity in the city. Scholar and author Irihapeti Ramsden was married at the Club in 1997 (NZFA PP JD Box 11 Ramsden, 1997). Ramsden said that she was the first of the urban born babies in the club, part of a new whānau, no longer based on kinship, as people came from all over the country to Wellington (I. Ramsden, quoted in authors notes section Grace et al., 2001).

70   "Although participation rates by Māori in universities have been extremely low, where Māori have participated they have been very successful as academics. Sir Āpirana Ngata, for example, trained at Canterbury University in the 1890s and as a Member of Parliament was one of the better educated members Māori or non-Māori. Sir Peter Buck trained as a medical anthropologist, taught at Yale University and was a foremost scholar of Pacific Anthropology" (Tuhiwai Smith, 1999/2012 p.133).

describe how Māori adapted to Pākehā systems, negotiating between two worlds (McCarthy, 2011 p.56). Harris was well aware of this negotiation as noted earlier, saying "my Māori world … my Pākehā world", an aphorism which continued to shape her throughout her life.[71] For Harris however her biculturalism was not related to power but to cultural experiences, experiences in the everyday.

Films of the tāngata whenua

Dennis and the NZFA curated a collection of early ethnographic and anthropological films and other archival materials in the mid to late 1980s for the *Te Maori* exhibition which travelled to the United States and subsequently returned home to an enthusiastic reception. He called the exhibition *He Pito Whakaatu A Nga Iwi Maori: Films of the Tāngata Whenua* (Dennis, J. 1987). Harris, Ngata and Buck were all involved in the making of those films which would become so important to the NZFA. Their experience is described below in order to provide the context for an analysis of the 1980s period in which these films were revisited, repurposed and recontextualised.

Although Harris' film experience was very different to the two scholar politicians, the films they were to be involved in were all recordings of representations of Māori peoples' cultural activities. The newest recording system on offer (cellulose nitrate film technology) was used nearly as soon as it was invented to record indigenous peoples, largely for non-indigenous audiences. These films would become part of a lively bicultural debate as they were preserved and presented by Dennis and the NZFA staff in the 1980s as people began to ask who had the right to exhibit, edit and control the material (Dell, 1987 p.3).

In the late 1910s and early 1920s Ngata and Buck had been involved in some of the expeditions of the then Dominion Museum in Wellington led by ethnologist Elsdon Best. These were recordings of trips to the Whanganui River, the East Coast and other locations to film Māori at iwi gatherings performing customary practices.[72] At that time, museums were largely controlled by Cambridge educated scholars who tended to collect Māori materials (including images) in order to "save them" because it was believed indigenous peoples would die out. This has come to be known as the "salvage paradigm" in museum studies (Clifford,

---

71 At Harris' funeral as is the Māori custom, photographs of her ancestors surrounded her casket – added to this was a full colour photo of Jonathan Dennis, "my Pākehā" as she called him (Harris in Fyfe & Dennis, 2001). Simon Dennis as the eldest living representative of the Dennis family was asked to sit with the Harris whānau at Witarina's funeral as a sign of the Harris' regard for Dennis and his whanau (Personal correspondence, S.Dennis 13/07/10).

72 A catalogue of the film exhibition by the NZFA of these works is appended to this study.

Seattle Bay Press/1987). The Polynesian Society published the papers which resulted from these filmed expeditions. Founded in 1892 and largely comprised of Pākehā scholars such as Elsdon Best (though Peter Buck was also a member), the Society represented an ethnographic attitude to indigenous peoples and materials. It was, however, perhaps an improvement on the common practice of settler societies of earlier times where local elites collected flora, fauna and indigenous materials (including mokomokai, shrunken heads) as curiosities which were displayed in glass cabinets with little attention to contemporary or past indigenous concerns or views (McCarthy, 2011 p.30). The fields of ethnology and anthropology treated indigenous materials as artefacts and evidence of cultural activity, and therefore organised and contextualised it as such. Best's work did not incorporate Māori perspectives often or appropriately. Writing of this period, McCarthy argues – "Despite the contact people like Best had with kaumātua, tribal elders ... there were no Māori staff working in museums, and few Māori visitors, and generally museums reflected the interests and perspectives of the dominant colonial culture" (McCarthy, 2011 p.33).

Best was involved in the films Ngata and Buck were to be associated with and therefore they have that ethnological feel to them which categorises Māori activity and presents practices such as kapa haka [a form of song and dance performance] as curiosities and representations of the "other". Cameraman James McDonald (1865–1935) originally proposed the first expedition of the Dominion Museum to film the Hui Aroha at Gisborne in 1919 as part of a proposed series of recordings.[73] Dennis wrote about this period in the catalogue for the 1980s exhibition – "The purpose of this and the three subsequent expeditions was to collect and record information on the crafts, activities, and tribal lore retained in the various areas. As well as the filming that took place, McDonald took many still photographs ... and made sound recordings" (Dennis, 1987 p.74).[74] In 1921 Dr Peter Buck accompanied the party on a trip to the Whanganui River, and in 1923 Āpirana Ngata, then Member of Parliament for Eastern Māori, supported an expedition to the iwi of the East Coast (Dennis, 1987 ibid.). Ngata and Buck's presence lent mana and prestige to these films and this implied that they were not exploitative of their subjects (Dell, 1987 p.3).[75] If this is the case, it is in

---

73 Dame Professor Anne Salmond is the great great granddaughter of James McDonald. She and Jonathan Dennis corresponded about his work and life at the time when the James McDonald films were presented by the NZFA (NZFA PP JD Box 11).

74 Sharon Dell and Jonathan Dennis curated an exhibition of these still photographs at the National Library in the 1990s (see appendices for further information).

75 There is debate about these issues – Michael King relates that politicians Maui Pomare and Peter Buck were later criticised for an attitude which suggested there was "no option but to become Pakeha" whereas Āpirana Ngata was perceived by some Pākehā as having a "chip" on his shoulder because he emphasised injustices experienced by Māori

contrast to the experiences of many indigenous peoples at this time. For example, Martin Nakata described a Cambridge anthropological expedition to the Torres Strait Islands in the late 1800s where there were no indigenous members of the party, nor does it appear that indigenous peoples were consulted about the expedition (Nakata, 2007). Nakata is critical of those who recorded images of his ancestors. He said their work helped develop the nascent discipline of Anthropology – "… in effect, the work of these scientists was … (to) … shape and inform disciplines". These reports are now "considered to contain data that provide accurate snapshots of a vanished culture". Nakata doubts that this is true (Nakata, 2007 p.28).

It is certainly true that the McDonald recordings informed research and the field of ethnological and anthropological work in NZ, although the evidence suggests that the films had few public screenings in the immediate years after they were recorded. Dell has noted that "information gathered has appeared in the articles of … Buck, Best, McDonald and Ngata" (Dell, 1987 p.4). Unlike the Torres Strait Islanders' experience Nakata described, there was apparently "considerable support among Māori leaders for ethnographic activities in Wellington in the 1920s, [including] the active research and collecting expeditions of Best at the Museum, the publishing undertaken by the Journal of the Polynesian Society and the Māori Board of Ethnological Research, and field trips such as the expedition up the Whanganui River in 1921" (McCarthy, 2011 p.35). Despite this support, few Māori themselves were able to take control of the recording process for many years to come.[76] In light of the lack of active iwi involvement in the making of these films there has been some reassessment of these recordings and other works by Buck, Best, McDonald and Ngata. For example, Judith Binney has described Elsdon Best's representations of the stories of one North Island iwi Ngāi Tūhoe (East Coast North Island) as being portrayals of "the epitome of the 'other', the 'untamed', unknowable human being: the savage living in a savage land" (Binney, 2009 p.31). Binney's description echoes Nakata's criticisms of non-indigenous

---

(King, 1985 p.10). Judith Binney describes Āpirana Ngata and James Carroll (Timi Kaara) as "the pre-eminent Māori members of Parliament" implementing the Liberal Government policies to open up land for settlement. She points out that both had a conflict of interest in their work as they were from iwi "steeped in histories of recent military conflict with Tūhoe", implying they were not appropriately distanced from politics in the area in which they worked (Binney, 2009 p.7). This failure by the government to recognize the conflict of interest reflects a still common argument in Pākehā circles that Māori all have common aims and perspectives when in reality different iwi have had hugely varying experiences and therefore hold very different viewpoints from one another in some specific situations.

76 An exception was a leader from the Waikato. In the 1930s Princess Te Puea Hirangi of the Waikato iwi Tainui and a leader of the Kīngitanga was to commission a film commemorating the art of canoe making (King, 1977) which Jonathan Dennis and the NZFA would become involved with in the 1980s. This film was to become *Mana Waka*, (Prod. Dennis, J., Dir. M.Mita, 1990) and will be analysed in a subsequent chapter.

scholars recording information from their own perspective and failing to take into account the indigenous view.

Although Ngata and Buck were apparently enthusiastic about the recording of performances and customs, Keith Sorrenson has recently suggested they were not completely comfortable with the Pākehā led process – "Despite a lack of formal training in anthropology, Ngata had a keen and critical appreciation of the subject, although, like Buck, he believed that Pākehā anthropologists lacked the ability to understand the inner emotions, heart and mind of Māori" (Sorrenson, 2012). Sorrenson's suggestion that in Ngata or Buck's view Pākehā lacked the ability to engage with a different understanding of ways of being and doing in the world is not so very different from views in the 1980s on the matter when calls for Māori to regain control of their own representation became more common and strident. Ngata and Buck were working biculturally in their own sense of the term, by navigating between two very different worlds. They were, in Sorrenson's view, aware of the limitations of the process, whereas the Pākehā anthropologists were not because they lacked the ability to understand the "inner emotions, hearts and minds" of Māori.

In Bourdieu's terms the Pākehā anthropologists from the Museum had their own cultural capital in its embodied state (as part of habitus). This was their "scholastic yield from educational action" (Pierre Bourdieu, 1986 p.2). This cultural capital ensured they felt themselves to have a superior aesthetic disposition and knowledge to Māori. Although Buck and Ngata also had European educational qualifications, which in Bourdieu's view provided them with an "institutionalised state of cultural capital" (Pierre Bourdieu, 1986 p.3) they had their iwi upbringing, knowledge, customs and lore which were unknown to or unappreciated by many Pākehā. For NZ historians of the late 19th or the early 20th century Māori were "savages" dying out, "unable to continue the pre-contact, communal savagism, and yet unable to participate fully in the new capitalist economy" (Pollock, 2005 p.67). It did not appear to occur to many Pākehā that Māori may have *chosen* not to "participate fully" or indeed to participate *differently* because of their own views, beliefs and practices.

Witarina Harris' experience of filmmaking was less scholarly in origin or intent than that of Ngata and Buck, but it also reflects the negotiation of differing points of view of the Pākehā and Māori worlds in which she was involved. It is possible that gender played a role in her experience too. Prior to her move to Wellington she had been employed as a typist at the Māori Arts and Crafts School near her home marae in Rotorua at Ohinemutu when two Americans came and asked her to test for a film. She had to sit on a rock by the lake and pose, and was selected to play the starring role of a princess in a dramatisation of an old Māori story for a European audience. She remembered the "special premier" at the Deluxe Theatre, Wellington, 1929, but then she "didn't hear anything more about it for another fifty-four years" (Harris quoted in Grace et al., 2001 pp.24, 25).

The film had a number of names including its official release title *Under the Southern Cross*, as well as *Taranga*, but was known by the NZFA as *The Devil's Pit* (Edwards & Martin, 1997 p.42). The film was part of a craze in the 1920s and 1930s for exotic South Sea Island adventure films made for North American and European markets. These tended to focus on exploiting the novel elements of the landscape – the bubbling geysers and hot water pools of Rotorua and the idea of "Māoriland" and its inhabitants. A previous film of this type was *Hinemoa* (Prod. & Dir. George Tarr 1914), usually referred to as New Zealand's first feature film and billed as *The Legend of the Pretty Māori Maiden of Rotorua*. Publicity for the film claimed "Specially Arranged Māoriland Music" accompanied it. In 1915, Australian Director/Producer Raymond Longford filmed *A Māori Maid's Love* in Rotorua and returned the following year to record *The Mutiny of the Bounty* (Pivac et al., 2011 pp.60, 61).[77] Dennis was to describe *The Devil's Pit* as an "appallingly banal Māori folk drama" (Dennis in Alley & Dennis 2002). Although Harris was the "star", she only saw the film once at the time it was released and never had further engagement with the filmmakers or the film world. She was ultimately an anonymous representative of the exotic female native created for a North American and European audience. It was not a partnership model of filmmaking.

Āpirana Ngata's interventions in Harris' life were positive and never forgotten. Harris said she was chosen by Ngata as secretary because she could speak and write te reo Māori, and that it was her language "that's put me into these important things, and from that time my Māori side really began to grow" (Grace et al., 2001 p.28). Harris became a founding member of the Māori Women's Welfare League (awarded "Whaea o te Motu" [Mother of the Nation] in 1979) and she returned to Rotorua in the 1970s where she continued this work. She was part of a movement to ensure that Māori values, cultural practices and beliefs were upheld. While this was her legacy from Āpirana Ngata and his ilk, it was also the work Māori women have quietly carried out for hundreds of years (Binney

---

77   "Certainly New Zealand has been often seen only as a set for productions attracted to exoticism" (Dennis, J & Toffetti, S. 1989 p.69).

& Chaplin, 1986).[78] Harris' experience with film was to bring her into contact with Jonathan Dennis and the NZFA. Her knowledge and experience (her habitus and doxa) were to affect Dennis personally and professionally to an enormous degree.

By the time Harris returned to Rotorua, a counter-culture had arrived in New Zealand which encouraged new arts to develop with a growing interest in indigenous cultures (Personal correspondence, R. Horrocks 25/10/11). Artistic collectives such as *BLERTA* (Bruno Lawrence's Electric Revelation and Travelling Apparition) were starting to make works reflecting the activism and new thinking of a younger generation. Many influential filmmakers of the late 1970s and 1980s would emerge from these collectives, including directors Roger Donaldson, Merata Mita, Paul Maunder (who ran the *Amamus* theatre collective) and others (Horrocks in Pivac et al. 2011 p.11). Roger Horrocks described this time in the 1970s as a turning point for NZ culture. He argued that film had a particularly important part to play in those "years of activism in politics as well as art, a time of Vietnam War protests, Māori activism, feminism and gay rights. More generally, the young took revenge upon the staid values of their parents' generation, challenging conservative New Zealand" (Horrocks in Pivac et al. 2011 ibid.). The films which began to be created at the time were often supported by the nascent NZ Film Commission.

Dennis was part of this challenge to the status quo of his Pākehā culture, trying to present stories of NZ through *Amamus,* the theatre troupe he was involved in, and by his work with the Film Society. But as this occurred, Māori began to challenge those Pākehā who believed themselves to be a younger generation of liberal thinkers who were "taking revenge upon the staid values of their parent's generation" (Horrocks, in Pivac et al. 2011 op.cit.). A modernist and cultural nationalist sentiment which developed into "the nationalist narrative", which supposedly would "unify New Zealanders within one discursive system" (Pollock, 2005 p.89), was challenged by young Māori, tired of either being relegated to the past, or pushed to belong to a version of NZ to which they could not relate. For them at least, the national identity narrative was not monocultural.

---

78   Harris also worked with Mātua Whāngai helping women in prison. She was involved in the te reo Māori movement, and was tipi-haere kuia, working particularly in pre-schools as a member of Awhina Whānau. Other Māori and Pākehā organisations she was actively involved in before becoming Kaumātua of the NZFA such as Zonta are listed in Grace et al. (2001 p.239).

Ngā Tamatoa: Young Warriors lay down a challenge

Harris' activities supporting her culture were part of a wider movement working towards greater freedoms for Māori. She navigated two worlds in the same way Ngata and Buck had before her.[79] As Horrocks suggested, both the Māori and Pākehā of the younger generation were less eager to work within their elders' respective paradigms. A generation or more younger than Witarina Harris, the group known as *Ngā Tamatoa* (Young Warriors) became active in the 1970s. They were largely urban Māori challenging their elders, whom they often regarded as having assimilationist tendencies (McCarthy, 2011 p.36).[80] For example, Ngahuia Te Awekotuku (Te Arawa, Waikato, Tūhoe iwi affiliations), a Ngā Tamatoa member and a student at the University of Auckland, was arrested for painting graffiti which demanded "Whakahokia mai ngā patu" (Give them back) on the Auckland War Memorial Museum (McCarthy, 2011 p.40). Te Awekotuku was to become a professional museum scholar herself and eventually sat on the board of the NZFA in the late 1980s and early 1990s (NZFA Board minutes, 1989–1992). Scholar and elder Merimeri Penfold (Ngāti Kurī iwi affiliations), remembered Te Awekotuku and others at the University of Auckland objecting to the fact that women were not traditionally permitted by Ngāti Whātua (local iwi of the area) protocol to make speeches at the paepae (speakers bench). Penfold was concerned at this challenge to tradition and the fact that the women were not speaking in Te Reo Māori. She said that much of what happened "wasn't right culturally" (Penfold quoted in Shepard, 2009 pp.117,118). Te Awekotuku commented on the "political minefield" of being a Māori woman working in the cultural heritage sector (McCarthy, 2011 p.67). Young Māori who took up public positions and challenged traditions were under great pressure from both their own elders and Pākehā.

The cultural heritage sector in New Zealand was influenced by these political and social tensions (McCarthy, 2011 p.56). As previously noted, Horrocks argued that "Film had a particularly important role to play because of its reach" in this

---

79 Frank Stark, former director of the NZFA points out Harris may have done important work but she was not of high status within her iwi – she was picked as kaumātua because she had starred in a 1929 film the Archive had "discovered", not because she had prestige within her iwi world (Personal correspondence, F. Stark 11/03/13). However, there is much anecdotal and published evidence that Harris was celebrated by her hapū Ngati Whakāue and the wider iwi of Te Arawa. For example, when Howard Morrison, a relation and well-known singer was asked to have his portrait painted, he instead suggested Witarina Harris be the subject, and this portrait is displayed at the Rotorua Council buildings (Personal correspondence, B. Harris 24/05/09). Harris also had connections to Peter Tapsell, another iwi relation and Government Minister who would call on Harris to do kaumātua duties for him and in turn Tapsell was also useful to the Archive (Dennis in Fyfe & Dennis, 2001).

80 Scholar Linda Tuhiwai Smith was part of the group. She says the aims were many, but two which were central were to gain recognition for the Treaty of Waitangi and secondly to implement "the compulsory teaching of our language in schools …" (Tuhiwai Smith, 1999/2012 p.13). The issue of compulsory Te Reo Māori in schools is still being debated today.

movement. A few feature filmmakers attempted to address the ideas and concerns of a younger generation. For example one of Dennis' favourite early filmmakers, Rudall Hayward, made *To Love a Māori* (1972) in order to explore themes of biculturalism. Hayward's wife Ramai was co-director and they described it as a "romantic documentary ... exploring love and racial discrimination in Auckland" (McDonald, 2011, p. 155).[81]

Pākehā filmmakers John O'Shea and Roger Mirams (Pacific Films), had explored similar territory in their 1952 film *Broken Barrier* (McDonald, 2011, p. 133) which "promoted the idea of biculturalism and acknowledged that racism was widespread in the Pākehā world" (Horrocks, 2011 p.10). Neither film was a box office hit, but Hayward was influential as the first feature filmmaker in New Zealand. John O'Shea was to become Dennis' mentor and an NZFA board member for many years (Dennis in Fyfe & Dennis, 2001).

As for television representation, Māori writer Patricia Grace wrote of the 1970s period – "there was no time any more for watching television, and not much liking for it because it did not define us. There was little indication through television that we existed at all in our own land" (Grace, 1986 p.105). However, in 1974 a new television series, *Tangata Whenua* (People of the Land) was produced which did indicate that Māori existed. Directed by Barry Barclay, produced by John O'Shea, and written by Michael King, Lawrence McDonald described *Tangata Whenua* as "one of the most important documentary series not only of the 1970s but also of New Zealand film history in general" (Pivac, 2011 op.cit. p.163).[82] The NZFA were to become the repository for these films in the 1980s which "paved the way for subsequent developments in Māori filmmaking and gave Pākehā a view into hitherto hidden worlds" (McDonald, 2011 p.163).

Barclay later commented on the climate in which the series was made in much the same tone as Grace, saying that the camera was alien to many Māori, distrusted and sometimes loathed. He felt this was because personal and significant matters for individuals and their communities are difficult to capture appropriately, as the "camera for most people, of whatever culture, remains an

---

81 Hayward had chosen Māori themes for his "epics" such as *Rewi's Last Stand* (1925), depicting the battle of Rewi Maniapoto and his supporters during the British invasion of the Waikato (Pivac et al., 2011 p.67), though at the time his reasons for making the film were not so much a desire to seek justice for Māori, but because he, like other filmmakers of the time saw possibilities in making New Zealand based frontier dramas similar to the popular Hollywood Western genre of the day (Pivac et al., 2011 p.63) or, as Horrocks has suggested previously in this chapter, wanted to play on exotic "Māoriland" themes.

82 Tangata Whenua 1, New Zealand 1974, 82m, Director: Barry Barclay *The Spirits and the Times Will Teach*. (Retrieved 26/05/14 http://tvnz.co.nz/2-movies/film-festival-09-tangata-whenua-1-2827426).

impersonal and often threatening mechanical presence, especially when in the hands of complete outsiders" (Barclay, 2005 p.99). To counter this viewpoint, while making *Tangata Whenua* Barclay sought ways in which to make the camera less threatening, by using a number of pioneering techniques when Michael King interviewed Waikato iwi elders such as Ngakahikatea Wirihana and Herepo Rongo.[83] Barclay had the camera placed as far away as possible so interviewees felt less self-conscious and disconcerted by the "impersonal and often threatening mechanical presence …" (Barclay, 2005 ibid.). Barclay started recording before the formal interview began so that the general chat could be included where appropriate. The interviewees spoke in Te Reo Māori with English voiceover translation added, and he ensured the settings for interviews were traditional spaces or in homes where people were most comfortable (Barclay, 1990, 2003). Barclay led these shifts in practice because he was an "insider". Though not necessarily with iwi affiliations to the interviewees, he was at least Māori which meant he was not a "complete outsider" (Barclay, 2005 p.99).

Barclay shifted the "rules of the game" as the first Māori television/filmmaker having control of the camera. He explained – "Every culture has a right and a responsibility to present its own culture to its own people …" He wanted to try and find "… ways to adapt the technology to suit our own purposes …" (Barclay, 1990 p.7). He felt that as a Māori filmmaker he needed to be a listener who did not interrupt, as "Māori debate tends to be cyclic" whilst Pākehā have a more linear style, "thrusting … forward … butting in … going one better …" (Barclay, 1990 p.14). As he talked to indigenous peoples across the world about his practice he developed a new language and method through which to represent Māori. He eventually came to call this indigenous approach "the fourth cinema" (Barclay, 2003).[84]

Despite his pioneering techniques Barclay was not comfortable with *Tangata Whenua*. Over time he became increasingly uneasy about the copyright of the images that had been recorded. The images were deposited at the NZFA as part of the production company *Pacific Films* collection, and so the issues for indigenous peoples, in relation to control of their images, came to rest with Dennis' institution. Barclay was concerned by how those images could be used after he

---

83 Michael King was later to be criticised for writing about the Māori world even though he felt he had an appropriate mandate (King, 1999). Dennis often quoted Michael King in his lectures (NZFA PP JD Box 2).

84 On travelling to Edmonton in Canada in 2010 I was very excited to see a "walk of fame" on the sidewalk with handprints of indigenous filmmakers, including those of Barry Barclay, outside the hotel I was staying in.

and Michael King were no longer able to exert influence over the archive in which they were held. This led him to argue for the concept of Mana Tūturu, roughly translated to indigenous intellectual property rights, in particular related to spirituality (Barclay, 2005).

In a radio documentary interview by Jonathan Dennis, the first Māori woman filmmaker Merata Mita, commented on Barclay's process and his changing focus over time –

> It's very interesting if you look back on the docos – starting with Barry Barclay/Pacific [Films] we [Māori] are explaining ourselves to white culture at large – then as Māori nationalism increased we took on the task of explaining issues to each other – Māori to Māori – and that trend hasn't changed. When you look back on Māori docos, [you are] tracing the rise of Māori nationalism and looking out to a more international perspective for our work, art, people (Mita, 1999).[85]

Mita understood Barclay's work as the beginning of a conversation which explained Māori to Pākehā and then shifted to an indigenous discussion about "Māori nationalism" before turning to an international perspective. This description is useful in thinking through the changes in institutions over this period of time when iwi based discussions became more common, moving away from the amorphous term "Māori" to something informed by specific iwi, hapū [subtribal] and whānau [family] values (Healy, 2013). At the same time Mita identified that the conversation also widened to the "more international perspective" to include other indigenous peoples and the development of transnational indigenous processes such as the concept of the "fourth cinema" (Barclay, 2003).[86] As Māori recognised an indigenous purpose and coherent practices which were sometimes similar across iwi, they also began to explore international indigenous perspectives and find support outside national borders. As they began to represent themselves they began to think about how their representations would be preserved and presented in the long term.

During the 1970s as the first representations of Māori appeared on television, there was still limited contact between indigenous and non-indigenous peoples in museums and archives. Conal McCarthy demonstrated that there was some, if rare engagement between Pākehā museum workers and Māori prior to the watershed of the *Te Māori* exhibition (1984–1987) (McCarthy, 2011 p.44). For

---

85 Box 9 NZFA JD's papers *Golden Kiwis Film Show* about NZ filmmakers, transcripts of recordings from 1999.

86 Little research has yet been done on the idea that Mita, Barclay and others were travelling during this period. They were looking back to NZ and seeing it differently through an international lens. When they returned home their thinking had shifted. Dennis also found the international perspective supported him to work differently in NZ. I think there is further work to be done on this notion.

example, McCarthy briefly mentions Pākehā curator Ron O'Reilly as someone working with Māori but does not elaborate (McCarthy, 2011 p.41). Although not particularly well known in New Zealand today, O'Reilly was an early champion of both indigenous and New Zealand modernist art as well as avant garde cinema (Personal correspondence, M. O'Reilly 30/11/09). His contribution is described briefly here as an example of a younger Pākehā interested in a new relationship with Māori materials, but also because he was Jonathan Dennis' uncle and as previously noted, had an early and strong influence on his nephew (Dennis in Alley & Dennis, 2002).

In 1964 O'Reilly travelled to Nigeria (his first overseas trip) and worked there for two years, becoming fascinated by the spiritual element of the Nigerian Yoruba carvings he collected (M. O'Reilly, 2009).[87] When O'Reilly returned to Christchurch in the mid to late 1960s Jonathan Dennis was a 15 year old at boarding school in Christchurch and would sometimes spend time on the weekends with his uncle as previously described. At this time, O'Reilly wrote two articles in *Ascent* magazine on the nature of Māori art (R. N. O'Reilly, 1968). Within these articles he argued for Māori materials to be shifted beyond the status of ethnographic object. His son Matthew O'Reilly argued that his father was "preparing the way for Māori art's normalisation as art and its entry into the art museum" (M. O'Reilly, 2009). Dennis was influenced by his uncle's taste in modernist painting and film. Ron's last two years were spent assembling a touring exhibition of Māori post-contact painted art under the aegis of the Govett-Brewster Art Gallery that would have pre-dated the watershed of *Te Māori* exhibition, but he died before it could be exhibited (M.O'Reilly, 2009 ibid.).

The work of O'Reilly and other Pākehā "cultural nationalists" raised questions regarding what national identity might mean, whose culture should be represented, and how that representation should be managed when the materials of Māori or other indigenous peoples were involved. The question which arises from the work of Ngā Tamatoa, O'Reilly or the early Māori filmmakers like Barry Barclay or Merata Mita, is *whose* cultural capital is to be valued in the art gallery, museum or archive or on the television or cinema screen?

Art Critic Hamish Keith argued that prior to the 1970s period Pākehā struggled to understand what their culture might be. They felt they were often lost in a

---

87   This interest is open to interpretation, as Ron O'Reilly was asked by some Nigerians not to take these carvings out of the country. He did so nevertheless, and so perhaps was not very different from the white collectors, the "elites" of earlier times. These carvings are now largely housed at the Canterbury Art Gallery as part of the agreement made when he took them from Nigeria (Hall, 2010) (Personal correspondence, M. O'Reilly 12/06/10).

"cultural wilderness" whereas Māori knew this to be a "despairing reality." Keith maintains that during this period Māori art was "invisible" to most Pākehā, existing only as representations of "an apparently vanished people, consigned by well-meaning elders and ethnologists to a largely fictitious past and a counterfeit chronology" (Keith, 2007 pp.200,201). In 1978, however, a small but not insignificant change occurred in the practice of the cultural heritage sector when Mina McKenzie became museum director at Manawatu Museum in Palmerston North – she was the first Māori Museum Director. She established connections with local iwi Rangitāne, and they blessed and advised the Museum in its role as "kaitiaki o nga taonga tuku iho – guardians of the treasures passed down" (McCarthy, 2011 p.41). McKenzie influenced a range of Pākehā and Māori curators who worked for or with her, and she contributed to national debates about the nature of Māori materials in the cultural heritage sector. Leading by example, McKenzie was an influential mentor for many younger Pākehā curators such as David Butts who also created a pre-*Te Māori* exhibition in a regional museum which incorporated local iwi views at Hawke's Bay Museum and Art Gallery, Napier (McCarthy, 2011 p.46). McKenzie's use of the phrase "kaitiaki o nga taonga tuku iho" may have been common in Māori circles, but it certainly was not part of the Pākehā cultural heritage sector discourse at that time. Professor of Museum Studies Paul Tapsell (Ngati Whakāue, Te Arawa iwi affiliations) describes the term "taonga" below. His definition is provided here in full as it has significance for Dennis and the NZFA:

> ...any item, object or thing that represents the ancestral identity of a Māori kin group (whanau, hapu or iwi) in relation to particular lands and resources (...) They are seen as the spiritual personifications of particular ancestors, either as direct images or through association. Descendants experience this wairua (ancestral spirit) as ihi (presence), wehi (awe) and wana (authority). Thus taonga are time travellers that bridge the generations, enabling descendants to ritually meet their ancestors face to face (Tapsell, 2006 p.17, translation Tapsell's).

This understanding of an "object" as carrying the ancestral spirit offers a very different conception of the material in a museum, archive or art gallery to that of most Pākehā archivists and curators. They generally saw their collections as containing individual objects to be catalogued and preserved in climate controlled environments which ensured the physical decay of the object is slowed or stopped. A *taonga* has a spiritual engagement with the whānau, hapū or iwi from whence it came. It has a dynamic reciprocal relationship to other materials and its iwi of origin. This requires an understanding and set of skills quite removed from the formal training of most Pākehā archivists or curators. It involves understanding one's role as a "kaitiaki" (guardian or steward) as opposed to a collector or owner.

It is "tuku iho" to be passed down – the curator or archivist is temporarily charged with caring for it for the peoples of the future. The material is never owned by the institution. The concept *taonga* makes manifest a reciprocal relationship between present and past.

Young urban Māori, "increasingly critical of images of themselves as 'primitive' rural folk living in the past" (McCarthy, 2011 p.36), knew that their relationship with nga taonga tuku iho was more dynamic and reciprocal than the museums were acknowledging. It was a more personal relationship. By the very definition of the term "taonga", Pākehā could not have the relationship that those descendants could, who would (as Tapsell puts it) "ritually meet their ancestors face to face" through the materials of the museum or archive.[88] This understanding requires a living relationship with the descendants from whence it came. These Māori assertions of a living relationship to taonga were to challenge and sometimes frighten Pākehā cultural heritage workers (McCarthy, 2011 p.64). It certainly changed the "rules of the game" for cultural heritage institutions including the NZFA.

The spiritual element: Ngā taonga – kaupapa Māori

To demonstrate the shift in understanding museum material which occurred in the 1980s, Professor Paul Tapsell tells the story of an ihupukupuku (cloak) from his iwi named Pareraututu (the ancestor for whom the cloak is a spiritual personification). It is worth noting here that Tapsell and Witarina Harris are relatives from the same iwi in Rotorua. Witarina and Paul knew each other well, and she was aware of this story (Personal correspondence, P. Tapsell 09/12/10). The story demonstrates the living descendants' relationship with the taonga. The narrative also functions as an illustration of Bourdieu's theory of competing values enacted in the struggle over the field of the exhibition space in the 1980s, though Tapsell does not use Bourdieu's philosophy himself.

Tapsell's Te Arawa relation Hari Semens saw an ihupukupuku at Rotorua in a travelling exhibition in 1982. He picked up the cloak and put it on his body, because it was not just a cloak, an item in a display, it was to him an embodiment of his ancestor. He felt the spiritual aspect of it; "People got upset, but they didn't

---

88   In fact, Colin McCahon, Dennis' hero, was to paint images related to Māori but get vital details wrong in the representation. This was to cause disruption and upset to Tūhoe and make the national news in 1997 (Binney, 2009 p.8). As early as 1991 artist Michael Parekowhai had boldly critiqued McCahon's work with a reappropriation of McCahon's *I Am* painting (1954). Parekowhai created a sculpture spelling "I Am He" in *The Indefinite Article*. There are various interpretations of this work, but "He" translates to "wrong" in Te Reo Māori.

understand, this was my kuia!" he said. Hari Semens asked Paul Tapsell as a member of his iwi (connected by social capital), but also as a recognised museum curator (with economic and cultural capital) to negotiate the return of the cloak. Tapsell has written how through this process he "began to understand why many Māori people have felt so alienated from their taonga held in large city institutions". The repatriation of the cloak to the iwi took many years (Tapsell, 2006 p.51). Tapsell's description describes a different world view from that of most Pākehā. For an object to be a spiritual personification of an ancestor seems impossible to the "rational" Western mind. And yet Hari Semens and Paul Tapsell, himself a trained Western archivist, believed this to be the case and indeed Tapsell's work since that experience has sought to honour Māori understandings in the face of Pākehā economic, social and cultural capital imperatives.

Bourdieu's theoretical framework suggests agents have an integral "social trajectory and disposition" which he calls "habitus" which in turn affects their "doxa" or beliefs and therefore their behaviour (Kloot, 2009 p.469). In Bourdieu's terms, Paul Tapsell was able to negotiate between his competing doxa. He chose to attempt to influence the field of museumship in NZ by changing the "rules of the game" or the field within which he functioned (Tapsell, 2010). In the case of Hari Semens, his doxa and habitus is imbued with a traditional Te Arawa iwi upbringing and he sits outside the field – the museum in this case. Semens seemingly had no choice over what he believed – the cloak before him *is* the embodiment of his ancestor and despite the rules of the institution, he must wear that cloak to honour her. Semens transgressed the regulative principles of the traditional museum space by touching what the museum staff would view as an "artefact" which they control and have ownership or entitlement to handle in certain ways. Hari Semens' behaviour on viewing his ancestor's cloak is arguably an example of his doxa and habitus, as is the response of the Pākehā museum curators who were upset and angry that he had put on the cloak. Their competing doxa, their different social, economic and cultural capital did not enable them to appreciate the perspective of the other party at that time.

Paul Tapsell, as both a trained museum curator and a member of Semen's iwi, was caught between the competing doxa of his upbringing and the field in which he was expected to behave as a curator who respected the boundaries between audience and "object" as they are understood in the Western museum, art gallery or archive context. Bourdieu's view that doxa and habitus are unable to change has been challenged (Kloot, 2009), but it is not without merit. Pākehā can acknowledge and accept Māori relationships to taonga (Semen's relationship to the cloak, his kuia) but they cannot feel that relationship themselves because it is not their cultural milieu. They cannot "time travel" to meet the ancestor face to face through the taonga. Semens is a representative of the social capital of the Māori person who has a connection through his networks and family to the cloak. Similarly Pākehā curators are imbued with their own social and cultural capital and may not be able to shift their view. Tapsell sits between the Māori and Pākehā position and must negotiate between these, much as Ngata and Buck did in Sorrenson's view many years before.

However, what is missing from Bourdieu's theory is an acknowledgement of the spiritual component (Semen's connection to his ancestor). It is this spiritual component which is by definition most difficult to measure or quantify in European (or Pākehā) philosophy. As Dennis was to complain to the International Federation of Film Archives in 1988, there is a fundamental inability in European archiving philosophy to engage with Māori perspectives (J. Dennis, report to FIAF Paris conference, 1988). Paul Tapsell said of Dennis that he listened and engaged with tangata whenua and he worked to ensure their tāonga were appropriately preserved and presented (Personal correspondence, P.Tapsell op.cit.). Tapsell was able to see first-hand how Dennis operated in his community in relation to the films which Dennis exhibited to his iwi. Tapsell argued that Dennis worked biculturally, and when asked what that meant Tapsell responded by describing the "twin streams" of hot and cold water near his (and Witarina Harris') traditional home at Ohinemutu in Rotorua. He said when you sit in the stream, the hot and cold water intermingle but are still separate, the cold reminding your skin that you are alive, while the hot is soothing, or sometimes even scalding. He sees Pākehā like Dennis as being like one part of these streams, existing side by side with Māori, but also remaining autonomous (Personal correspondence, P.Tapsell op.cit.). Tapsell's view of the semi-autonomous but co-mingling "hot and cold", has echoes of Harris' reference to "my Māori world" and "my Pākehā world". Both are aware of the negotiation between two autonomous spheres of influence and can co-exist between them.

In the 1970s there was a growing awareness of Māori rights and knowledges demonstrated by the work of Mina McKenzie, and later Tapsell, Semens and others which moved towards a practice which incorporated Māori beliefs and practices. Simultaneously, the activist campaigns of the likes of Ngā Tamatoa, and the influence of film and television works encouraged significant legislative changes which would have an impact on cultural heritage practices. In 1975 changes to the Antiquities Act occurred to control the sale of carvings to overseas collectors and to encourage repatriation of Māori materials in overseas collections (McCarthy p.40).[89] Other important social and cultural movements of that time included the 1975 Hikoi Land March led by Whina Cooper from Northland to Parliament and the 1978 occupation of Bastion Point which would be recorded in Merata Mita's film *Bastion Point: Day 507* (Prods. & Dirs. M. Mita, & Pohlmann, G. 1980). The introduction of the Waitangi Tribunal through The Treaty of Waitangi Act (1975) began to allow the stories of colonisation and their impact over time to emerge in the wider community. These changes began to have an impact upon staff and practices in the government sector in the late 1970s and 1980s period (McCarthy 2011).[90]

These significant political and cultural changes towards a biculturalism arguably had less popular impact however than a sports game, which for many has defined national identity and the sense of being a "New Zealander" for many years. In an exhibition at the NZFA looking back at this time, curator Campbell Farquhar recognised the significance of rugby as a tool of propaganda for a "united" nation. Farquhar argued that:

> The story of rugby and the story of NZ have been intertwined since the game was first played here in 1870. In NZ rugby is one of the cultural touchstones for ideas about masculinity, toughness and giving things a go. In cinema and on television this has been exploited to tell stories, sell products and generate community spirit (Farquhar, 2011).

Other authors also recognise the specific geographical and socio-political significance of sport in relation to biculturalism. For example the Ministry for Culture and Heritage includes the following on its website:

> Sport was an aspect of the "cultural power" through which the British Empire imposed and maintained itself more cheaply than it could have done by military might alone. In colonial New Zealand, rugby football rather than cricket came to perform such a function. It both encouraged loyalty to the Crown amongst white emigrants and helped assimilate a Māori elite into the "British way of life" (Ministry for Culture and Heritage website, 2011).

The game of rugby has been used to regulate behaviours without ostensibly needing to enforce discipline or control. Rugby has become a kind of representation of NZ identity which many people are reluctant to disrupt (Brady,

---

89 Barry Barclay was to make a feature film about an iwi trying to repatriate their taonga from a German Museum. This was entitled *Te Rua* (Prod. O'Shea, J., Dir.B. Barclay, 1991).

90 The Treaty of Waitangi itself and the discussions and debates around it at this time are described in detail in Claudia Orange's book *The Treaty of Waitangi* (Orange, 1987) as well as in the work of many others including Mason Durie (Durie, 2005), and Ranginui Walker (R. Walker, 1990).

2006, 2012). This "cultural touchstone" was to be a focus for a clash of multiple perspectives in relation to biculturalism and national identity when the 1981 Springbok (South African Rugby team) Tour of NZ was announced. This event became a galvanising force for many New Zealanders prior to the 1984 *Te Māori* exhibition. Both the Springbok Tour and *Te Māori* forced people to realise how little had changed since Ngata and Buck's experience of Pākehā being unable to engage with the "emotions, hearts and minds" of Māori or Witarina Harris' representation as an exotic "Maoriland" princess. Both the Tour and the exhibition had a great influence on representations of the nation. These cultural historical events were to impact upon the newly formed NZFA in its founding decade when debates about the nature of biculturalism were underway. McCarthy suggested that in the 1980s period influenced by these events, the argument that biculturalism was a negotiation or a power sharing exercise shifted to an exploration of "how the system itself could change" to incorporate Māori values (McCarthy, 2011 p.56). By changing the system itself it was thought that the doxa and habitus of both Māori and Pākehā could be honoured.

Chapter 5

The New Zealand Film Archive become Guardians of the Treasured Images of Light/Ngā Kaitiaki o ngā Taonga Whitiāhua

Wᴵithin its first decade, the NZFA developed from its "very European" origins (Dennis, 1989 p.10) into an institution which had a working document called The Constitution/Kaupapa in which the Treaty of Waitangi principles were incorporated and acknowledged as the founding document of the nation.[91] In particular the Archive developed an understanding of Article Two of the Treaty which referred to "taonga", as we have seen, a concept which would alter the manner in which institutions in New Zealand would engage with Māori materials (McCarthy, 2011). As set out in the previous chapter, in the 1970s there was a re-evaluation of socio-political processes in the cultural heritage world, with small and incremental shifts eventually leading to changes in institutional practices. Because the NZFA was not a government department it was not obliged by legislative changes or ministerial decree to shift its practice. But the staff were aware of the changes occurring both inside and outside bureaucratic regimes. They were also becoming attuned to the needs of their multiple audiences, informed by Witarina Harris, Merata Mita, Barry Barclay and others.

During the 1980s, Dennis and the Archive staff became involved in a process they called "Returning", which was a way for the Archive to make its material more accessible to those who would not necessarily feel comfortable coming into a Western institution (Barclay, 2005 p.105). It was also an effective tool through

---

91 The Constitution/Kaupapa is an appendix to this work.

which to gain subject expert knowledge from descendants of the people in historic films; both Māori and Pākehā. The audience's skills, knowledge and experience of the images previously unavailable to archivists within an institution, were important to a better understanding (and therefore cataloguing and presentation) of the films (Dennis, 1989 p.10). The doxa and habitus of descendants of Māori in films held by the Archive, for example, ensured they had cultural and social capital previously unavailable in a predominantly Pākehā institution. Dennis recognised this as a change in the "European" style of the Archive. However there were ethical issues here as Pākehā gained from Māori knowledge, and this became increasingly problematic during the 1980s period.

Screening films to audiences in regional cinemas and traditional meeting places proved to Dennis that a fundamental shift in the framework of the Archive was necessary in order to address the fact that the institution had remained firmly in Pākehā control, even as engagement with Māori had increased. This led Dennis and the Archive towards structural changes as the understanding of Māori films as artefacts, in the ethnographic sense, changed to a re-understanding of these materials as artworks in their own right. This meant presenting Māori materials in context and with appropriate accompanying information. Subsequently, there was a further shift towards seeing these materials as ngā taonga. The corresponding shift in the structural framework which was required, led Dennis to more creative practices and responses to the materials housed in the Archive through an increasingly reciprocal relationship with the audience. This shifted the power of the Director of the Archive, who had previously been the expert, and now became the pupil.

Springbok tour protests, the NZFA opens

The NZFA was founded in 1981 – the same year as the Springbok tour of New Zealand which caused protests across the country, described by Bruce Babington as "nation-splitting" (Pivac et al., 2011 p.202). According to his diary, Jonathan Dennis attended at least one Wellington protest on Friday 1st May, 1981 (NZFA PP JD Box 20).[92] The protests began as an all white Apartheid era South African national rugby team came to tour the country and play the All Blacks, the New Zealand national team. There had previously been a history of protest from (largely) Māori people who felt it was unacceptable for the New Zealand Rugby Football Union to send only white or "honorary white" players to matches in

---

92 Dennis' sister Simon also remembers him attending "anti tour protests" (Personal correspondence, S. Dennis 13/07/10).

South Africa.[93] By 1981 the protest movement included Pākehā. There were competing perspectives, but the purpose – to halt the current tour – was sufficiently galvanizing for people to stand under the same banners; at least for a time. The protests successfully halted the game at Hamilton and disrupted every other match played in the country. They encouraged a wide and passionate debate about the role of politics in sport, Pākehā responsibilities for the continuing aftermath of colonial occupation of the country, and brought to the surface ongoing anxieties and concerns in a country which liked to present itself as enjoying racial harmony.[94]

Scholar and activist Ranginui Walker remembered that in Māori political circles the Springbok tour protests were an important moment, describing how "In the wake of the tour, an argument adopted by some – that Māori should not be reliant on Pākehā and that Pākehā had no role in Māori political campaigns – gained ground" (Walker quoted in Spoonley, 2009 p.109).[95] The "argument adopted by some" is articulated in Merata Mita's film of the Springbok protests, *Patu!* (Prod. & Dir. M. Mita, 1983) (which translates to strike, beat, hit or subdue) in which we see protest meetings where Māori speakers ask Pākehā why they are willing to stand for the rights of Black South Africans when they had never protested about the inequities of the indigenous peoples of the country in which they lived. This film used footage Mita had collected and edited, together with that of other Pākehā filmmakers who donated their materials.[96] The film would be deposited in the NZFA and Dennis personally appointed by Mita as its distributor even after he had finished at the NZFA (NZFA PP JD Box 11).[97]

The tour and the film *Patu!* were very important for the cultural history sector, with almost the whole of the film industry joining the protests and providing footage to Mita while helping her "keep the footage out of the hands of the police, who were attempting to requisition it for 'evidence'"(Horrocks in Pivac et.al.,

---

93   "Māori had long held concerns over sporting contacts with apartheid-era South Africa, but protests began in 1960. Prior to this, New Zealand Māori teams played against South Africa in 1921 and 1956" as "honorary whites" (Keane, 2012).

94   For a discussion of this topic from a Pākehā perspective see Pollock 2004.

95   For further discussion of the impact of the Springbok tour protests there are many texts, including Ranginui Walker's *Struggle Without End Ka Whawhai Tonu* (R. Walker, 1990).

96   These included co-ordinators Gaylene Preston, Gerd Pohlmann and Martyn Sanderson. Photographers were Barry Harbet with W. Attewell, C. Barrett, A. Barry, J. Bartle, A. Bollinger, P. Carvell, R. Donaldson, M. Fingel, E. Frizzell, C. Ghent, A. Guilford, R. Long, Leon Narbey, R. Prosser, and M. Single all contributing (Edwards & Martin, 1997 p.91). Many of these people were or went on to have prominent careers in the film industry in NZ and/or overseas.

97   NZFA JD PP Box 11 correspondence on distribution of *Patu!* through the 1990s in folder labelled "Merata". Annie Collins private papers at Wadestown accessed 2009 included requests addressed to Dennis asking to screen the film (AC PP).

2011, p. 14). Annie Collins was the editor of *Patu!* She was a young Pākehā woman, who felt her "eyes were opened" regarding the history of colonialism by working on this film.[98] She said Merata Mita was a key part of this education for her – "it was on *Patu!* that my comprehension shifted. It was on *Patu!* I realised that I did not understand the land that I was born in" (Personal correspondence, A. Collins 26/01/09).

Collins was also aware of the police presence around Mita's house, and heard about the harassment of Mita's sons and the attempts made to seize the film footage to use in the prosecution of protestors. They decamped at one point from Auckland to Waiheke Island in the Hauraki Gulf in order to avoid the disruption to the edit caused by police activity. They did not have a lot of money, and Collins vividly remembered eating home-made pizzas with gritty sand from the pipis (shellfish) they had gathered (Personal correspondence, A. Collins op.cit.). As Dennis noted in his own presentations later in the decade, Collins' knowledge was to benefit the NZFA when she ran anti-racism workshops for the NZFA staff and quickly became a key ally for the NZFA (Dennis, 1989 p.11).

Merata Mita was one of only two Māori feature filmmakers to emerge in the 1970s/1980s period; the other was Barry Barclay, previously discussed as the director of the *Tangata Whenua* series in the 1970s. Both were involved in the development of the NZFA as it began to incorporate indigenous perspectives into its practices. For many years though, Barclay campaigned from outside, with Dennis commenting that he was "banging on the walls but we had already opened the door." Mita on the other hand, was seen by Dennis as a "key supporter" (Dennis in Pivac & Dennis, 2000).[99]

As Barclay described it – "During the 1980s, a very significant contest developed within the [New Zealand Film] archive, a struggle of conscience, if you like, in which there were many players, to all of whom we are greatly indebted" (Barclay, 2005 p.103). This "contest" involved Māori and Pākehā debates on how archiving should be undertaken. The issues raised in Mita's *Patu!* and exemplified by Ranginui Walker's description of a particular viewpoint, "Māori should not be

---

98 Annie Collins worked as editor on *Patu!* because of her previous experience with other film productions: "I'd cut *Keskidee Aroha* for Martyn [Sanderson] and she [Mita] was co-director of that, although she wasn't around when that was cut. And from there I was passed to Gerd Pohlmann, her husband, for *The Bridge*, and Gerd said 'try Annie Collins [for *Patu!*]' to Merata" (Personal correspondence, A. Collins 26/01/09).

99 There is some contention about Barclay's influence at the NZFA. Barclay believes his interventions resulted in the Kaupapa of the Archive being established. Others including Dennis argue that the Kaupapa was already in place and what Barclay contributed was the phrase and understanding of "mana tūturu", a spiritual guardianship aspect (Dennis in Pivac & Dennis, 2000). Barclay was certainly influential in ensuring that the NZFA post Dennis' tenure as director continued to maintain a bicultural partnership agreement (Barclay, 2005).

reliant on Pākehā and that Pākehā had no role in Māori political campaigns", were indicative of the debates, tensions and difficulties at the Film Archive and in the wider cultural heritage sector as attempts were made to move towards the incorporation of Māori perspectives.

Because they hold the cultural materials of the nation, "museums are at the centre of arguments about culture identity, history, restitution and social inclusion" (McCarthy, 2011 p.2). A bicultural discussion was inevitable at the NZFA because of the nature of the film medium which "cries out to be shared" (Dennis, 1989 p.10), and the fact that "The wealth of the NZ Film Archive is actually the indigenous material" (Personal correspondence A. Collins, op.cit.). If the NZFA staff were taking indigenous materials out to the public then they were going to have to engage in discussions about rights and privileges in relation to control of those materials. The debate can be seen as an early discussion of kaupapa Māori methodology. Like Barclay's experience of archiving the *Tangata Whenua* films, the attempts to have Māori people in control of the process within filmmaking and the subsequent archiving of those materials, is part of the discussion of Māori self-determination.

During the 1980s the term "bicultural" appears to have been variously understood by people and organisations in the sector. For example, Sharp argues that "bicultural reformism" was one approach which caused an adaptation by existing institutions which largely remained under Pākehā control, whereas "bicultural distributivism is the development of specifically Māori institutions to share the authority defined by the Treaty" (Sharp, 1997 p.230). The latter understanding equates to the concept of Nga Pūna o Maumahara (marae based repositories of knowledge). This idea has been discussed and debated at various conferences including the Archivists and Records Association of New Zealand (ARANZ) *Ngā Taonga Tuku Iho* national conference in 2004. At this conference, Māori speakers expressed frustration at the lack of genuine progress in relation to the maintenance and cultural safety of indigenous materials in mainstream institutions (ARANZ, 2004).

Eagle has described the government department or state response to biculturalism as ideally a "journey". The institution begins as monocultural. It then moves to a decision to be bicultural and introduces a Māori perspective. Next it encourages active iwi involvement and engenders trust, then finally creates a bicultural partnership which incorporates the values of the Treaty of Waitangi (Eagle, 2000). Eagle critiqued this process, acknowledging that for most government departments the journey had not been either smooth nor successful and in fact in most cases had stagnated by the end of the 1990s (McCarthy, 2011 p.12).[100]

During the early 1980s there were few Māori staff within the cultural heritage sector. Those few were the only people able to advise on appropriate management of indigenous materials until Ken Gorbey established a national scheme for employing Māori after the *Te Māori* exhibition (McCarthy, 2011 pp.42,43).[101] There were no Māori staff at the NZFA in the early part of the decade.

Te Māori and its implications for biculturalism

Influenced by the many changes in practice and philosophy which were occurring during the 1980s, Roger Neich of the Wellington National Museum – previously called the Dominion where Elsdon Best had worked – curated two exhibitions: *Māori Art for America* and *Nga Taonga Hou o Aotearoa: New National Treasures* in 1983 and 1984 respectively. The 1984 exhibition was regarded as particularly innovative for displaying Māori carving as art rather than artefact. Displaying indigenous materials as art had become common practice overseas but not yet in NZ and echoed Ron O'Reilly's suggestions in his 1968 *Ascent* articles. Neich's exhibitions also used the word *taonga* as a bilingual term for the first time (McCarthy, 2011 p.42). This predated the *Te Māori* exhibition which is generally understood to be the first national exhibition in which Māori taonga had been treated in a way which incorporated Māori values and perspectives.[102]

The 1983 exhibition is significant in that Jonathan Dennis and the NZFA were involved for the first time with the museum in these early exhibitions. McCarthy makes a fleeting reference to Dennis when he writes:

> Rare films shot by James McDonald of the Dominion Museum in the 1920s, preserved by the NZFA, were shown together for the first time in June 1983 in association with this [Māori Art for America] exhibition. Director Jonathan Dennis demonstrated through an active public programme and community outreach how a small cultural organisation such as the Archive could begin to take on board Māori values and practices (McCarthy, 2011 p.42).

---

100 This discussion of biculturalism in museums and archives owes great debt to Conal McCarthy's work (McCarthy 2011).

101 This scheme no longer exists (Bloomfield, 2013).

102 This is not to say that Te Māori was considered an exemplary exhibition by all Māori peoples. Not all iwi agreed to allow their taonga to be involved in the exhibition (including the Whanganui iwi because of their negative experiences with museums including museum staff tossing shrunken heads at visitors in earlier times) and some Māori women were upset that only men's art (carvings) were included (Merimeri Penfold quoted in Shepard, 2009 p.115).

These are the same films Ngata and Buck had been associated with, as described in the previous chapter. They were the ethnographic and anthropological studies which Dennis and the NZFA had inherited from the National Archives in 1981 now generally known as the James McDonald films (McDonald, J. 1919, 1920, 1921, 1923 NZFA collection). When Dennis and the staff began to process the film they had noted elements they "didn't understand", and so began to ask Māori people such as Bill Cooper to advise them, and then others became involved (Dennis, 1989 p.10).[103] In response to this advice they began to take the films to their communities of origin for screening, realising that to be a truly national institution they had to respond to regional interests and could also encourage feedback and information on the films (Davy & Pivac, 2008). At first Dennis was the only NZFA employee and so he was accompanied by Clive Sowry, the only other trained Film Archivist in the country (Pivac & Dennis, 2000).[104] They would load up projection equipment and drive around the country, showing films to anyone interested in seeing them.[105] Merata Mita described the practice as "giving us insights into ourselves of which we would normally be bereft ... .These showings demonstrate a process of retrieving and restoring history, heritage, pride, consciousness and Māori identity" (Mita, 1996 p.50).

This practice, as Mita notes, was reminiscent of the days of the travelling picture showmen in the late 1800s and early 1900s before purpose built cinemas were common. As early filmmaker Edwin (Ted) Coubray would later describe it in a film directed by Dennis, these men would travel through towns setting up their equipment in a local hall or empty building and charge a small fee for the local people to see images of interest. Sometimes children were so astounded by the images their mouths would fall open and they would toppled backwards off the wooden benches they were sitting on (*Mouth Wide Open*, Prod. Collins, A., Dir. Dennis, 1998). In the 1980s the revival of this practice became increasingly exciting to Dennis, as local Māori people responded with not only passion and interest, but also a "subject expert knowledge" to the films they were seeing (Dell,

---

103 The catalogue for the collection includes a list of those involved in the preservation and contextualisation of these films and is as previously noted appended to the thesis.

104 Although their relationship eventually soured, Sowry worked closely with Dennis in the late 1970s and early 1980s to champion the idea of the NZFA, even writing the first and second monograph for the NZFA (Sowry, 1984). Dennis acknowledged Sowry's important role when he said "the notion of a film archive certainly didn't come to me, it wasn't a blinding flash that I had, it was Clive Sowry that initiated I suppose my understanding that the films that I clearly liked, the Hayward films and the others were in some kind of danger" (Dennis in Pivac & Dennis 2000).

105 Dennis himself never learned to drive, so always needed someone with a car or van to accompany him (Personal correspondence, S. Dennis 13/07/10).

1987 p.3).[106] The responses of these audiences helped guide how the films were catalogued, edited, and eventually managed in the Archive. For example, Dennis described how in 1985, "The Māori and Pacific Island weavers invited us to two of their national hui and we showed the weaving sequences from the [McDonald] film" (Dennis, 1989 p.10). This national weavers hui at Te Teko was an opportunity for the weavers to help the Archive understand the sequence of shots through the order of the weaving patterns in the film.[107]

It was becoming clear to the Archive that their own expertise in preserving and presenting films was growing, but their knowledge of Te Ao Māori, or "taha Māori" (often translated as the Māori side) as Dennis sometimes called it, was lacking.[108] Dennis and his small but growing Pākehā team had a formal European training in archiving but lacked the cultural capital of Māori who may have grown up in traditional environments where the stories of their ancestors were shared. They could not have a spiritual engagement with ngā taonga o ngā iwi [the treasures of the tribe]. They were constantly reminded of this as they made mistakes. For example when the NZFA returned to the weavers' next hui, having followed their advice for editing the film, the weavers' feedback was that it was now an accurate edit, but "what a shame" that dialect appropriate intertitles for that region had not been created. "We hadn't even thought of that!" said Dennis. The NZFA then had those intertitles translated appropriately (Dennis 1989 p.10).[109] In this manner, screening to audiences all around the country encouraged the appropriate experts who were unavailable in a Pākehā dominated Wellington archive, to support and improve the contextualisation of the archival object or taonga.[110]

---

106 As Dr Susan Healy said at a presentation about Ngā Puhi philosophy, "the knowledge rests with the people it belongs to" and may or may not be shared with others depending on whether relationships develop which encourage trust and reciprocity (Healy, 2013).

107 NZFA JD PP Box 19 (loose in box).

108 Turoa Royal notes that Graham Smith calls "taha Māori" a Pākehā invention (Royal, 2010). Dennis used the term in the catalogue of an exhibition in 1989 (Dennis Jonathan & Toffetti Sergio, 1989).

109 Sharon Dell completed an early draft translation of the McDonald film from Whanganui. Ruka Broughton, Taranaki Te Reo Tohunga then did a further translation (Personal Correspondence, S.Dell 13/04/15).

110 This process could be understood as either reciprocal or exploitative. Presumably the weavers did not get paid for their expertise and advice to the NZFA. It is not clear if others who helped with intertitles were paid for their time as I do not have access to NZFA financial data. Cushla Parekowhai was the first Māori employee of the NZFA, but did not begin in the role until the end of the 1980s (Dennis in Pivac & Dennis, 2000). Witarina Harris as kaumātua was paid various stipends and travel expenses for her work but she was a "figurehead" and was not involved in the day to day archiving processes. In 1987 on the 10th of February, a letter was written by the then Minister of Recreation and Sport Mike Moore awarding her a "retainer" of $5,000 (net) to be Cultural Ambassador of NZ Films for the year in London, Paris and Bonn (NZFA JD PP loose in Box 19). Dennis appears to have funded many Māori associated activities with "one off grants" from Ministers of the Arts, Recreation, and (later) Internal Affairs (Dennis in Pivac & Dennis, 2000).

Unlike screenings in museums and archives which tended to follow a Pākehā protocol, regional screenings at marae were very different. Dennis' developing practice was a crude and early form of kaupapa Māori in that it acknowledged that Māori people held the expert knowledge about their materials. However, the film archivists were still Pākehā and therefore from some perspectives, it could never truly be kaupapa Māori practice.

Pākehā Sharon Dell was the Māori Materials Subject Specialist in the 1980s at the Alexander Turnbull Library and began to accompany the Film Archive on these "returnings" in 1986.[111] She described her observations of marae screenings in some detail. One of the James McDonald films, *He Pito Whakaatu I Te Noho A Te Māori I Te Awa O Whanganui/Scenes of Māori Life on the Whanganui River* (1921) was first screened locally at Matahiwi in 1985, and since that time had several further screenings. In 1986 a MASPAC [Māori and South Pacific Arts Council] sponsored conservation hui at Koroniti, provided another opportunity to show the film and she wrote of the "profound and moving" experience as the films opened up "a direct communication … between the living and the dead" (Dell, 1987 pp.3,4). She described audience members identifying family, and even ancestors of the animals in the village. "Most are known by name and some are greeted as if they stood before us … Personal characteristics are laughed at, family likenesses in the present generations are pointed out – even amongst the pigs and dogs which still wander around the village" (Dell, 1987 ibid.).

As Dell described it, the response and critique from iwi audiences suggested a living relationship with the ancestors in those images, a living memory of those on the screen, and also an understanding of the playfulness of the film when "the people themselves face the camera with self-possession and confidence. They are aware of the artificiality of some of the reconstructions (when obviously dead fish are scooped all too easily into a net, the 'actors' perform with wry comic glee)" (Dell, 1987 pp. 3,4). Dell was able to learn that the performances were not necessarily authentic but they were important nonetheless. She described how some of the scenes in the film were set up for the camera "where they are using digging sticks and things that they hadn't actually used that way for a long time … I think there is that sense that iwi were presenting what they wanted to present …" but said the screenings were still "magic" occasions (Personal correspondence, S. Dell 10/09/10).

---

111 Dell also helped Dennis a great deal in an advisory capacity and they worked on exhibitions of James McDonald's still photography as well as the aforementioned Hocart collection of Fijian images (Personal correspondence, S. Dell 10/09/10).

Dell and Dennis observed the reactions of the audiences, spoke to them and listened in turn to their interpretations of the films. As Dell notes, this was not a simple process of assuming an authenticity in the films, but an acknowledgement that these were constructed representations of indigenous peoples. However this did not detract from a passionate engagement by the audience. Working with these films and experiencing audience reactions, Dennis and the other staff began to learn from contemporary Māori people and their relationship to the films made so long ago. This was an extremely labour intensive and time consuming process. Dennis said – "… we tried to take films out of the archive and return them to people which meant we had to engage in dialogues with people and communities and at the time we could not find much of a precedent for this – but [it] gave us extraordinary insight" (Dennis in Mita & Dennis, 1991). Dennis' friends and colleagues recognised that the passion he felt for films was finally matched by the audience, as Māori responded with enthusiasm to films of their ancestors (Personal correspondence, M. Wall 01/10/10). Dennis described another screening, this time in an urban setting in the capital city Wellington – "… an old lady who remembered the filming back in 1921 and who'd seen the film already at Matahiwi and at the Museum, stood and began to karanga, to call out to the ancestors, to welcome them back" (Dennis, 1990 p.3).

This elder was responding to taonga as described by Paul Tapsell – she was calling to the wairua of the films, to the ihi and wana with wehi.[112] Because of these kinds of responses, rituals and ceremonies of the tāngata whenua came to be incorporated into the screenings of the films, and Mihipeka Edwards (iwi affilations to Te Arawa and Ngāti Raukawa), Lily Amohau (iwi affiliation Ngāti Whakaue) and Witarina Harris were all elders who "warmed" the films by accompanying them to various locations and contextualising them for audiences through introductions, prayer, song and talk (Dennis in Fyfe & Dennis, 2001). Conal McCarthy describes warming as "an essential element in the care of taonga" referring to "the bond between people and treasures that is activated and maintained when they come together" (McCarthy, 2011 p.133).

This was exciting progress for Dennis and the NZFA, but it did pose many questions for the formal Western film archive model they were part of. In his

---

112 A reminder of Paul Tapsell's (Te Arawa) description of the term taonga: "any item, object or thing that represents the ancestral identity of a Māori kin group (whānau, hapū or iwi) in relation to particular lands and resources … They are seen as the spiritual personifications of particular ancestors, either as direct images or through association. Descendants experience this wairua (ancestral spirit) as ihi (presence), wehi (awe) and wana (authority). Thus taonga are time travellers that bridge the generations, enabling descendants to ritually meet their ancestors face to face" (Tapsell, 2006 p.17 translation Tapsell's).

1988 report to the Federation Internationale des Archives du Film (FIAF) Congress, Dennis expressed his concern with the lack of progress internationally in working with indigenous peoples to better catalogue materials. Dennis described the difficulties the NZFA encountered as they prepared a catalogue for the sixty films accompanying the return of the Te Māori exhibition of taonga from the United States of America. It was becoming increasingly difficult to follow the "European" model where the normative practice did not account for indigenous perspectives. The difficulty of ensuring appropriate process which could honour the Māori perspective as well as satisfy European archiving protocols was an issue for the international community in his opinion (Dennis Jonathan, 1987).[113] He felt that although some "basic descriptive cataloguing" progress had been made, the "process cannot be sustained in isolation". He was concerned by this and felt that "the inability of present cataloguing philosophy and practice to acknowledge the contribution and status of indigenous peoples ought to become the subject of much larger and more vigorous debate" (FIAF report of NZFA, Paris, 1988).

In this report Dennis is signalling a tension between geographically specific practices and processes developed with iwi which were alien from the international codes of film archiving. He is naming a failure in European "cataloguing philosophy" and calling for an international response to this dilemma. He was also asking for help from the international film archiving community. In the presentation of the films, Dennis had been able to follow the lead of elders such as Witarina Harris to ensure appropriate practice. But Harris was not an archivist and therefore was unable to advise him on the practice of appropriate cataloguing or long term preservation of the films in the care of the NZFA. Nor were Barry Barclay or Merata Mita archivists themselves. The International Federation of Film Archives, dominated by European and North American interests were not engaged by ihi, wehi, wana or wairua. The "magic" Dell described in relation to these films was not part of the traditional view of the Western archivist. These concerns were not resolved by the time Dennis resigned from the Archive, and in fact these ongoing difficulties were part of the reason he departed from the Archive (Dennis in Pivac & Dennis, 2000).

Dennis was able to continue to engage with indigenous materials throughout the 1980s because Witarina Harris supported his work. The alliance with a Māori elder was his entré into Māori communities where an unknown Pākehā and

---

113 The NZFA gained membership of FIAF (Federations Internationale des Archives du Film) in 1985. The archive was audited regularly, and if found to be failing the standards of FIAF's code they would be expelled (FIAF, 2002).

Director of a Wellington institution could not otherwise go: people's private homes, Black Power hui [Māori gang gathering], whare nui events and Māori film screenings (Alley & Dennis, 2002; Fyfe & Dennis, 2001; Pivac & Dennis, 2000). He had no social or cultural capital in these spaces and relied entirely on hers.

Harris' influence on Dennis' practice was profound. He sought her out when his international colleagues indicated that a copy of the 1929 film *The Devil's Pit* might be available for repatriation from a private collection in the United States. Dennis had heard that the star of the film might still be alive, so just as he had sought out other stars and icons such as Lillian Gish, Len Lye and Mary Meerson, he arranged to meet Harris in 1982 (NZFA PP JD Box 19). She began to have an impact on his practice immediately, but Dennis said in later interviews that it was the 1984 response to the films with Witarina Harris at the Rotorua Festiv'Art which really had a great impact on the Archive's direction. He described how she organised "a private screening [in someone's home] and all the old people came. It was the first time we had shown the films in that context … when we showed the films at the festival, hundreds of people came. It was quite extraordinary …" (Dennis, 1989). It was this screening which encouraged him to realise how much more engaged Māori people were by their films, and how the NZFA could be part of that engagement.

Dennis notes it was the first time they had shown the films in a private home. It was Harris' influence which allowed this to happen since she had arranged the screenings in her hometown. It opened Dennis' eyes to new possibilities which would engage this passionate audience. Dennis said that when the films were shown privately to the elders they wanted to see each film fragment "*at least* twice" (Dennis, 1990 p. 2, Dennis' emphasis). In another interview he said "a thousand" came to the film screenings at the festival (Dennis in Fyfe & Dennis, 2001). Dennis described the "terrific sense of excitement at being able to greet these images. It was like a whole tribe and city's home movies had been returned, were now known about and accessible (even though still only through the Archive). The occasion was deeply felt by both Māori and European alike…." He said although he did not realise it at the time the films and their reception were starting to change the archive, which needed to be "responsible for offering balanced and equitable services at local, regional and tribal levels – not just in the city where we were based" (Dennis, 1990, p.2). Dennis was clearly excited and the responses he saw were motivational in trying to engage people who really responded to the NZFA screenings. However he also notes that the films were only available through the Archive, signalling his awareness of the concerns iwi had over the control of their own materials.

Harris' knowledge and iwi based relationships afforded Dennis many advantages and opportunities he would not otherwise have had. Harris had a wide network, she had full command of her language, and knowledge of her culture. This allowed Dennis to invite other Māori to become involved through her influence. But ultimately, as Ngā Tamatoa (the Young Warriors of the previous chapter) and other younger activists began to pressure cultural heritage institutions, it became clear that Harris' support was not enough. The younger generation of activists were not content to work in a supporting capacity for Pākehā, as (arguably) Ngata, Buck and Harris had done. They wanted control (arguably the kaupapa Māori mode). Dennis as a Pākehā did not understand the (as Sorreson described it of other Pākehā) "inner emotions, hearts and minds" of Māori (Sorrenson, 2012). He did not have the cultural capital required, nor did he feel as a non-Māori that he had the networks or support (which would have been provided by social capital) required. As Dennis said, without Harris' "generosity and love" he could not have undertaken many of the screenings they did. He acknowledged that although "she, and the others of her generation ... were there for the Archive and for me, [ultimately they] were not enough" (Dennis, 1990 p.4).

Dennis was ostensibly European, being of a line of English/Irish settlers. And yet he was a Pākehā too – a New Zealand born European with strong ties and links to his country. He was in the same position as many Pākehā working in cultural heritage institutions in the 1980s. While he was willing to learn and take on the values of indigenous peoples, this was not enough to satisfy those who felt that in order to adequately redress the many wrongs of the past it was necessary to take back control of their own images. In addition, he could never experience ngā taonga as face to face encounters with the ancestors, because they were not his ancestors. Māori had a different kind of cultural capital than Dennis did; they had a relationship to their taonga which he could not have. They did not, like Bourdieu and some Pākehā, see their taonga as "primitive" (Pierre Bourdieu, 1984 p.3). For Māori, who had social capital through iwi networks, they had a knowledge and experience very different from the Pākehā Director of the NZFA.

Dennis' experience is certainly reflected in the wider development of the kaupapa Māori movement during the 1980s. The debates, such as "do you have to be Māori to do this?" were rife and Dennis was, as the Director of a national institution holding Māori materials, asked this himself. By the 1980s the "rules of the game" were changing and Pākehā were being challenged to give back the power they had held since colonisation. The kind of concerns about Māori materials being screened by the Archive were encapsulated in an experience Dennis described which occurred while presenting the McDonald films at the old museum in Wellington on Buckle St (formerly the Dominion Museum where Elsdon Best and James McDonald had worked). With an audience of about 300 people, but without Witarina Harris present, a young Māori man demanded to know "what was a Pākehā doing with this material in the first place and what were we doing with it and how much do I earn, and you know, what gave us the right to preserve this material, and did this as a complete, really, aggressive challenge at me" (Dennis in Pivac & Dennis, 2000). Dennis said this was "early days" for these kinds of challenges, and the Pākehā people in the audience "curled up in horror" but the Māori people in the audience sat and watched "as one would do on a marae"(Dennis in Pivac and Dennis, ibid.).[114]

In this instance, Dennis was describing culturally informed responses which depended upon the habitus and doxa of the individuals. The young man was openly speaking to Dennis in a public forum, challenging his right to hold this material of Māori origin. He was questioning Dennis' power, his cultural capital in relation to these materials, which this man, like many others, responded to as ngā taonga, as a direct encounter with the ancestors. If Dennis had been on a marae and working within a framework for that space, it may have been a very different engagement.

As indicated by his observation that Māori sat up and watched as one would do on a marae where particular protocols and responses were normative, Barclay's argument that Māori debate is nonlinear and cyclic arises here. Dennis was outside his own field, the Archive, and the young man was (possibly) outside his traditional field, the marae, where there would be rules of engagement quite different to those at the Museum where the films were screened. This young man was expressing sentiments similar to those which Mita's film *Patu!* had shown and Ranginui Walker had alluded to. For this man, "biculturalism" meant self-determination, tino rangatiratanga. Dennis said he had "rarely felt so exposed

---

114 Merimeri Penfold, a Māori scholar described similar criticism leveled at Judith Binney, a Pākehā historian and Anne Salmond, a Pākehā who had been chosen by Māori iwi elders to tell their stories: "Anne Salmond and Judith Binney were approached by Māori women protestors demanding them to 'Stop. Stop writing about us.' Judith was working on *Ngā Mōrehu: The Survivors*, her book of oral history interviews with Māori women elders associated with the prophet Rua Kenana and the Ringatū faith. She replied 'The writing has been done with the permission of the Māori women elders. Are you saying I should not accept the permission they gave me? Are you challenging their decision?' … These women protestors were much younger and for the first time they had to confront real issues. They needed to respect that Judy and Anne were working with the approval of the elderly Māori women" (Shepard, 2009 p.128).

... The generosity of my reception in places around the country never eased the vulnerability, or the hurts and rejection that seem to be part of the painful process of disempowering oneself. Without blueprints, the process of finding and providing some kind of adequate framework to empower others is immensely slow and difficult ... But it can also be ... a time of real awakening". Although hurt, Dennis still respected the young man for making his feelings and views known, and he ensured that he told others what had occurred (Dennis, 1990 p.6).

Another Pākehā working with taonga (and the descendant of James McDonald who was the cameraman for the films Dennis was screening above) felt there was an irony to a situation where in the 1980s period "Pākehā people ... were bringing Māori things to public attention because Pākehā were in a position of advantage and privilege. They had better access to education over generations, so I could understand the force of Māori criticism" (Dame Anne Salmond quoted in Shepard, 2009, p. 182). Dennis was clearly not the only one criticised for engaging with Māori materials at this time. Pākehā privilege meant they were in a position to bring "Māori things" to public attention.

Dennis responded to the criticisms encapsulated in the young Māori man's attack at the museum by attempting to change the institutional structure to reflect genuine power sharing. For example he invited Annie Collins, editor of *Patu!* and an anti-racism trainer with *Pākehās Against Racism,* to carry out workshops with the staff.[115] This group was undertaking "Pākeha to Pākehā" efforts to challenge racism. Collins did two workshops with the NZFA staff and they redrafted the constitution into the kaupapa (Personal correspondence, A. Collins op.cit.).

The rewriting of the Constitution/Kaupapa of the Archive occurred around the same time as the name of the Archive was changed from the *NZFA* to the *NZFA Ngā Kaitiaki o ngā Taonga Whitiāhua* (The Guardians of the Treasured Images of Light). Sharon Dell created the Te Reo Māori translation. These actions were intended to be steps toward a final goal of a restructured Archive with fifty percent Māori and fifty percent Pākehā Board (Dennis in Dennis & Pivac 2000). The change of name began to appear on official documents of the Archive in 1987 (for example, the FIAF report to congress) and on its newsletters around the same

---

115 By this time Annie Collins had worked again with Merata Mita as Senior Editor on *Mauri* (Prod.& Dir. M. Mita, 1988), and returned to Wellington where she had been working with others in the anti-racism movement. A report came out of the Department of Social Welfare in 1985 (Department of Social Welfare, 1985, *Institutional Racism in the Department of Social Welfare, Tamaki-Makau-Rau* [WARAG] revised edition, Auckland) which set out the institutional racism in that department. Groups like Annie's were seen as useful in training staff to respond to the concerns raised in the report. Collins made a film *Double Take* about racism at this time which she used in her training (Personal Correspondence, A.Collins op.cit.).

time.[116] The rewritten Constitution/Kaupapa states that the Archive aims to be a "storehouse/pataka tuturu of moving image materials/taonga whitiahua in accordance with the Treaty of Waitangi/Tiriti o Waitangi principles of partnership" and the objectives are – "To acquire and receive all moving image materials/taonga whitiahua of permanent national and cultural significance in fulfilment of the above aims, with due regard for and reference to mana tuturu and the rights of the materials themselves, the rights of the copyright owners and the rights of the depositors".[117]

This revised Constitution/Kaupapa made the NZFA different from any other Western archive in the world at that time (Personal correspondence, M. Labrum 08/08/11; R. Horrocks 21/10/08). It incorporated indigenous rights into its infrastructure and acknowledged the rights of the materials *themselves* as ngā taonga, as living entities with relationships to people. This was significant, and despite various changes since Dennis' time at the archive which are outlined in Barclay's book *Mana Tūturu* (Barclay, 2005), the Constitution/Kaupapa still operates in 2015. But the written statements of the Archive were not enough. Māori people needed to be employed in the NZFA in order to provide their perspectives on the work to be done.

The first Māori staff member was employed as the Māori materials cataloguer in the late 1980s, but as Dennis had signalled in his reports to the International Federation of Film Archives, this work could only be "experimental" without wider inter-institutional support. Dennis acknowledged that this staff member was under immense pressure (Dennis, 1989 p.11) and she resigned after a short time. The next Māori staff member also resigned.[118] In 1991, NZFA Board member Te Aue Davis observed that Māori employed or asked to support appropriate Māori practice in mainstream institutions often become overworked (NZFA Board minutes, 1991).

In March 1990 Dennis had also resigned from the Archive, stating in lectures,

---

116 This title is first used in a FIAF report in 1987 (NFSA collection NZFA report to FIAF 1987 Dennis). Sharon Dell created the title as a symbol of the ongoing attempt to create a bicultural institution (Personal correspondence, S. Dell 13/04/15).

117 Dennis was to write in his FIAF report in 1990 that the Kaupapa was the first "major step toward becoming an institution that is fully bi-cultural in image and practice, has affected every level of the Archive and has given a place to stand on issues confronting our operation and activities. While sometimes progress toward real structured change – at staffing and Board levels particularly – has seemed slow, the commitment has not waivered ... .This Film Archive is, we hope, a living archive and we want to keep it that way" (FIAF Congress report of NZFA 1990).

118 Both former staff members declined to be interviewed for this work (Personal correspondence with author). This is a silence in the discourse which is hard to interpret without their input and I do not want to try and explain their positions for them.

presentations and articles for various journals, that he recognised that as a Pākehā, he was not the appropriate person to be in control of the Archive as it moved towards bicultural practice (Alley & Dennis, 2002; Dennis, 1989, 1990). Dennis was working at the Archive at a time of wide and ferocious debate about the role of Pākehā in bicultural endeavour. As the philosophy of kaupapa Māori, which (often) asserted Māori control was becoming more popular, Dennis felt his position was increasingly precarious.

The minutes of the NZFA board state – "Ngahuia Te Awekotuku confirmed that the first Director of the Film Archive had taken personal responsibility for bicultural matters. His departure left a critical muddle which had been difficult to deal with" (55th meeting of the NZFA Trustees 17/11/91 NZFA Board minutes, 1989–1992 p.3).

In terms of Eagle's "journey", Te Awekotuku's statement suggests that Dennis and the NZFA had indeed moved from the monocultural to a decision to become bicultural, but this had only occurred thus far by individual "kanohi ki te kanohi" [face to face] relationships and not permeated the entire structure of the Archive. However, the rewriting of the Constitution which included the Treaty of Waitangi as its basis had already occurred, so there was a foundation for a general bicultural process as the infrastructure was being altered. This was not always acknowledged or perhaps even understood by all NZFA board members (Dennis, 1989 p.11). As the elders of Ngāpuhi argue in a 2012 report, it may be that "bicultural" relationships are only possible "kanohi ki te kanohi" and although institutional changes can be made, unless people are willing to come together face to face, trust will not be developed between them (Kuia and Kaumātua of Ngāpuhi Nui Tonu., 2012).

In the 1980s the power struggles which were occurring between groups such as Ngā Tamatoa, younger Māori outside institutional walls and Pākehā within the institution demonstrated that many Māori were not interested in Pākehā re-understanding their "primitive" materials as "art", but instead wanted to obtain control of their own materials and have a different kind of relationship with them (McCarthy, 2011). Indeed, in the Māori understanding of cultural capital, an entirely different set of values have eminence. In European culture, written documents are often considered superior evidence of truth or value (for example, in the written descriptions of the provenance of an art or cultural object), whereas in Māori culture in the pre-colonial contact era, whaikōrero (elaborate and allusion filled speeches in the whare nui and the accompanying complex protocols) or traditional tattooing, are two examples of erudite and rich cultural information sources completely undervalued in Pākehā culture (Kuia and Kaumātua of Ngāpuhi Nui Tonu., 2012). Two cultures with two different sets of understanding of "cultural capital" were talking past each other. Dennis described the views of some, such as Barclay, in an article in which he said that although he tried to "work these issues through" it was difficult because "even our terminology was different … The Archive's structure allowed for tangata whenua window dressing, without a shared power base, and still without power at the decision making level" (Dennis, 1990 pp.4,5).

By 1990 there were many Māori critics of state-sponsored biculturalism, one of whom was Irihāpeti Ramsden, who was soon to start work with Dennis and author Patricia Grace on the oral histories (and the eventual book) of Ngāti Pōneke Young Māori Club (Grace et al., 2001). She remarked at a talk at the National Museum in 1990 that "to her, biculturalism meant 'bye-bye culture!'" (McCarthy, 2011 p.84).[119] Ramsden, Dennis and Patricia Grace were going to have many conversations about "biculturalism" over the next ten years or so as they worked together. Some of these fascinating discussions were recorded by Dennis and are available in the Alexander Turnbull Oral History Library (Ramsden, Grace, & Dennis, 1995).

It is possible to see the "journey" of the NZFA in the 1980s as being typical of government departments of the period. Pākehā historian Jacob Pollock described the bicultural era, which "emerged alongside the reformist fourth Labour Government in the 1980s, following more than a decade of social unrest" (Pollock, 2005 p.21). He suggests that in hindsight "Pākehā biculturalism … appears to be thoroughly engaged in the impossible task of achieving indigeneity" (Pollock, 2005 p.28). This is something akin to Bourdieu's argument, that one cannot completely remove oneself from the doxa and habitus within which an agent in the field has been raised. However Kloot argues that although Bourdieu is often understood to be pessimistic and "social reproductionist", a more "optimistic, transformative" reading is possible in which human agency is adequately accounted for (Kloot, 2009 p.473). Yet Pollock argues that the national identity narrative is "intimately bound up" with the project of "cultural colonization" (Pollock, 2005 p.3). Māori scholar Dominic O'Sullivan concurs, arguing that the

---

119 Ramsden wrote her PhD thesis in the 1990s on "cultural safety", then a new concept developed by Māori nurses. Jonathan Dennis was one of a group of friends who made regular payments to an account to support her studies (NZFA PP JD Box 11). Ramsden invited Dennis to her wedding in 1997, and there are a number of warm letters and cards from her in his archive (NZFA PP JD Box 11). Ramsden was to die of a brain tumour about a year after Dennis died of cancer, but they both managed to be at the launch of their ten year effort with Patricia Grace to document the Ngāti Pōneke elders in late 2001 (Personal correspondence, S. Dennis,. op.cit).

enthusiastic embrace by state institutions of biculturalism was a liberal strategy of managing resistance while actually denying self-determination (D. O'Sullivan quoted in McCarthy, 2011 p.77). Ultimately, Māori are still the subjugated partner in the relationship.

Dennis never found moving towards biculturalism easy, and often found it "scary" (Dennis, 1990), as did many others, Māori and Pākehā. What Dennis did do was listen to the criticisms that the Archive was receiving and try to respond appropriately to address Māori concerns. Mita, a strong critic of Pākehā who did not respect Māori views, allowed Dennis to be the distributor for her films and to work with her for the rest of his life, suggesting that she felt his work was appropriate. The elders Witarina Harris, Lily Amohau, Mihipeka Edwards and others supported Dennis to the end and were even an important part of his funeral, sitting with him on the stage at the Paramount Theatre ("The Last Film Show; Funeral of Jonathan Spencer Dennis", 2002 January 29). Barry Barclay, a passionate and astute critic of Pākehā institutions, said that the signing of a 2011 NZFA memorandum regarding the returning of films to iwi "somehow vindicated Jonathan's stumbling prescience back in the first years of the archive, and showed, at least in film archive circles, how he was much ahead of his time" (Barclay, 2005 p.107).

Dennis' ten years at the NZFA saw him experience the excitement of founding a new national institution, working with the everyday development of a Film Archive while adapting to social and political movements which were impacting upon concepts of the nation. He adapted as best he could, but felt it inevitable that he must step aside in order to allow for ngā taonga to have a relationship with Māori people unimpeded by Pākehā gatekeepers. This was part of the narrative of his own life and work in relation to biculturalism but also a significant aspect of how others understood him.

Chapter 6

Narrative of Jonathan Dennis' archive

W hen filmmaker Peter Wells made an audiovisual recording of Jonathan Dennis at his house as Dennis was dying of cancer in late 2001, he used a small hand-held digital camera which he felt was less intrusive than a film camera which would have required a crew. Wells admits this made for "an amateurishly shot home video", but felt "it wasn't that kind of massive invasion that you used to get with film. I was just there as a friend, really, and it was part of the privilege of being there" (Wells cited in Cardy, 2004). The edited footage from this recording was later interwoven with an oral history recording made by other friends (Elizabeth Alley and Gareth Watkins) and eventually the film *Friendship Is the Harbour of Joy* was screened at the New Zealand International Film Festival (Prod. & Dir. P. Wells, 2004). The film was then seen by a number of people and it in turn became one of the texts of the narrative of the life of Jonathan Dennis. This film is tangible evidence of Dennis' life: his house, his friendships and interests. It bears testament to Wells' and Dennis' friendship, which was partly based on a mutual fascination with film as a medium – not just for transmitting audio visual images, but as an artefact in and of itself. Using a camera, Wells is able to capture recordings of verbal and non-verbal information. These sounds and images represent the "languages of the unsayable ... negations, erasures, revisions, smokescreens and silences" through which a narrative is told (Sorsoli, 2007 p.306). The title refers tacitly to Wells' own friendship with Dennis, but more explicitly it depicts the friendship of Dennis and Witarina Harris.

By collecting images and sounds of Jonathan Dennis and his friend, as well as the house in which Dennis lived, "ephemeral physical manifestations" (Grishakova & Ryan, 2010 p.1) such as the sound of wind chimes, of kitchen business, and the spoken word were recorded. Sound engineer Gareth Watkins also deliberately recorded the sounds of Dennis' house after the collection of an oral history with colleague Elizabeth Alley (Alley et al., 2001). These recordings enabled later works about Dennis' life to use these rich ambient sounds as layers in the text, to add depth and substance without the need for verbal or written description of these ephemera. They are a library of sounds which, decontextualized, mean nothing. But attached to the name Jonathan Dennis, they are filled with memory for those who knew him and had spent time with him in his house. For those who did not know him, they evoke various impressions to the audience depending on their perspective.

Wells' film is just one of a number of attempts to record the narrative of Jonathan Dennis shortly before his death, using various modes of oral history narrative co-construction which will be explored in this chapter. These recordings were also attempts by his friends to try and understand their relationship to Dennis' living and dying time. They are multiple co-constructions of a life and death. Within Wells' text there is a representation of friendships which express the "intimate public" and a "queer" perspective.[120] They are examples of Foucault's "heterotopias", folds within the normative world "where one can encounter the positivity of being otherwise ..." (Berlant & Prosser, 2011 p.181). These are particularly present in Peter Wells' documentary of a gay man, by a gay man, at a time when they were both aware of the importance of documenting their own lives as the first generation of "out" and legal gay men in NZ. Dennis was also quite consciously shaping a narrative of his life from his own memory. How he told his story, and how he interpreted the events of his life, are fundamental to his narrative of self.

Oral histories

A popular method for collecting life histories is through the oral history interview, which since the 1960s has been a relatively low budget method for recording life narratives (Mellor & Haebich, 2002). Oral history philosophy has been affected by poststructuralism, and it is therefore often understood that the purpose of the recordings is not to collect a verifiable truth. In fact, "oral history has made us uncomfortably aware of the elusive quality of historical truth itself" (Portelli, 1991 p.ix). Although facts can be established, verified and triangulated and the aspiration towards reality is essential, "certainty is bound to escape us" (Portelli, 1991, ibid.).

---

120 In using the term "queer" I do not imply any homosexual tendencies in Witarina Harris, but instead offer "queer theory" as a way in which to think about Dennis and Harris' unusual relationship.

An oral history records the voice of the person, which is a form of truth: the intonations of that voice, the pauses and sighs, the sounds of the space in which they are recorded. Roland Barthes has referred to the "grain of the voice", which Siobhan McHugh pursues as a concept in her analysis of the oral history and its significance in the narrative co-construction (McHugh, 2012). What interpretation is possible from those spaces is different for each interviewer, each transcriber, listener, or reader. These are Sorsoli's "languages of the unsayable" which add richness to the text, but are open to interpretation by the listener/reader/viewer (Sorsoli, 2007). Yet the various oral history interviews undertaken with Jonathan Dennis form an autobiographical arc that suggests a narrative "co-construction, an interactional achievement, a joint production and/or collaboration between the interviewer and interviewee" (Petraki et al., 2007 p.108).

Many of the texts which are evidence of Dennis' life are spoken word and therefore are "ephemeral physical manifestations" (Grishakova & Ryan, 2010 p.1). However, as soon as they are recorded and potentially transcribed they "become part of a more 'stable' historical record for future generations" (Binney, 2010 pp.323,324). However, as Binney suggests in the title of her collection of essays, *Stories Without End…*, the meaning conveyed by words still have an "'original' fluidity of metaphor and meaning. Our understanding of them is not fixed by the act of writing. Contradictory meanings coexist …" (Binney, 2010 ibid.). Dennis' oral histories and other recordings have become the evidence through which he is understood, constructed and co-constructed by listeners and readers. But they are still open to various interpretations, they contain "contradictory meanings" and they are "fluid" in their "metaphor and meaning".

Many interviewees for this research commented on Elizabeth Alley's interview with Dennis, which was edited by Paul Bushnell and played on Radio New Zealand after he died (Alley & Dennis, 2002). They said they had not understood certain aspects of his personality until they heard that recording (for example, Personal correspondence, S. Dell, 10/09/10). The interviewees believed they had received some new truth or clarification about the personality of Jonathan Dennis through hearing the interview/oral history. Indeed, that narrative of his life became part of how they remembered Dennis posthumously. Because by the time they heard this new information Dennis was dead, it has become "fixed" in their minds as fact, but also gelled with something they already thought – or explained something they had not previously understood. They were not able to ask him questions themselves, follow up and clarify his meaning or explore his ideas after hearing this interview. Therefore, those who edited that oral history for broadcast are privileged because they cannot seek further clarification from the subject; their interpretation is final. Yet other edits of that same material could offer a different perspective entirely depending upon which elements were emphasised or edited out of the broadcast or text.

Narrative co-construction through oral history

"A sense of self is difficult without myth" (J.C.Davis 1985 p.7).

Davis suggests that the process of constructing the self and narrating one's actions shifts the discussion away from the authentic nature of the subject to something other and perhaps more intriguing. Similarly, Virginia Woolf said in *The New Biography* that truth and personality do not always sit easily together and that for a writer of biography "in order that the light of personality may shine through, facts must be manipulated; some must be brightened; others shaded. Yet, in the process, they must never lose their integrity" (Woolf, 1967 p.229). Just what "integrity" might mean in this context is left unexplained. The reader must interpret Woolf's statement, and thus the challenge of retelling or presenting a life. It is quite possible that, as she suggests, by the end of the biography "the figure which has been most completely on display is that of the author" (Woolf, 1967 ibid.) echoing David E. Gray's warning of the potential narcissism of the reflexive approach (Gray, 2009 p.499). In narrating one's own life history or that of others, facts are "manipulated", some "brightened", others "shaded" as Woolf has described. Foucault's description of the archive itself resonates here – the enunciable will "... shine, as it were, like stars ..." (Foucault quoted in Merewether, 2006 p.29). The author will choose to focus on some elements of a life and not on others for their own ends.

Fischer and Goblirsch (2007) claim that people construct a narrative through a "creative process of self-constitution"; through interaction, accessing memories and co-constructing through talk (Fischer & Goblirsch, 2007 p.38). People do this every day in informal conversation. This process of self-constitution becomes more pronounced when people are interviewed and specifically asked to reflect on their lives. Jonathan Dennis gave repeated interviews for radio and newspapers throughout the 1980s in order to publicise the NZFA (Dennis in Pivac & Dennis, 2000). From 1990, the focus of these interviews changed from the NZFA to his own creative practice, his resignation from the Archive, and later still, his overall career. Finally the focus moved to his attitude towards his life, his experience of cancer (from which he suffered for six years), and his imminent death (For example Fyfe & Dennis, 2001). Through this process certain milestone stories about Dennis' life and work begin to be repeated, which function to offer a narrative coherence, a discourse in "a privileged mode … tying together existent analogies between life, biography, and story" (Bamberg, De Fina, & Schiffrin, 2007 p.5).

Mieke Bal's *Theory of Narratology* is useful here in considering the versions of the narrative of Jonathan Dennis' life which have been produced by himself and others. In summary, Bal's approach considers many modes, including film, video, comic strips, oral stories and written texts as "narrative artifacts" or "narrative texts" which tell the reader a story (Bal, 2009 3rd ed., p.5). In Bal's theory, a story is the content of the text, but the text is not always identical; there are potentially many versions. For example, the story of Tom Thumb may appear in an adult and children's version. Some of the content will be altered as appropriate for the audience. All of these are versions of a narrative; the same story but a different text. According to Bal, a narrative contains fabula which are a "series of logically and chronologically related events that are caused or experienced by actors" (Bal, 2009 3rd ed., pp.5,6).[121]

The "fabula" of Jonathan Dennis' narrative are told in two major autobiographical oral histories (Alley & Dennis, 2002; Fyfe & Dennis, 2001).[122] In addition there is a further interview which focused largely on his work and was recorded by a fellow film archivist Diane Pivac (Pivac & Dennis, 2000). These interviews were undertaken by three women who understood the value of recording stories, but each came from a different perspective.

Firstly, Diane Pivac, who has worked at the NZFA since 1990, interviewed Jonathan Dennis. She had liaised with him after he left the Film Archive as he organised various exhibitions and film screenings nationally and internationally (Personal correspondence, D. Pivac 26/11/09). Because she had access to the administrative records of the Archive and knew the Archive well, her interview is rich with specific technical questions about the decade in which the Archive was founded. A particular kind of "co-construction" is apparent in her interview which seeks to clarify information about the founding years of the Archive, some of which was later used in a publication (Davy & Pivac, 2008).[123] Secondly,

---

121 "Actors" being those who perform an action (Bal, 2009, pp. 5, 6).

122 Malcolm McKinnon has pointed out that the Alley and Fyfe interviews may be markedly similar because Dennis was very tired from his illness and had to be conservative with his energy, therefore perhaps he provided simple and more practiced answers (Personal correspondence, M.McKinnon 14/07/10).

123 At the National Film and Sound Archive in Australia, key staff members oral histories are recorded and added to the Archive to develop and support its own corporate history (Personal correspondence, C. Guster, 05/07/11). This is not the usual practice at the NZFA.

Elizabeth Alley, veteran radio broadcaster and interviewer recorded Dennis' oral history not long before his death. She undertook this interview with sound engineer Gareth Watkins who had worked alongside Alley and Dennis, making *The Film Show* (film review show broadcast on Concert and then National Radio) for a number of years (Personal correspondence, G. Watkins op.cit.) Both Alley and Watkins had begun working with Dennis as colleagues, but were firm friends by the time this recording was undertaken (Personal correspondence, E. Alley op.cit.). This interview explores Dennis' feelings and the impressions he made on others in some detail.

Finally Judith Fyfe, a significant figure in the New Zealand oral history movement was asked by a group of friends to record a film and sound interview not long before Dennis died. Fyfe did not know Dennis previously (Personal correspondence, A. Collins 26/01/09). Annie Collins filmed the Fyfe interview. For much of the interview the image is one fixed shot of Dennis and Fyfe. In the background the bright colours of his walls can be seen as well as Dennis' Colin McCahon painting, *Paul to Hebrews* and a window across which is an elaborate iron artwork. These are discussed during the course of the interview. The impression is of an artistic house of a well-established person. Later, Dennis is recorded with Witarina Harris by his side and she also speaks. All three recordings were deposited in the NZFA. Fyfe accessed Pivac's interview before meeting with Dennis, so to some extent her interview follows the fabula of Pivac's previous work, but then explores the idea of his imminent death (Fyfe & Dennis, 2001).

There is perhaps something akin to the confessional in the Fyfe and Alley interviews with Dennis. In both he accepts that he is going to die, although he does not know how soon that will be. He reviews his life and tries to explain aspects of his behaviour and personality. This kind of oral history at the time of someone's diagnosis with a terminal illness is perhaps a specific mode of narrative and storytelling which is quite different from (for example) the interviews I have gathered about Dennis, which did not focus on the interviewee's life story, although aspects of that were often offered and always accepted (Examples include Personal correspondence, R. Grover op.cit.; B. Sheat op.cit.; D. Eckhoff op.cit.)

Within the narratives created by these three interviews are recurring motifs and moments in which Dennis indicated incidents which he understood to have shifted or developed his thinking. These paint the picture of his personality, of his life and interests and works. They are neither true nor false, being simply stories through which Dennis and others (including myself) understood and understand him as a coherent personality. This collection of materials offers an insight into the role of storytelling in the making of meaning for the understanding of "a life" of Jonathan Dennis. The narrative arc remains remarkably consistent across these three interviews, with commonly recurring milestones or "fabula" which identify it as the same story even if it were not attached to the voice of Jonathan Dennis or to his name. These are Foucault's "said and unsaid" moments, or Virginia Woolf's facts polished to reveal certain aspects and not others. Before these edits and representations are possible however, the original raw recordings were undertaken. These too involved an editing process in the mind of the interviewee who chose what to reveal or conceal.[124]

Interviewees themselves also actively engaged in the meaning making of the story of Jonathan Dennis in discussion with me as interviewer and biographer. Ricoeur argues that "narrative coherence" is important for all of us, helping us make sense of life and how it has been lived in meaningful ways (Bamberg et al., 2007 p.5). Themes emerged from the interviews unprompted by the author's questions. For example, many interviewees discussed Dennis' appearance at some length, expressing amusement, fondness, and at times, bewilderment or embarrassment. For example, Lindsay Shelton, who was then Marketing Director of the NZ Film Commission described walking down a mall in Milan in the early 1980s with Dennis who was dressed in his usual colourful apparel. A group of very formally well dressed young Italian men were walking towards them and "parted like the red sea" on seeing Dennis (Personal correspondence, L. Shelton 07/12/09). Many felt that Dennis' presentation of self through his choice of clothes reflected his performance of a public persona, a use of metaphorical masks which helped him negotiate his way through often difficult and confrontational public experiences. A close friend remarked – "I often used to think that the thread that linked all of Jonathan's activities was that they were performances of one kind or another" (Personal correspondence, M. McKinnon 23/11/09). This understanding of Dennis as being performative, for some interviewees at least, may have been prompted by the interview most had heard between Alley and Dennis in which they discussed his "personas" (Alley & Dennis, 2002).

However, many people had experience of the performances for themselves. A close friend who had been part of the *Amamus* theatre troupe described how

---

124 As part of my own practice in being interviewed, I reflected on the process of myself and my father being interviewed by Gareth Watkins for an online archive both reveal and conceal facts about our lives – we did not do so to "lie" but one finds oneself quite necessarily developing a narrative which fits the purpose of the interview as one understands it at the time. In asking my father about this afterwards, I clarified that some of the events he had described had been "edited" in his head before he explained them to the interviewer. Interview available from http://www.pridenz.com/emma_and_john_kelly.html.

performance seemed to her an intrinsic part of Dennis' own family dynamic. She related her experience of the Dennis family dinner table – "… for the outsider it was like watching *Who's Afraid of Virginia Woolf*…a theatrical performance almost that they put on" (Personal correspondence, D. Young op.cit). Many others described these family dinners as exhausting, with guests and family alike being expected to take a position in the argument and see it through to the "bitter" end (Personal correspondence, K. Dennis 13/07/10). Gubrium and Holstein argue that "family is not so much a concrete set of social ties or bonds as a way of attaching meaning to interpersonal relations. Like other social objects, family is a project that is realized through discourse" (Petraki et al., 2007 p.108). The charged atmosphere at the Dennis family dinner table was reminiscent of some interviewees' views on Dennis' personal interactions, particularly when he was angry. Dennis did not hide his opinions or emotions well and perhaps had learned to behave this way through his family interactions, supporting Gubrium and Holstein's view of the role families play in the attachment of meaning to interpersonal relations and discursive practices.

Some interviewees described Dennis by linking back to the stories they knew of film archiving history. For example, British Film Institute (BFI) archivist Elaine Burrows remarked that she thought Dennis had a similar passion and flamboyant enthusiasm to Henri Langlois, founder of the Cinémathèque Française (Personal correspondence, E. Burrows 07/07/10) while others said they were reminded of Len Lye (Personal correspondence, G. Watkins 21/11/09). Bill Gosden thought Dennis perhaps modelled himself on Edith Kramer, film archivist for the Pacific Film Archive at Berkeley (Personal correspondence, B. Gosden op.cit.). Edith Kramer was certainly a strong influence and became a good friend to Dennis and Paolo Cherchi-Usai (Personal correspondence, E. Kramer 02/04/12; P. Cherchi-Usai 14/05/09).

Other interviewees described the theatricality of Dennis' behaviour. Elizabeth Alley remembered a phone call in which she had told Dennis that their radio show was nominated for a New Zealand Radio Award for the first time and that he needed to wear "black tie" [formal wear] for the ceremony – "He went out and he bought the most rare pair of blue, peacock blue trousers, brightest blue I'd ever seen really, with a gorgeous orange shirt. I can't remember if he bothered with a tie and a long jacket in another colour, it all sort of blended, and he looked like a peacock. It was wonderful. In this boring sea of black. I was thrilled. I knew exactly what he'd do. But I couldn't resist saying to him 'black tie' just to see what the reaction was [laughs]. He was not a corporate animal" (Personal correspondence, E. Alley op.cit).

Alley's description signals her understanding of Dennis as someone defiant of convention but also her amusement and delight in the performance of his blue trousers (note she repeats the name of the colour three times). She also says in an understatement for anyone who knew him that Dennis "was not a corporate animal". Roger Horrocks interpreted Dennis' appearance as "camp" after the style of Susan Sontag's *Notes on 'Camp'* (Sontag, 1964); he felt there was an element of stylistic play, and a careful statement of identity in his apparel (Personal correspondence, R. Horrocks op.cit.). Wells used the phrase "better blatant than latent" to describe Dennis' outfits (Personal correspondence, P. Wells 30/06/09).[125] This phrase recalls the gay rights movement, as Alley's serves to remind us that Dennis was not a person who enjoyed the boundaries of mainstream society or institutions.

Fabula in the narrative

In relation to his professional rather than his personal life, there are two fabula of Dennis' narrative which speak to his internal understanding of his formation as a film archivist. These involved receiving advice from people he regarded as significant in their fields of practice. He stated that these experiences were influential for his own thinking. Dennis recounted for all interviewers in very similar words the following story: "I'd written to Len Lye [early NZ ex-pat filmmaker] and … he wrote back and said he'd be happy to meet me, it was a very gracious letter, but said something like 'oh you scholarly chaps with your archives … will it aid creativity?' And I had no idea what he meant. I couldn't fathom what he would mean by such a question" (Dennis in Pivac & Dennis, 2000).[126]

The letter has become part of the mythology of the Archive's development and Dennis' place within it where he argued that being "creative" was the key. It is

---

125 Previous director of the NZFA Frank Stark jokingly wondered who came first: Jonathan Dennis or Freddy Mercury? (Personal correspondence, F. Stark 11/03/13).

126 Aerogramme from the United States sent on February 28 1979, from Len Lye: "Dear Jonathan: Thanks for your letter and news of the NZ National Film Archive … all you scholarly chaps! Good luck for your study and hope it helps creativity … that's the rub. We, my wife Ann and I will just be getting back to NYC from Puerto Rico in April and sorry we can't put you up, but if you get a chance to come to the Nitty NYC Gritty, take it. We'll delighted to see you and help in any way poss … Old Paul Fiondella will be here and he can wise you up on my material. You seem to have a life's work with your millions of feet and news reel backlog. All best Len Lye ps. If ever acquiring film prints I suggest animation film students would get benefit out of UPA's Robert E Cannon's 10 min film work – Christopher Crumpet, Gerald McBoing-Boing, Billy the Kid. I don't know who has the rights but you could find out when you're here? L" (NZFA PP JD Box 2 Folder "Len Lye").

part of the discourse of Dennis and Lye as author functions (Foucault, 1969 p.11) in that the story had impact on others and influenced their lives and behaviours. For example Sarah Davy, an employee of the Archive, was influenced by Dennis' passion for Len Lye in her choice of Master of Film Archiving project. When asked how she came up with her thesis topic she replied that it was because of the neon sign outside the Film Archive at Tory Street – "I loved that sign, and it was my first exposure to Len ... that whole you know 'hope it aids creativity' famous letter that was written" (Personal correspondence, S. Davy op.cit.). As Davy notes, Dennis actively promoted an association with Len Lye by framing the letter and by using Lye's writing from the letter on the neon sign for the NZFA. Len Lye's words became one of the founding myths of the Archive – it functioned to remind those who saw it that creativity was an important part of the ethos of the Archive. Other interview subjects felt that Dennis' personal aesthetics and energy were also influenced by Lye, guessing that he "based a lot of himself on Lye ... that zany, zappy, all that thing ... it's just that amazing energy that Len had, and you look at his age and you think man I want to be doing that when I'm that age, you know, just amazing" (Personal correspondence, G. Watkins op.cit.).

Watkins refers to himself in relation to his view of Dennis and then talks about the energy Len had – "I want to be doing that when I'm that age". Watkins in turn was influenced by what he felt were the best traits of Dennis' behaviour and life such as his aesthetic sense, creativity, ethical approach, archiving integrity, passion and determination (Personal correspondence, G. Watkins op.cit.).

Dennis' second story of an influential moment, a fabula which affected his life, was also recounted in each interview. He recalled his arrival at the Cinémathèque Française (the first film archive in the world established in the 1930s) on his late 1970s archive tour. Dennis described a conversation with Mary Meerson not long after her partner and founder of the archive, Henri Langlois had died. "Mary continually talked about films as living objects that for them to have a life they had to be in front of people. It was people that brought them to life and that if you didn't show them then you might just as well have some cupboard full of whatever, but it was of no value. You had to put them in front of people" (Dennis in Pivac & Dennis, 2000).

Later, when Dennis was to take films up the Whanganui River and see the reactions from descendants of those in the films who would call to the screen, laugh, weep and talk passionately, he was to remember Meerson's words, as did Di Pivac when she interviewed Dennis and commented on this "living" aspect of the films (Pivac & Dennis, 2000). Meerson's passionate engagement with films as "living objects" as Dennis recounted it, became related to his understanding of film as taonga in later life (Dennis, 1987). The idea of the living archive links "biculturalism" through the notion of "living objects" or ngā taonga. [127]

Both these stories as fabula in the narrative of Jonathan Dennis' life have a number of functions. Firstly, they were links of association to two icons of film history. Others often told stories of Dennis' association with people well-regarded in the film world – Kenneth Anger, his meeting with Lilian Gish, Len Lye and Mary Meerson. Secondly, these are important moments in which he and others made sense of the process of developing the NZFA, creating its founding myths and supporting its vision. It also reflected Dennis' own desire not to just archive things, keeping them in a "cupboard" tucked away, but to present them to people and justify the less traditional approach he took to archiving.

In addition these film figures lent a cinematic glamour to the dry and arduous work of archiving and linked that work to the films which inspire the behind the scenes efforts. They are presented by Dennis and others as catalytic moments in which the subject and others, through telling and retelling of the story, aid the development of a sense of the Archive's identity and its function as a creative enterprise supported by filmmakers and film personalities from both the national and international arena. It is not a "quiet" vault in which Dennis is "bottling away" preserving the films (Dennis in Fyfe & Dennis, 2001) but a living and creative entity. These are two moments in which Dennis feeds a narrative about himself and the Archive and the way in which he wants to be understood and remembered.

Versions of the story

1. If I dreamed of anything I dreamed of being a film star

In one of the two substantial oral history interviews undertaken before his death, Jonathan Dennis was asked by Elizabeth Alley about his sense of his own persona over the course of his life.[128] Bamberg et al. (2007) assert that – "… narrative

---

127 Fax August 1993 from JD to Alain Marchand, La Cinémathèque Français – to Antonio Rodrigues, Lucy and Renee Lichtig from Jonathan Dennis: "I wanted you to know that my thoughts will be with you all at the funeral on Monday. My friendship with Mary was incredibly important to me and I loved her dearly. She was (and remains) an inspiration. She took me in when I was struggling to shape my ideas for setting up a film archive in New Zealand. What eventually grew into The NZFA would have been poorer, and certainly less creative, without Mary's generosity" (NZFA PP JD Box 11 Folder "Mary Meerson").

128 Oral History by Elizabeth Alley (interviewer) and Gareth Watkins (sound engineer) Interview with Jonathan Spencer Dennis. Recorded 6th December 2001 at Dennis' home 14 Edge Hill, Wellington, NZ.

functions as the glue that enables human life to transcend the natural incoherence and discontinuity of the unruly everyday ... by imposing a point of origin and an orientation toward closure, and thereby structuring the otherwise meaningless into a meaningful life" (Bamberg et al., 2007 p.5). In this context when Dennis and the interviewer are aware that he is dying, the importance of meaning and closure seem to be more pressing matters than in the normal oral history situation.[129] Dennis discussed at some length his life story and the use he had made of public and private personas. He recounted how he quite consciously used his knowledge of performance to endure difficult situations which his private self did not feel capable of managing. Within this discussion a number of components of Dennis' narrative are referred to, including his self-perceived skills and failings, his work experiences and his perceptions of others:

> EA (Elizabeth Alley) – ... *as director, as critic, your perception and understanding of the human condition ... you make finely tuned summations of films and people*
>
> JD (Jonathan Dennis) – *sometimes too finely tuned. I was surprised when I'd find someone was scared of me*
>
> EA – *are you not aware of your two quite clear personas?*

Alley challenges Dennis to think about the various ways in which he is understood by others which might not cohere with his sense of self. In the full interview she takes him through his life story, from childhood through to adulthood, and as someone who clearly knows him well, is able to do so in an intimate mode. When she asks about his "two quite clear personas", she does so as someone who knows this about him – it is not a question an oral historian would generally ask. Dennis clearly trusts Alley to answer this question as honestly as possible. The interview continues:

> JD – *yes, public and private. I became aware of inhabiting a different persona probably at school. I know the boy practising invisibility at boarding school in Christchurch, that what I was presenting to people there was in some ways an outer shell to protect the more vulnerable inner ... In the 80s I felt very strongly I created a public persona, and then there was me ... It's a protection thing for me to really keep strong the things that are important to me in whatever I'm feeling or doing I need another layer of protection I suppose. And I've created quite a good one* (Dennis in Alley et al., 2001).

Many interviewees heard the edited version of this interview broadcast after Dennis' death and remarked as Sharon Dell did, that these comments made sense

---

129 Although it is becoming increasingly common to collect oral histories of patients if they wish it in NZ at Hospice [hospital for the dying] (Unrecorded discussion at Auckland National Oral History Association of NZ Symposium May 2013).

of the fact that Dennis insisted on travelling with a "retinue", which could be quite tiring for those who felt they were expected to attend. Once she knew he felt the need for "protection" it became much more understandable to her and she was able to reconcile her previous perception of Dennis as being at times demanding as she realised how important his friendships were to him (Personal correspondence, S. Dell op.cit.).[130] Dennis then explains this a little further:

> JD – *In the training perhaps, all those years of being an actor … I feel like a lot of what I have done in the '80s and '90s was a performance, but the difference now was I was the director … Film Archive in '80s, '90s* Film Show [Dennis' film review show on Concert FM and then National Radio]. *That suited me to have someone else I could inhabit in the public sense. I feel absolutely tongue tied and scared and feel ungainly in any public sense where I feel I've got no friends or protection around me.*
>
> EA – *and yet most of us see you as fearless*
>
> JD – *(laughs) yes, it's weird* (Alley et al., 2001).

With the help and support of his interviewer, Dennis is doing what we perhaps all would do in similar circumstances. He is creating the narrative of his life as he wants others to hear it but he is also being honest about his sense of self. He knows he is dying and that this is one of the last chances he has to leave a record that he has some control over. Rubby Dhunpath says that in telling our life history we "make our existence into a whole by understanding it as an expression of a single unfolding story" (Silverman, 1997 p.545). This is particularly important if you are (relatively) young as Dennis was when he was dying. He had enjoyed a public and varied career, and was well-known by many in New Zealand and by the film archiving community through Europe and North America, as well as "Oceania" as he liked to call the South Pacific (Dennis in Fyfe & Dennis, 2001). Therefore, having the opportunity to describe his own life seems to have been important to him – or perhaps to his loyal friends who wished to have him represent his own story before others, like myself, started to interpret it. Perhaps understandably, he fails to mention in any of his interviews his infamous ability to snub people who he felt were not worthy of his attention or had slighted him, instead referring to it obliquely when he says he was "surprised" when people were scared of him.

Dennis refers in the interview to the theatre work with *Amamus,* which he understood as having enabled him to perform a part, to have a separate public persona which he could utilise in order to protect the self who struggles to communicate with strangers. He felt this was reasonably successful, but also

---

130 Dell has since commented "… he was always so kind and generous – had things prepared for you when you went to stay etc so it was deeply moving to hear that we were doing something important for him too" (Personal Correspondence, S.Dell 16/04/15).

recognised that a "tight band of friends" was important in order for him to feel safe. Interviewees who heard this interview were often taken aback by these details which took them by surprise (Personal correspondence, G. Watkins op.cit.). For others it came as no surprise, including for his niece Kirsten Dennis who knew he was an introvert (Personal correspondence, K. Dennis op.cit.). It is unlikely Dennis would have spoken quite so frankly unless he was near death, however this is purely speculation. In the Pivac interview from 2000 he also revealed some frank personal feelings although at the time he certainly did not think he was dying even though he was aware that he had cancer (Pivac & Dennis, 2000).

2. 24 Frames: The Greatest Love Story Ever Told

There are now a number of versions of the above oral history narrative in various edits of the original Alley recording. The Elizabeth Alley and Gareth Watkins' interview with Dennis on 6th December, 2001 exists as a raw recording (Alley et al., 2001). That interview was initially edited by Paul Bushnell for a broadcast played after Jonathan Dennis' death in 2002 on Radio NZ under the title *If I Dreamed of Anything I Dreamed of Being a Film Star*. The title refers to a quote from Dennis in the interview (Alley & Dennis, 2002). Excerpts from that same recording were then used by Peter Wells as the voiceover in his film *Friendship Is The Harbour of Joy* (Prod. & Dir. P. Wells, 2004). In 2012 the original recording was re-edited by Gareth Watkins, commissioned by Kate Mead and Roger Smith for RNZ Concert, and additional broadcasts played on RNZ National. This version was called *24 Frames: The Greatest Love Story Ever Told* (Watkins, 2012). An accompanying article I wrote appeared in *OnFilm* magazine under the same title as the Watkins' edit (E. J. Kelly, 2012). The various versions of the sound recording, the broadcast, the film and the article about Jonathan Dennis utilise fabula from within the original text that are considered by the various editors/authors to be important parts of the narrative. They choose to let certain words shine or be hidden.

One of the chief differences between the Paul Bushnell edit of the interview and the subsequent edits by Wells and Watkins is that Elizabeth Alley, a consummate professional interviewer with many years of experience in radio, is heard to break down and cry in both Watkins' and Wells' edit. Paul Bushnell created a formal professional presentation of Dennis' life (rather like an oral obituary) whereas Watkins and Wells choose methods perhaps less "professional" (in the formal sense), but certainly more emotionally engaging. The ambient sounds from Dennis' house on the original recording were not used in the Bushnell edit.

Similarly to Wells, Watkins wanted to remember the house as a "portrait of the man" (Wells, 2004). In Watkins' edit of the Alley interview he includes these sounds and narrates using his own voice to explain their inclusion as a way for himself to be able to remember Dennis. He narrates his choices within the text, giving the story a changed emphasis and making transparent the co-construction of narrative by the author/editor (Watkins, 2012). This shift in emphasis perhaps reflects a different time period in which the edits were made, the later edits perhaps adhere to a less traditional style of broadcasting with a self-reflexive influence. The effect is a more personal tone. The various edits become new co-constructions of the narrative of Dennis' life, utilising various modes of sound, including the ephemeral and non-verbal. They demonstrate not only the role of the editor in making important decisions about emphasis in the narrative, but also how the original recording becomes part of a discursive practice related to the author function "Jonathan Dennis". In other words, the impressions and conversations about Dennis shift and change over time, as they do about any of us.

3. Friendship Is the Harbour of Joy (2004)

The film documentary *Friendship is the Harbour of Joy* further develops the non-verbal and interweaves this into the narrative artefact of Peter Wells' story of Jonathan Dennis.[131] Although originally it was to be a record of Jonathan's house itself, it developed into a piece about the friendship of Jonathan Dennis, a 49 year old Pākehā man and Witarina Harris, a kuia in her 90s (Personal correspondence, P. Wells 22/04/10). Wells, like Watkins, weaves himself into the narrative, but rather than doing so with his voice, he uses silent cinema style cards and sometimes he is seen in the frame.[132] The film opens with the sound of laughter, and a date on the screen, "18 November 2001". There is a close up of an orange and teal house, and then the next shot is of a cushion on which is written – "Friendship is the Harbour of Joy". Images of slippers and then a crutch are seen, and the writing appears again – "A portrait of the friendship of Jonathan Dennis and Witarina Harris". The next card reads – "During the last months of his life I asked my friend Jonathan if he would like me to make a little film about the interior of his house … . Once I began filming it changed into a portrait of

---

131   What is not clear within the recordings is the considerable effort a number of people made in order to ensure Dennis could die at home. Ferry Hendriks, Dennis' long time companion organised a number of people to cook, clean, sit with Dennis and organise everything as he died. Hendriks had by this time nursed a number of friends with HIV AIDS through their dying (Personal correspondence, F. Hendriks 28/11/09).

132   The use of title cards nods to Dennis and Wells' love of silent cinema (Personal correspondence, P. Wells 22/04/10).

what happened within the house." Wells is seen at one point in the film in a shot with Dennis. He's heard to laugh and comment on the small size of the camera he is using. He weaves himself into the film, asserting his right to be there by making a statement about his friend Jonathan. Like Watkins' edit of the Alley interview, the form is self-reflexive. It also follows the oral history tradition of recording the stories of those who are traditionally marginalised – in this case a gay man and an older Māori woman.

In the production notes Peter Wells wrote while making the film, he asks himself, "Where do I stand?" (Wells, 2001–2004). He struggled to know if and how he should include himself within the text of the film he was creating, but clearly decided in the final edit that it was important he was present. Wells recalled – "Someone, having seen the film, said they felt it was the most personal film I've ever made and it was a real expression of my own character" (Wells in Cardy, 2004). He says he disagreed with the statement, but the fact that he repeated it to a journalist writing a piece about the film suggests he thought the idea had some merit, or at least was worthy of discussion.

The following outline of an excerpt of the film demonstrates how Wells blended the narrative texts of the oral history interview (by Alley and Watkins) and the film recording, skilfully interweaving verbal and non-verbal cues to tell the story of Dennis' life and work with Witarina Harris.

A shot of Witarina is shown as she reads on the sofa. Jonathan then walks into the shot while diegetic music is playing in the background, presumably from a stereo. Witarina starts to sing along to the music as Jonathan looks at her and smiles.

Dennis' voice from the Alley interview – "I really had no contact with taha māori, I didn't even go onto a marae until about 1978 for the first time, and it was a revelation to me, I had no idea there was this separate world, I was completely ignorant …"

Cut to Jonathan and Witarina sitting on the sofa together

"… and I'm appalled by that ignorance when I think of it now, that I could be in my mid-twenties before any sense of anything Māori began to permeate, but what really happened, what really triggered …"

Camera swoops across room, close up on mantelpiece with photos and decorations

"… my involvement in any sense was the films again. We had found a print of a film called 'The Devil's Pit' …"

Shot from "The Devil's Pit" is intercut

"… an appallingly banal Māori folk drama …"

Shot of kids from film cheerfully performing a playful version of a haka [war dance]

"… made by Universal Studios here in the late 1920s. We regarded it as completely lost because Universal was one of the studios that burnt all of its original nitrate from that period …"

Shot of Witarina and Jonathan on sofa, Jonathan yawning

Jonathan goes on to describe calling Witarina Harris whom he had heard had starred in the film. This was the beginning of their relationship – "… we met and formed the most astonishingly deep friendship very very quickly, to the point where she became the kaumātua of the Archive, to the extent that she travelled with the films both Māori and Pākehā …"

Close up shot as Witarina sings, cut to medium shot of Jonathan and Witarina holding hands

"… to warm them, basically, to bring some of the life to these films, to be the conduit between the audience and the image …" (Prod. & Dir. P. Wells 2004).

This sequence which intercuts the sound from Alley's interview and the images from Wells' film demonstrates verbally and non-verbally the intimacy of Dennis and Harris' relationship. The images and the soundtrack describe a friendship which is both cross-cultural and intergenerational. Wells' film brings together the warmth of the Alley interview with the visuals which emphasise the platonic love Dennis and Harris felt for each other. It is demonstrated how their intimacy had a huge impact upon both their lives and on Dennis' passage towards his death, as Harris guided him in his dying time (Personal correspondence, S. Dennis op.cit.). According to this text, Dennis wanted this "bicultural" story told. In the film sequence shot after he died, we see unnamed Māori women dressed traditionally for a funeral welcoming mourners into his house. Dennis was proud of his engagement with "taha Māori" and the influence it had on his work ever after he stepped onto that first marae in 1978. He described how it was not until after his meeting with Witarina Harris that he was able to start usefully employing that engagement within his work at the NZFA. This is an intrinsic part of his "narrative arc", the fabula of his story in every oral history recorded.

The intimate public – silences in the narrative

Much of the "text" of this film is silence; revisions and negations are present within the recorded footage. Dennis' imminent death is not discussed in the video recordings made by Wells, but through the post-production edit the topic is introduced via the interweaving of Alley's interview as the voiceover, and also through the images of medical paraphernalia around the house and via the footage of his wake. Dennis and Harris are seen in the film enjoying their time together as the camera pans from their various activities to the walls of the house, the shelves covered in knick knacks and decorations. We can hear Dennis and Harris talking and singing. Their story within the narrative text is one of peace and happiness in their friendship. But Dennis and Harris are not a couple, and their relationship is in no way a traditional one. The very fact they are together in this intimate setting is unusual.

Dennis and Harris' relationship is certainly a "queer" one in the sense of the term derived from queer theory. Annamarie Jagose describes queer as a conceptual position – "Broadly speaking, queer describes those gestures or analytical models which dramatise incoherencies in the allegedly stable relations between chromosomal sex, gender and sexual desire" (Jagose, 1996 p.3). Harris and Dennis' relationship sits outside the everyday assumptions of intimacy and coupledom. Their relationship is not "nameable" in the traditional sense. "Queer ... has proved a useful category for scholars who seek to discuss sexuality outside the organising dichotomy of heterosexuality/homosexuality" (Jagose, 1996 p.136). It is in this sense that Peter Wells' film about Jonathan Dennis and Witarina Harris is a *queer* narrative text, a version of the story of Jonathan Dennis which highlights the "unusual" angles – his close friendship with an older Māori woman, and his non-heterosexual lifestyle. Dennis was literally gay, but that is an identity category which "queer" avoids. Queer does not assume an essentialist gay perspective. Queer is a moving beyond gender and sexuality categorisation, challenging heteronormative assumptions about the roles of male and female, about what a life might be and who may have a right to "have a life". The film speaks to Lauren Berlant's idea of the intimate public as offering moments within the folds of the heteronormative world in which being "otherwise" might be positive (Berlant & Prosser, 2011).

Dennis and Harris' relationship defies categorisation. Although Harris is female and seems elderly and vulnerable, it is the younger of the two, Dennis, who is dying. It is Harris who leads Dennis with her knowledge and experience through the journey towards his death. The hand holding, the intimate warmth between Dennis and Harris, signals the behaviours of the everyday couple. Bernard claims that "the correspondence between lovers, between a husband and wife – are the very stuff of the archive" (Bernard, 2011 p.102). Is Harris and Dennis' relationship not the "very stuff of the archive" even if they are not lovers? Or is this not possible because they are not a heterosexual couple?

Wells was initially determined to document a gay life (Personal correspondence, P. Wells 30/06/09). He was bearing witness and creating evidence of the lives which are often left unrecorded. The title of the film refers to a friendship which was unusual and often referred to by others (for example, Personal correspondence, D. Pivac 26/11/09; N. Brand 13/07/10; S. Davy 08/11/10). Italian film archivist, author and curator Paolo Cherchi-Usai described their friendship:

> I think they were kindred souls ... I don't think I've ever witnessed such a fusion between two souls ... in some respects the nature of this spiritual intimacy between Witarina and Jonathan is a mystery, and it should remain a mystery because it's something between Witarina and Jonathan (Personal correspondence, P. Cherchi-Usai 14/05/09).

Indeed, their relationship is a mystery, but one that has been recorded on film and is therefore a text available for analysis. Yet interviewee Sister Loyola's words to the interviewer off camera in the NZ documentary *Gardening with Soul* (Prod. Pope, V., Dir. J. Feast 2013) echo – some things are "beyond words". The story of the narrative text is certainly one which piques the interest of those who see it.[133] It is also painfully intimate and can feel voyeuristic when the camera follows mourners up the stairs into Dennis' bedroom where he lies in state.

Lauren Berlant's re-evaluation of representations of intimacy offers a lens through which to consider this friendship. Berlant's notion of the "intimate public" calls for a re-understanding of the heteronormative assumptions of relationships and intimacies:

> Rethinking intimacy calls not only for redescription but for transformative analysis of the rhetorical and material conditions that enable hegemonic fantasies to thrive in the minds and on the bodies of subjects while, at the same time, attachments are developing that might redirect the different routes taken by history and biography. To rethink intimacy is to appraise how we have been and how we live and how we might imagine lives that make more sense than the ones so many are living (Berlant, 1998 p.286).

This redirection of routes of history and biography is an apt description of the relationship of the couple who are not a couple within the film narrative text. They love each other, they support one another, they sleep in the same bed and both refer jokingly at various times to being "girlfriend" and "boyfriend". But they do not have a sexual relationship, which would make their intimacy comprehensible to a film audience accustomed to seeing heterosexual couples of comparable ages in intimate circumstances within the home environment.

Berlant states that "desires for intimacy that bypass the couple or the life narrative it generates have no alternative plots, let alone ... laws and stable spaces of culture in which to clarify and to cultivate them" (1998 p.285). In Mieke Bal's

---

133 When I was an image archivist I attended the International Film Festival in Auckland in 2004 and watched *Friendship Is the Harbour of Joy*. This was the first time I had heard of Dennis or Harris.

terminology, the fabula that make up the narrative artefact are not familiar. Peter Wells is representing something queer, yet it is not once stated in this film that Jonathan is gay. Nor is it hidden, and in fact from the opening sequence it can be guessed that if not gay, Dennis certainly does not hold to any set of masculine gender assumptions, at least as far as interior decoration of his home is concerned. For example, there is a shot of a stone with the name "Jonathan" carved into it. That shot then pans to an image on the wall of a beautiful young man (James Dean) with a cigarette in his mouth. Other images of Dennis' house include shots of a ledge with four tiki (Māori symbols representing the first human) in a row, pacific style necklaces, three images in a row of black and white female movie stars of the past, and a shot of "Be Here For the Cure" literature.[134] The images are perhaps best described as camp, and could be considered quite stereotypical of the gay man. They are non-verbal signals; code which can be read by the astute viewer. Wells was quite deliberate about showing these images so that although it is not stated that Dennis is gay, it is quite clear for those who can read the signs that he is (Personal correspondence, P. Wells op.cit.).[135] The film echoes David Halperin's idea of masculine "Tacit codes of conduct" and those who resist them. This is significant in Dennis' narrative in terms of heteronormative assumptions about what constitutes a normative portrait of a private setting.[136]

This film is a curious hybrid; a home movie, a diary, an attempt to portray the intimacy of Jonathan Dennis' life and friendships. There were some family and friends who felt ambivalent about the film which they understood as "invasive" because it showed mourners in Dennis' house and left people feeling exposed or vulnerable (Personal correspondence, B. Gosden op.cit.).[137] Yet it was Dennis who asked Wells to record even the moment of his death (Wells, 2004). For Dennis, an avid and passionate film goer, the ultimate compliment was to be

---

134 HIV AIDs awareness literature. People who did not know him well often made the assumption that Dennis died of AIDs, being at a moment when those deaths among gay men had been reasonably common for a decade. He died of cancer, the diagnosis and prognosis of which is discussed in the film by Dennis. There is also correspondence in his personal papers in which a correspondent asked whether he had HIV AIDs (NZFA PP JD Box 11).

135 This "signalling" through objects is common in any culture which has been forced to be discrete and there is a large body of literature about it. The word "camp" itself suggests a positioning of self to suggest ones' sexuality through attitude, clothing and style and is most often associated with male homosexuality. As Stephen Fry puts it – "Camp is queer. (Mostly)" (Fry, 1997 p.127).

136 Stuart Harris one of Witarina Harris' sons, read an early draft of my paper for a conference on the "Intimate Public" and *Friendship Is the Harbour of Joy* and found it offensive. He felt the use of the word "queer" in association with Witarina Harris was inappropriate. Therefore I have only used material about Harris already available in the public sphere and that not gleaned from my one interview with her daughter-in-law. Since this early discussion I did write another paper and submit it to the Harris whanau. They gave it their blessing and it was published in April 2014 in the International Federation of Film Archives journal. However this present chapter is not approved by Harris' family.

137 Wells took an edit of the film to Witarina Harris' house and got her blessing for it to be screened before it was shown at the International Film Festival. She loved the film (Personal correspondence, P. Wells 22/04/10).

recorded on film. Ever the archivist, he wanted a record of his story, a narrative of his life and his passing.[138] Through recording the banal everyday domesticity as well as the friendship of Dennis and Harris and the death of Dennis himself, Wells is presenting a biography of gesture, of friendship and events leading to a death in a manner which he felt was respectful. It is an ephemeral moment captured on digital video, evidence of sorts of a gay life. As Wells said in an interview at the time the film was broadcast on television – "Nothing is as transient as the interior of a house. That transience becomes particularly poignant when someone is dying or has died. You are aware of a world that is about to vanish completely. It's not only the person, but everything about them. The way they haphazardly arrange dishes in the kitchen or really think about what they put on a mantelpiece" (Wells in Cardy, 2004). Much of what Wells is trying to describe is unspoken – it is the visual and non-verbal which paint the picture of Dennis and Harris.

Representing gay men's lives: Folds in the heteronormative world

Peter Wells has described the ways in which he survived his childhood through creative attachments and fantasy in his own works (Wells, 2001). He also discussed them privately. Wells said, for example, that he and Dennis discussed at length the experience of cinema going in the 1950s and 1960s and what it meant to them. Wells described in detail the mutual understanding he and Dennis had of their childhood pleasures in going to the cinema. It is recounted in full here because it is difficult to do justice to such an articulate passage by summarising it:

> …sitting in the dark and watching alternative lives was a way of avoiding what amounted to the compulsory heterosexuality of our … mutual childhoods … you could sit and dream and experience a notion of freedom which seemed to have great depth – you looked into a space and it offered both diversion and a contradictory reality – contradictory to the one you were imprisoned in, outside the cinema. You could also fall in love with the beautiful faces and bodies of men on the screen. You always imagined they were going to kiss your lips as the camera moved in a pre-clinch close-up (Personal correspondence, P. Wells 30/06/09).

Like Dennis, Wells is a gay Pākehā man from a working class background. They were virtually the same age, and therefore grew up in a similar era (the 1960s). For many years now, Wells has contributed to a public conversation about male

---

138 Many interviewees emphasised that Dennis was very angry that he was dying. He did not want people to think he had accepted his death as inevitable. It was also very physically painful and frightening (Personal correspondence; S. Dennis op.cit.; S. Dell op.cit.; S. Bartel op.cit.).

gay narratives in NZ through visual and written media (For example Main & Wells, 1993; Wells, 1997, 2001). Dennis felt a kinship with Wells' work, their correspondence in the NZFA attesting to the warm regard and support Dennis felt for Wells' films and books (NZFA PP JD Box 11). As Wells describes it, they were both cinephiles who used cinema as an escape from their heteronormative upbringings, revelling in the films and their gorgeous images. As a child and as an adult, Dennis engaged with cinema as a way to escape the everyday difficulties of boarding school and a crippling shyness in social situations which he described in his interview with Alley (Alley & Dennis, 2002). As previously noted Eve Kosofsky Sedgwick's work describes a similar theme of gay youth alienation, survived through identifying cultural objects which have some hint of homosexuality about them (Sedgwick, 1993 p.3). Dennis and Wells "survived" through cinema and fantasy at a time when heteronormative culture did not allow an explicit homosexual reality to exist in the everyday.

As the director of a national archive, as a lifelong archivist with an acute and conscious sense of the public and private spheres, Dennis more than many biographical subjects sought to be the narrator of his own story. He understood the power of the archive intimately, and he chose what was to be deposited in his collection of personal papers. Dennis also chose to allow Peter Wells, a man known for his representations of gay stories and his activism into his home at the time of his decline; he chose for the oral history interviews to be recorded. Dennis knew Peter Wells' work, and he knew that Wells sought to claim a public space for the gay story, for the marginalised, and for the man dying before his time. He wanted the queer narrative to emerge. Dennis had also previously chosen to create a soundscape about artists who had been diagnosed with or had died of HIV AIDS with Elizabeth Alley (this will be analysed in the following chapter). That work supports the view that he was interested in representations of folds within the heteronormative world which expressed the possibility of being otherwise.

Although an intensely private person, Dennis also had the abilities of the performer and the knowledge of the archivist. He knew or hoped that researchers would be interested in his story, and so he took the opportunity to present it. Or to put it another way, he chose to narrate the first distortion of the truth before others began to (re)interpret his life.[139]

---

139 Comment by John Reynolds, NZ artist, on the reason for creating a book about his work himself, rather than allowing someone else to interpret him in a monograph (Reynolds, J. 2010).

Chapter 7

Beyond cinema, beyond the NZFA

The previous chapter examined Dennis' narratives of his life, while this chapter takes the threads of Dennis' experience and knowledge of social injustice and relates these to the presentation of archival materials which he undertook. It will demonstrate how Dennis' practice was a creative endeavour and a collaborative venture which sought, through remembering rather than forgetting the colonial history of NZ and the South Pacific, to trouble the contemporary moment. Stephen Turner's analysis of settler culture and its effects is employed to consider Dennis' practice.[140] In addition Homi Bhaba's concept of hybridity is investigated in relation to one of Dennis' final soundscape works, *Ocean of Time* (2000).

As we have seen, Dennis had worked with Māori and helped develop a "kaupapa" for the Archive which incorporated Māori values into its framework. He explained in a lecture and a subsequently published paper that his aim was "uncovering and releasing the images" from the Archive to find ways in which Pākehā and Māori could work together (Dennis, 1990). This could be interpreted as an attempt towards "kaupapa Māori", an indigenous centered perspective and practice which engaged face-to-face with Māori in order to enable the descendants of taonga to respond to them (McCarthy, 2011; Tapsell, 2006; Te Awekotuku, 1991). This perspective required not only a strong sense of place and self, but imagination to create new ways of presenting archival materials in a culturally appropriate manner. It involved cooperation and engagement with others. Dennis' work from 1983 onwards increasingly took materials outside the Archive walls into the wider world. In doing so he incorporated the values and practices he had learned from Witarina Harris, Barry Barclay, Merata Mita and the

---

140 Turner has not analysed Dennis' work but he has considered Dennis' colleague Barry Barclay's filmmaking and writing in depth in relation to colonialism (S. Turner, 2002).

audiences for the films he had screened (Dennis, 1989). It also utilised his international contacts and knowledge, his cinematic sensibilities and theatrical flair.

Like Italian oral historian and political activist Alessandro Portelli, Dennis knew to "never turn your attention off, and always show respect for what people choose to tell you" (Portelli, 1991 p.x). This enthusiasm for being an active recorder and presenter of history rather than a passive keeper, was fundamental to Dennis and he continued pursuing this idea after his time as Director of the NZFA. It is certainly one of the reasons he was engaged with and by people from film, arts, and other communities outside the direct radius of the Archive itself (Personal correspondence, P. Wells 22/04/10). He was never regarded as a "gatekeeper" but as an enabler and "the unsung hero of the film culture" (Personal correspondence, R. Horrocks 21/10/08).

Dennis retained his passion for his first love, silent cinema. He was nostalgic for and engaged by early cinema, believing that the silent period had offered a more "pure" form of cinematic expression and a superior art form to that which came after it (Dennis in Alley et al., 2001).[141] As described in Chapter Three he was part of the 1960's and 1970s "feverish age of movie-going, with the full-time cinephile always hoping to find a seat as close as possible to the big screen ..." (Sontag, 1996). Dennis had a "particular sense of film aesthetics – he loved film-as-film" as well as specific filmmakers who he understood as auteurs, such as Robert Bresson (Personal correspondence R. Horrocks 21/10/08). He took these influences into his radio programmes, television and film works and soundscapes in unexpected ways, which will be analysed in this chapter.

He also added an element to his work which seemed alien to many white European and North American audiences; he was actively supporting indigenous peoples to have a voice in exhibitions, books, radio works, television and film projects. As he learned from his many collaborators, Dennis could no longer see images of indigenous peoples in the kitsch light of camp, but instead viewed them as a representation of their ancestors, which signified not so much a truth in their representation, but a truth about how they were perceived by filmmakers at the time of the recording. For example, he was realistic about *The Devil's Pit* in which Witarina Harris had starred, calling it as we've seen "an appallingly banal Māori

---

141 Others have spoken and written in detail about what was lost when sound was introduced to cinema. A different aesthetic was required once verbal explanation was possible and the sound equipment itself affected the visual nature of cinematography. See Kevin Brownlow *The Parade's Gone By,* first published 1969 by Secker and Warburg, London.

folk drama ..." (Dennis in Alley et al., 2001) yet he valued the film because it was his opportunity to meet Harris herself. It also functioned as a telling example of how European filmmakers of the 1920s and 1930s had exploited New Zealand as an exotic location to tell inaccurate tales of Māori people for box office purposes (Dennis, J. NZFA PP JD Box 2 Folder "Lectures").

Dennis believed that he was led by his "heart not his head" in the work he did (Dennis in Fyfe & Dennis, 2001). This meant an emotional and personal engagement. He became committed to exploring a "sense of place" within NZ and the wider South Pacific through the NZFA (Davy & Pivac, 2008), attempting to engage with the people in the place in which he lived rather than reaching for a European ideal. The *Mana Waka* film production was an opportunity to test the new biculturalism of the archival structure and was a demonstration of a commitment to archival material being accessible to people who were not "archive literate". Finally it was a chance to demonstrate how a cultural heritage institution could be "active rather than passive" (Dennis in Fyfe & Dennis, 2001). Director Merata Mita was enthusiastic in her praise of the process when she and Dennis presented the film at a conference in Australia, saying – "... as an archive working in partnership with Māori people [the NZFA] has a lot to teach the world. That's not to say it was easy – but the fact that Jonathan and I are still friends [laughter] reflects that it worked" (Mita in Mita & Dennis, 1991).

Mana Waka consisted entirely of archival footage donated to the NZFA by the Manly family in the 1980s. The footage depicted the building of war canoes commissioned by Princess Te Puea of the Waikato iwi Tainui in the 1930s. Te Puea was one of the leaders of the Kīngitanga, a collective inter-iwi movement based in the Waikato in the North Island, and she commissioned the making of the film by Jim Manly, a Pākehā photographer.[142] When the Film Archive had repaired and restored the footage as much as possible, Dennis approached Merata Mita to suggest she direct an edit of the material. She agreed, and in turn she approached Te Arikinui Dame Te Atairangikaahi, the Queen of the Kīngitanga who gave her permission for the edit to begin (Personal correspondence, A. Collins 26/01/09).

This was a kaupapa Māori process with the indigenous players in the film production leading. By appointing Merata Mita as director, Dennis demonstrated how the "bicultural" structure of the Archive could function, with Māori

---

142 Manly went bankrupt during filming. Te Puea had tried to rescue the situation by selling some land to create more capital, but the film was never completed in their lifetimes (Mita & Dennis, 1991).

people in control of their own materials. He acted as producer and was "immensely proud" of the work (Dennis in Pivac & Dennis, 2000). Merata Mita in turn hired Annie Collins who had previously worked with her on *Patu!* They based themselves at Turangawaewae [home of the Kīngitanga] in the Waikato for the edit. This was highly unusual – there was no editing suite there and they were away from the resources of the main cities. They were eight hours drive from the NZFA. This was necessary because of Merata Mita's commitment to a process for making the film following Māori practice, where the film was regarded as taonga and needed to be edited in the place in which it had originated, surrounded by the people who were originally present or their descendants. There was a process for the handling of materials and traditional methods undertaken in relation to prayers and other blessings following a Māori based kaupapa (Personal correspondence, A. Collins 26/01/09). Supporting this, iwi elders had an open invitation to attend the edit. Some described the birds that were singing as various sequences were shot back in the 1930s. The sounds the elders remembered were recreated for the soundtrack when the edit was completed (Mita & Dennis, 1991).[143] This augmentation of the film with a soundtrack recalls Dennis and Ferry Hendriks' careful presentation of silent films back in the 1970s as described by Bill Gosden, where they would "play DJs" to ensure the correct and appropriate sound accompaniment to the film they watched (Personal correspondence, B. Gosden 08/12/09).

As producer, Dennis was the negotiator with the NZFA and the Manly family over aspects of the production. There were confrontations between Māori and Pākehā perspectives as the Manly family became increasingly uncomfortable with the bicultural emphasis Mita placed on the footage. For example they did not want a discussion of the Treaty of Waitangi included in the film. Dennis recalled that Jim Manly had written a rough script, which was an "exotic Māoriland adventure" style movie, exploitative in its tone, and that his descendants wanted to use that script (Dennis in Pivac & Dennis, 2000). The NZFA Board were also uncomfortable with the process, as Dennis strongly encouraged them to financially support the production, particularly once a working print was stolen by the Manly family (Dennis in Dennis & Pivac 2000). Some people also said Dennis was physically away from the Wellington Archive helping with the edit which caused tension with the staff (Personal correspondence, D. Pivac 26/11/09). Clearly, working in this manner was not without its challenges.

---

143 The sound of wood being chopped is frequently heard in the film. Annie Collins remembered the meticulous work required to create the sounds the elders described, and laughed as she said "I never want to hear the sound of chopping wood again!" (Personal correspondence, A. Collins op.cit.).

Despite the difficulties it entailed, Dennis felt this process was part of living up to the kaupapa and rewritten constitution of the NZFA which incorporated the Treaty of Waitangi and the idea of film as taonga of the iwi of NZ. Dennis felt *Mana Waka* was a chance to try and live up to the Archive's Māori name and he said that it was a "peak of creativity" for the institution (Dennis in Pivac & Dennis, 2000). It is of note that Dennis viewed this as a creative endeavour for the Archive and an "active rather than passive" practice (Dennis in Fyfe & Dennis, 2001). It was certainly unusual for an archival production to follow an indigenous inflected editing process on a marae rather than in an editing studio. And yet by doing so the NZFA was able to actively expose and present its material to a much wider audience than would otherwise view it at its city base. In addition it was a chance to work with a foremost indigenous filmmaker such as Mita. It demonstrated the NZFA commitment to indigenous perspectives and highlighted the role of the film archivist as "framer of the kept" (Wisniewski, 2007). It explicitly addressed concerns that archivists as predominantly colonial descendants tend to control the presentation of indigenous materials (Jimerson, 2010). The process acknowledged the colonial origins and purpose of much early film and sought to empower Māori to reinterpret the footage as they chose. It offered Mita and the iwi the chance to be the "framers" of their own material.

Dennis found this process exhilarating and also "frightening" (Dennis in Pivac & Dennis, 2000). It responded to Mary Meerson's urging that in order to live, films from an archive needed to be shown to an audience and it also made reference to Len Lye's support of creative endeavour by the Film Archive (Dennis in Dennis & Pivac 2000). By employing a film director to edit the archival material anew into a feature length documentary, the NZFA was able to submit the film for exhibition at multiple venues as a new work. It played for the 1990 Commonwealth Sesquicentennial Celebrations, at the New Zealand International Film Festival, at festivals and conferences in Australia and screenings in the United States (Mita & Dennis, 1991). This ensured multiple audiences for the film who never would have known to make the journey to the NZFA in Wellington in order to access the images from there. It allowed creative people to engage with the material to produce something new from its fragments and from the memories of the elders and also to "uncover and release the images" held at the Archive. This work used materials (film) and memories (of the elders during the edit) to create a new work and audiences for it into the future. It acknowledged both colonial and indigenous efforts to preserve moments in history and re-presented them in new formats for a contemporary audience.

Honouring the ancestors

Dennis' practice in making *Mana Waka* sought to encompass and acknowledge the "tenacious historical memory and insistent presence of Māori" (S. Turner, 1999 p.22). The film was an example of archival material creatively re-presented. In other projects he continued to work with archival principles to preserve materials but ensured an active mode by also collecting new recordings in the form of the stories of older people both Māori *and* Pākehā. He then found ways in which to not only archive those stories, but present them to audiences.

One example of this practice is the only film he would write and direct which recorded the memories of Edwin (Ted) Coubray, a Pākehā filmmaker of the early period of New Zealand film production.[144] The film was entitled *Mouth Wide Open* because it described the astonishment of audiences seeing film for the first time in the early twentieth century (Prod. Collins, A. & Dir. Dennis, J 1998). Dennis explained his purpose for making the film in a later interview in which he stated that Ted Coubray was "somebody who had not only done things I thought were wonderful, but he remembered them, and still cherished the memory of them ..." Dennis felt that the filmmaking Coubray had been involved in during the 1920s and 1930s was "wonderful". He said he had no desire to be a film director, but wanted Coubray's story to be acknowledged and particularly to ensure that his story "existed into the future ... [these] things are really immensely important to me" (Dennis in Alley et al., 2001).[145]

Analysing Dennis' exuberant language, it seems he was following his "heart not his head", recognising fellow Pākehā like Ted Coubray and Len Lye as *his* artistic ancestors and engaging with their work and memories in such a way as to celebrate them as Pākehā taonga. The Coubray film was an example of this, as is Dennis' championing of Lye wherever possible. For example, Dennis contacted French film archive colleagues to suggest a screening of Lye's work in Europe and said – "To have an ancestor of this kind – someone who maintained a lifetime commitment to experiment – has been particularly important for us. His films are ... dazzling and, wherever they're shown, are incredibly popular with audiences ..."

---

144 Dennis also worked with Annie Collins on what they envisaged to be a series of archival shorts for television starting with *Girls' Own Stories* (Dennis, 1993) for the Work of Art Series on TVNZ, Executive Producer Caterina de Nave. They were not successful with subsequent pitches (NZFA PP JD Box 2). This could have been related to a very long fax Dennis sent de Nave complaining of the late night slot the programme screened in. He had believed it would be played earlier when a larger audience was possible (AC PP).

145 Ted Coubray had worked both in Australia and New Zealand in the silent film period and into the 1930s. Graham Shirley, Australian film historian also collected oral history recordings with Ted in the 1980s and Dennis and Shirley shared information and eventually films between their respective archives in Australia and New Zealand (Personal correspondence, G. Shirley 29/07/11).

(NZFA PP JD Box 11 Letter J.D. to Marco Muller and Marina Mottin 24/01/96). He also wrote a chapter in a book on Len Lye for an exhibition held in Paris (Bouhours & Horrocks, 2000) and produced a video compilation of Lye's work (Lye, Re-release 1996). By championing the films of Coubray and Lye, but also by producing new texts analysing them and compilations of their work, Dennis demonstrated a commitment to supporting older generations of "ancestors" to be acknowledged and known long after they had finished their own careers.

For Dennis, Lye was the first of many older people associated with the NZFA with whom he would create a personal connection, and Lye demonstrated a manner in which New Zealand filmmakers might be experimental and creative in their approach. At the end of his life, Dennis reflected on the projects he had been involved in and the friendships he had. He said that people often commented "on this strange attraction to collecting elderly people, but I find such richness in the friendships." He felt that he had learned so much from the "sheer generosity" of Witarina, and had "such fun". With others – "… our connection was film. I loved these people for what they did …" (Dennis in Alley et al., 2001). His personal experiences of friendship crossed over into his work, motivating him to exhibit and share older peoples' memories and works from the past.

Dennis maintained the archivist's drive to preserve the memories of these older people, but he took this a step further by actively recording stories rather than simply receiving them into the archive, and further, by finding ways to ensure people would engage with those memories. He said he had "no desire" to be a film director, but in order to tell the story of Ted Coubray he became one (Dennis in Dennis & Alley 2001). He refused to be just "bottling away somewhere" in a basement with films. He wanted archive materials exhibited and therefore had to create platforms and opportunities to allow this to occur (Dennis in Fyfe & Dennis, 2001). This drove him to his own creative practice through collecting new archival materials and then writing, directing, producing and editing that material into various formats for audience consumption.[146]

Dennis championed other "ancestors", including NZ filmmaker John O'Shea by supporting and editing his biography (O'Shea, 1999) as well as contracting him to produce a short film for the Centenary of Cinema (O'Shea, 1996). These types of works were sparked because he wanted to "acknowledge" the life and work of

---

146 Before he finished at the NZFA, employee Jane Paul remembered a conversation with Dennis in which he described a plan for the NZFA staff to begin actively collecting audiovisual recordings of street scenes for the archive collection (Personal correspondence, J.Paul 03/02/11).

these "ancestors" "into the future". In lectures and interviews, Dennis said "we take our films personally" (NZFA PP JD Box 2 Folder "Papers"). Dennis certainly felt a keenly passionate and personal relationship with films of the "ancestors" and attempted to respond by honouring their work with new presentations of it, or supporting his elders to create new works themselves. This supports the description of many interviewees of Dennis as an enabler (Personal correspondence, R.Horrocks op.cit.) or catalyst for the works of others.

A further pan-iwi Māori historical project which would eventually include a book, oral histories and the re-release of a musical recording from the archive was instigated by two Māori authors who knew Dennis' work by reputation. When Irihapeti Ramsden and Patricia Grace asked Dennis to be involved in the project which would become *The Silent Migration, Stories of Ngāti Pōneke Young Māori Club...* (Grace et al., 2001), he said they imagined a small publication which members of Ngāti Pōneke and their families would buy. Instead it took ten years and became something quite different – "... part of this was that the stories of these old people were stories we hadn't heard, and they were stories that deserved to be told, and documented richly ... those things are really wonderful and fulfilling to me in a way that is exciting and palpable" (Dennis in Alley & Dennis, 2002).[147] The book is a form of curation of the recordings gathered by the authors and presented as a text. Similarly to the work with Coubray, Dennis wanted the stories of the old people to be heard. In order to do that in an "exciting and palpable" way, Dennis, Grace and Ramsden produced a text which they felt "documented richly" the lives of these elders who were both Māori and Pākehā.

Dennis recorded some of the extensive discussions he, Ramsden and Grace had during their research and analysis of the materials they were collecting, and he deposited these audio recordings in the Alexander Turnbull Oral History Centre at the National Library of New Zealand (Ramsden et al., 1995). This provides a valuable group of materials that were not published in the book but offer a window on the thinking of the authors who produced it and their developing sense of purpose.[148] The recordings of the authors offer an analysis of the materials they were collecting which is not included explicitly in the publication itself. For example, we hear Irihapeti Ramsden discussing the past as well as the

---

147 Ramsden was Ngāi Tahu and Rangitāne, born 24/02/1946 died 5/04/2003. She was known throughout the indigenous world as an important champion of 'cultural safety' which was translated into practice in Canada and other countries (Sweetwater, 2003). The Kaua Whakaruruhau (Cultural Safety) Committee at Auckland University of Technology was started after a visit by Ramsden (Personal correspondence D. Payne 17/08/13) and still functions today. Ramsden's PhD thesis is available at: http://culturalsafety.massey.ac.nz/thesis.htm.

148 Dennis similarly archived all full interviews from which he took extracts for his radio work. They are available through the NZFA.

contemporary climate, in which she says Māori are still being defined as warriors. She says this is purposeful in that it allows Pākehā to justify brutal actions against Māori. She offers the example of the introduction of British soldiers during the early years of colonisation to control indigenous people and argues this continues today– "… they're [Pākehā] afraid of rough justice – the gangs, Mongrel Mob … I think it's a very deep dark vein in NZ society; more than 'vein', I think it underpins it in lots of ways" (Ramsden & Grace, 1995).[149] Ramsden, Grace and Dennis are reflecting on the contemporary New Zealand situation "it's a very deep dark vein in NZ society …" and how people understand (or fail to understand) each other across cultures in NZ.

The tone of the publication they were working on does not refer to this kind of perspective at all or only obliquely. It is only by listening to the recorded opinions of the authors that a darker analysis of the current climate in which the book was published is possible. It is unclear why the editors' personal reflections were not included, but it certainly follows Dennis' practice in later years where he eschewed the formal narrator's voice and relied instead upon the raw materials gathered from interviewees. The recordings of the editors themselves offer the possibility of another project which analyses their views in relation to the text they created.

Accompanying the book, which was eventually published by Huia Publishers, is a sound recording of the music of Ngāti Pōneke. This was produced by Dennis (Producer J. Dennis Ngāti Pōneke Young Māori Club, 2001).[150] It offers another manner in which to engage with the content gleaned from the oral histories and presented in the text based work, providing the sounds of the music which Ngāti Pōneke members created so many years ago. It also reflected Dennis' interest in sound and his ability to think outside a narrow view of the presentation of archival materials. Between the recordings of the author/editors, the oral histories of the participants in the project, the text based publication and the re-released recording, Dennis, Ramsden and Grace managed to produce a multiplicity of materials to stimulate various senses and commemorate the past, but also present these stories in such a way that they would last "into the future". Multiple access points to the material are possible through aural, visual and archival means.

During the period he worked on *Mana Waka* and then with Ramsden and Grace on the *Ngāti Pōneke* project, Dennis was also developing two large scale interna-

---

149 The Mongrel Mob are a pan-iwi Māori gang.

150 Dennis also produced other re-releases of historic sound recordings of Māori music for the National Library: *Ana Hato with Deane Waretini* (Hato & Waretini, 1995); *The Tahiwis* (Tahiwi, 1998).

tional exhibitions of NZ film which reflected this desire to disseminate and share the resources of the archive widely and prove their value as art works in their own right, but also as taonga.[151] Dennis' large network of international contacts instigated by the late 1970s study tour, now came into play as these people continued to be a source of encouragement and a "lifeline" after his time at the NZFA to help him continue his film archiving presentations (Dennis in Pivac & Dennis, 2000).[152] Both exhibitions were held in Italy – the 1989 Torino exhibition *Te Ao Marama ...* and the 1993 Pordenone Silent Film Festival Australia and New Zealand retrospective *Aotearoa and the Sentimental Strine*. Both reflected Dennis' desire to curate NZ film and display his developing creative signature style which used juxtaposition, montage and humour to unsettle the notion that NZ had a unified national identity. Matthew Leonard, who would work with Dennis in the late 1990s, commented that he and Dennis were heavily influenced in their creative practice by Irihapeti Ramsden. He felt Dennis and he both "riled against boring Pākehā stuff", wanting to challenge the "dominant cultural voice" (Personal correspondence, M. Leonard 01/04/10).

Te Ao Marama, Il Mondo Della Luce, Il Cinema Della Nuova Zelanda (Dennis Jonathan & Toffetti Sergio, 1989) was (and remains) New Zealand's largest ever international film retrospective. It included 78 features and short films and a substantial book publication. The then manager of marketing for the NZ Film Commission Lindsay Shelton commented in his book on selling NZ films – "*Te Ao Marama* was accompanied by a book ... edited by Jonathan and Italian film historian Sergio Toffetti in three languages: Italian, Māori and English. The book's overview of New Zealand culture went beyond cinema, with quotes from literary legends ... and reproductions of paintings by artists Ralph Hotere and Colin McCahon" (Shelton, 2005 p.101). Dennis' desire to go "beyond cinema" reflected an attitude similar to that of one of his heroes, Derek Jarman (Hendriks, F. Personal communication January 2012) who believed that all life was art, and that no art form should be elevated over any other (Jarman, 1996 2nd ed. p.163).

Te Ao Marama is the name of one of the whare nui/meeting houses at Ohinemutu where Witarina Harris was born, but is also a phrase from Māori culture which

---

151 Dennis said in 1984: "The [Film] Archive is to moving images what art galleries and museums are to artefacts and paintings, and libraries to rare manuscripts and books: a guardian of national works of cultural value placed in its trust, a show place, dissemination centre, and study resource" (Introduction by Jonathan Dennis in Sowry, 1984). The view was not Dennis' alone, but that of FIAF, the Federation of International Film Archives (Bowser, 1991).

152 After Dennis resigned in 1990 there was a three year period of relative upheaval at the NZFA with two directors appointed in quick succession, both of whom also resigned. In 1993 Frank Stark took up the role which he continued to hold until 2014 (Personal correspondence F. Stark 11/03/13). Stark argues that during Dennis' tenure the archive took the role of "treasure hunter" whereas under his directorship they were "asset managers" (Stark, 2006).

translates very roughly to "into the world of light", the world between Ranginui (sky father) and Papatuuaanuku (earth mother) where mortals dwell ever since Rangi and Papa's children forced them apart (Te Papa Tongarewa, 2011). It is the world of mortal life (Binney, 2010 p.33). The title of the exhibition is also a play on the idea that films can only be screened when light is shone through them.[153] Film, like mortal life, only becomes animated with the addition of light. This also supports Langlois and Meerson's assertion that in order for films to live, they must be screened.

The views of John Grierson, founder of the British documentary film movement (and one time employer of Len Lye) who visited NZ to report on government filmmaking in February and March 1940 are quoted in the *Te Ao Marama* publication. Grierson said – "… if you want to show New Zealand's importance to the world you should show the things which make New Zealand important. This sounds a simple proposition, but I am afraid you have not been doing it and we have all been missing a great deal. So when you send us your films never send merely the scenic ones. Put in something about the real things you do" (Dennis, Jonathan & Toffetti, Sergio, 1989 pp.81,82). The editors comment that "his recommendations were not implemented" (Dennis, Jonathan & Toffetti, Sergio, 1989 p.81). Dennis repeated this quote from Grierson in at least one other exhibition booklet (Dennis Jonathan & Cherchi Usai, 1993). He was certainly not the first to pick up on Grierson's recommendation. Film critic and filmmaker John O'Shea also quoted Grierson (O'Shea, 1999) as did others in earlier times when arguing the case for government support for local filmmaking (Sigley, 2003). Yet until the *Tangata Whenua* television series previously described played on state television in the 1970s, there was little representation of "the real things you do" until the Film Commission formation in 1978.

Presumably in response to Grierson, the *Te Ao Marama* publication presents a multiplicity of examples of the "real things you do". For example, in a section entitled *The Long White Cloud*, Pākehā painter Colin McCahon's *A Landscape with too few lovers* is quoted, translated into Italian as well as being written in English – "I hoped to throw people into an involvement with the raw land, and also with raw painting ... I hope you can understand what I was trying to do at the time – like spitting on the clay to open the blind man's eyes" (Dennis, Jonathan & Toffetti, Sergio, 1989 p.23). McCahon's romantic relationship with

---

153 There had also been a "large and successful" exhibition of Māori artists work curated by Te Rangihiroa Panoho at the Sargeant Gallery in Whanganui in 1986 with the name "Te Ao Marama: Seven Maori Artists" (McCarthy, 2011 p.88). It is unknown whether Dennis was aware of this exhibition.

the land is contrasted with Donna Awatere's statement of Māori sovereignty also included in the exhibition book – "In essence, Māori sovereignty seeks nothing less than the acknowledgement that New Zealand is Māori land, and further seeks the return of that land" (Awatere, D., First published 1984 in Broadsheet, Dennis, Jonathan & Toffetti, Sergio, 1989 p.25). McCahon and Awatere's views are juxtaposed through the fact that Awatere's essay excerpt sits adjacent to Colin McCahon's painting *One* in the exhibition book (1965 – Collection of National Art Gallery, NZ). Arguably McCahon's "involvement with the raw land" suggests no one has had a relationship with the land before him, while Awatere reminds the audience that Māori inhabited the land long before Pākehā, contradicting McCahon's view of the land as "raw".[154]

Dennis was a fan of Eisenstein, Vertov and the other early Russian filmmakers who used juxtaposition for political effect (Personal correspondence, R. Horrocks 25/10/11). He was to use this technique consistently in his exhibitions to highlight indigenous and other marginalised peoples' perspectives through ironic juxtaposition of materials such as that described above. The work recalls Judith Binney's suggestion that stories cannot be amalgamated but they can be juxtaposed as illumination occurs "in the juxtaposition" (Binney, 2010 p.329). The editors continue to juxtapose coloniser and colonised perspectives in the exhibition book, placing celebrated Pākehā expatriate writer Katherine Mansfield's letter to Sir Harold Beauchamp, 18 March 1922, in which she says – "New Zealand is in my very bones. What wouldn't I give to have a look at it!" (Dennis, Jonathan & Toffetti, Sergio, 1989) alongside the writing of Tuini Ngawai of the iwi Ngati Porou who warns that "Pākehā knowledge/sucks you in then confiscates land/Be strong friends,/Land is all we have/to rest a throbbing heart" (Dennis, Jonathan & Toffetti, Sergio, 1989 p.22).

These contrasting narratives – Pākehā feeling a kinship with the land (" in my very bones") and Māori feeling enraged by Pākehā assumptions ("Pākehā knowledge … confiscates land") is a tense dynamic in the exhibition book. It responds to John Grierson's call for a representation of the real people of the land and their desires and practices by moving beyond the "merely … scenic". It is a montage of text and images, a collection of opposing viewpoints which presents a nation at odds with itself. These images from the archive expose "the underlying currents of power … [which] … are hard to detect, except through the shock of montage,

---

154 Dennis did not write about his intentions with this publication to my knowledge so the interpretation is my own. The juxtaposition does echo his practice in a number of creative works where he seems intent on exposing contradiction, hypocrisy or disjunction.

when pictures from antagonistic categories are juxtaposed ..." (Sekula, 2003 p.445). They confront the reader/audience in a way which requires interpretation and engagement in an active manner. The materials presented in this manner suggest race relations are imperfect and that NZ contains many tensions and disparate views. It presents a vastly different perspective to some other representations of NZ. For example the scenic and resplendent images in the triple screen presentation of snow covered mountains in a NZ film presented at an earlier international exhibition, Japan Expo in 1970 *This Is NZ* (Dir. H. Mac-Donald 1970).[155]

At the time of the *Te Ao Marama* exhibition Dennis was working on *Mana Waka* – by his own description a "terrifying" time for the archive and himself, in which the bicultural process they had established was tested in the making of a film from archival footage (Dennis in Pivac & Dennis 2000). The process demonstrated how the ideology of biculturalism was extremely difficult to implement in the everyday. The striking divide between Māori and Pākehā sensibilities had been something he was well aware of since the first screenings of the James McDonald films – Dennis was not trying to hide this divide in this exhibition in Italy. There is nothing of the tourist version, the marketable, about this presentation of NZ, its art and artists. It appears Dennis was more interested in stimulating debate than he was in any presentation of NZ as an idyllic country.

By the time of this exhibition, NZ's filmmaking was thriving compared to the dearth of films prior to the 1980s, and this meant there were a wider variety of materials to offer at such an exhibition. Filmmakers represented included Barclay and Mita, but also Peter Wells (*Little Queen* 1983), Vincent Ward (*The Navigator* 1988), and Geoff Murphy (*Utu* 1983). All were making films which challenged assumptions about what life in NZ might really be like beyond the "scenic" views Grierson described.

The second large scale Italian cinema exhibition by Dennis, *Aotearoa and the Sentimental Strine: Making Films in Australia and New Zealand in the Silent Period,* was co-curated with Paolo Cherchi-Usai, who is a founding director of *Le Giornate del Cinema Muto* (known in English as the Pordenone Silent Film Festival). This exhibition was also supported by a publication, but a self published

---

155 "Directed by Hugh Macdonald, *This is New Zealand* was made to promote the country at Expo '70 in Osaka, Japan. An ambitious concept saw iconic NZ imagery – panoramas, nature, Māori culture, sport, industry – projected on three adjacent screens that together comprised one giant widescreen. A rousing orchestral score (Sibelius's *Karelia Suite*) backed the images. Two million people saw it in Osaka, and over 350,000 New Zealanders saw on its homecoming theatrical release" (Retrieved NZ On Screen 08/29/14 http://www.nzonscreen.com/title/this-is-new-zealand-1970.)

one of modest means compared to the lavish text of the former (Dennis Jonathan & Cherchi Usai, 1993). Dennis had suggested the theme of Australian and New Zealand silent film for the festival to challenge the "very Eurocentric and North American" tradition of the film festival in previous years (Dennis in Labrum & Dennis, 1993). As co-curator, Cherchi-Usai visited New Zealand and Australia for the first time and met Dennis and began to look at films. Encouraged by Dennis he also met with Witarina Harris.[156]

This was to be the first of a number of collaborations between the two archivists. Cherchi-Usai came to see Dennis as more than an archivist. He felt Dennis' work was a great influence on his own (Personal correspondence, P. Cherchi-Usai 14/05/09).[157] Although Cherchi-Usai said Dennis had an "acute awareness of archival procedure", he was also someone who understood that the procedure had no value except in "how it functions for the collection". He said that Dennis was "archivist, curator, a cultural agent, but … also a cultural agit-prop, he was an activist. And so he was all these things together … I myself would not know how to define Jonathan in one word, but curatorship, the word curator, are the first things in my mind" (Personal correspondence, P. Cherchi-Usai op.cit). Cherchi-Usai acknowledged the social justice perspective from which much of Dennis' work arose. Dennis was an "activist", someone who responded to the archive by recognising its inherent flaws as a biography of the nation – the exploitative tone of some of the films, the importance of acknowledging the films as taonga with relationships to living people who were the descendants of those in the films. Cherchi-Usai noted at the time the vast gulf between the indigenous engagement at the NZ Film Archive compared to the Australian equivalent where there was little or no understanding from the archivists beyond a "knee jerk" desire not to offend anyone (Personal correspondence, P. Cherchi-Usai op.cit).

Dennis contextualised the films appropriately by having Witarina Harris or Lily Amohau accompany exhibitions to "warm" the films.[158] As Dennis described it, the role of kaumātua was "to warm them, basically, to bring some of the life to these films, to be the conduit between the audience and the image …" (Dennis in Alley & Dennis, 2002). Dennis' mother Pat, Di Pivac and Bronwyn Taylor

---

156 Witarina Harris gave Paolo the name "Paora" and he stayed with her when he visited New Zealand. He also called her regularly on the telephone until she died (Personal correspondence, P. Cherchi-Usai 14/05/09).

157 When Cherchi-Usai created his own film made of archival materials entitled *Passio* (2007) it originally debuted at the Adelaide Film Festival dedicated to Jonathan Dennis and is a montage of images from archives. It was accompanied by a live choir and orchestral performance (Personal correspondence, B. Ikin 05/11/10).

158 The first time they did this was for the *Te Māori* exhibition in San Francisco in the 1980s. This was Harris' first overseas trip. She was in her eighties at the time (Dennis in Fyfe & Dennis 2001).

from the NZFA also attended the Pordenone Silent Film Festival (Personal correspondence, D. Pivac 26/11/09).[159] Although Dennis' mother and the staff of the NZFA were Pākehā they also "warmed" the films by singing songs with Harris and Dennis and provided information to festival goers. They were supporting Dennis and Harris (Personal correspondence D. Pivac op.cit.). Dennis was presented with the Jean Mitry Award for service to silent cinema at the festival that year (Pivac & Dennis, 2000).[160]

Aotearoa and the Sentimental Strine sought to represent Māori and Pākehā filmmaking and filmmakers appropriately to contextualise these early silent films. These were creative responses to the films in the sense that Dennis undertook a non-European archiving practice when he chose to support and present indigenous responses to the films exhibited. It was not creative in the sense of creating something new, but instead was an approach which opened up the space for Māori ways of being and doing to become incorporated in archival presentations in a way that had not been done before. Dennis was reframing the works. The kaumātua were in fact the highlight of the festivals for some people.

Cherchi-Usai remembered the 1993 festival with a "great deal of emotion". Witarina spoke, sang and danced and taught the audience songs, some of which he and his colleagues still remember. Witarina and Jonathan "became the ambassadors of NZ cinema, and they were extremely effective at this … they were providing the context …" Cherchi-Usai recognised that without indigenous representation accompanying these films, their "context" would have been lost. As "ambassadors", Harris and Dennis were able to provide appropriate support to the films for an audience who would otherwise have found them potentially confusing to engage with (Personal correspondence, P. Cherchi-Usai op.cit).

Neil Brand is a silent film pianist based in London who played at the *Aotearoa and the Sentimental Strine* exhibition. He remembered the New Zealand section with delight, describing Dennis' presentation and the "theatricality of the Māori content … [and] Witarina, this tiny little lady in the spotlight singing and talking beside enormous Jonathan … It was phenomenally exotic in that extremely austere company …" For Brand, the presentation was "exotic" in the European setting and exciting for him. "All the fun and colour and theatricality of the film was to be had from that Māori culture … I'm parroting what Jonathan obviously

---

159 Pat Dennis became close to Witarina Harris, and learned te reo Māori herself in her seventies (Personal correspondence, S. Dennis 13/07/10).

160 Since his death, the Jonathan Dennis Memorial Lecture is held at each Festival (Personal correspondence, P. Cherchi-Usai 14/05/09).

felt, that the Pākehā culture had their own inbuilt neuroses ..." (Personal correspondence, N. Brand 13/07/10). Brand, like Cherchi-Usai, recognised that the Māori cultural context complemented and drew out the films on the screen. They both recognised that the difference between the NZFA and other archives around the world was the indigenous materials and how the staff responded to them. By working with Māori people, Dennis allowed the "colour and theatricality" of the films to flourish. This was a new meaning for the word "exotic" which was not exploitative in tone. Dennis' own theatrical background helped him understand how the performance of the archive was important but Harris created the appropriate context for the performance (Dennis in Alley & Dennis 2001).

Dennis was committed to not just preserving but also curating and presenting materials to the widest possible audiences in New Zealand and overseas. The "inbuilt neuroses" of Pākehā culture could be countered by the warmth, colour and theatricality of Māori and Dennis knew how to exploit that in the "austere" company of the European silent film festival audience. The film archive could be "performed" for an audience in such a way that it could come to life. This was the creativity of the archive for Dennis – finding ways in which to present the films to multicultural audiences in a culturally appropriate manner.[161] Dennis found these experiences of presenting the films outside NZ with Harris (and occasionally Lily Amohau) very rewarding and also screened film presentations in many other countries including North America, Hawai'i, Poland, France and Australia (Fyfe & Dennis, 2001).

Cinema for the ears

After a few very busy years of projects and a great deal of personal upheaval with the cessation of his role of Director, Dennis was in need of a regular income by

---

161 It is not surprising that the biggest exhibitions of NZ films have been in Italy. Italians seemed to have received the films particularly well – in a similar presentation in London Sef Townsend described a much more muted response from the audience. Townsend suggested (as others have done before him) that Māori and Italian cultures hold much in common in terms of practices around hospitality, music and performance and family connection (Personal Correspondence S. Townsend 05/07/10). The Māori Battalion soldiers had spent time in Italy and many brought back the language and interest in cultural practices such as opera which have been passed down generations. I personally know a man brought up in Rotorua by his Te Arawa grandparents who taught him Māori, Italian and finally English as his third language. His grandfather was a Māori Battalion soldier in WWII. New Zealand artist Michael Parekowhai represented New Zealand at the Venice Bienalle in 2011 and similarly commented on the Italian people's interaction with his art work which reminded him of that of Māori (M.Parekowhai inaugural professorial lecture University of Auckland 28/11/13). Actor Wi Kuki Kaa commented in a radio program by Jonathan Dennis and Meredith Stephens that when he accompanied Barry Barclay's *Ngati* (1987) to Italy, his mihi (greetings) at the press conference were a cause of great excitement to the Italians who recalled in his greeting "from my mountain to yours, from my waters to yours" the old Sicilian greetings of their own country. There was such interest in fact that his words were reported in the newspapers, much to Kaa's surprise and pleased bewilderment (Voices on Film IV, NZFA collection).

1993. Just as his film reviews on Radio 2ZB in the 1970s had led to Lindsay Shelton, programmer for the Film Society and founder of the Wellington Film Festival, offering Dennis a role in programming the Festival, in the 1990s after the Italian film festival of 1993, opportunities arose again through radio.[162],[163]

Elizabeth Alley, Executive Producer of Spoken Word programmes at Concert FM, recognised the value of Dennis and Bieringa's new publication *Film In Aotearoa NZ* (Dennis & Bieringa, 1992/1996). The book was edited by Dennis and Bieringa and is a collection of essays written by various filmmakers, academics and critics. Alley interviewed Dennis about the book for her radio show *Anthology* (Personal correspondence, E. Alley 11/06/10). Subsequently she suggested Dennis turn the publication into a series for radio (Alley et al., 2001). Dennis said at the end of his life – "Radio in the last ten years has been the most creative part of what I've done. The sense of freedom that existed for me in radio was unexpected" (Dennis in Alley et al., 2001). Much of his previous work with various film personalities at the NZFA was to continue in this new medium – he was to record new interviews with Merata Mita, Barry Barclay, Witarina Harris, Bridget Ikin, Neil Brand, Paolo Cherchi-Usai and many others to use in his radio shows.[164] He continued to incorporate juxtaposition, irony and playfulness in his work with a strong sense of place (Hurley, 1998). Indigenous voices continued to feature. He said he began to understand the creative possibilities of radio in the early 1990s, that "the creative side was wide open. You could do just about anything. The idea of trying to make a moving image form work as cinema for the ear was, I thought, incredibly exciting" (Dennis in Alley et al., 2001).

Dennis uses the term "creative" repeatedly when describing his sound work, more often than in describing the moving image works he had previously focussed on, with the exception of *Mana Waka* which he saw as a "peak of creativity". Once more he uses superlatives which describe his emotions as he undertook these

---

162 Both Lindsay Shelton (Personal correspondence L. Shelton 07/12/09) and Jonathan Dennis (Pivac & Dennis, 2000) mention this in interviews and books (Shelton, 2005). In Dennis' archive there is a letter from Lindsay Shelton of the Wellington Film Society dated January 6 1976 inviting Jonathan (who was then living with his parents at 19 Central Terrace in Kelburn) to become involved in the organisation of that year's film festival (NZFA PP JD Box 7). Through the 1990s and until his death, Dennis also annually curated a silent film with live orchestra for the NZ International Film Festival (Personal correspondence, B. Gosden op.cit.).

163 One of Dennis' earlier film review broadcasts from the 1970s was a critique of *Star Wars* (Dir. Lucas, G 1977). It reflects a fearless style which did not waiver during his career as a film reviewer. In part it reads: "I don't wanta be the Grinch (or whatever it was) that stole Christmas, the blue meanie spoiling everybodies fun – but really, Star Wars is just not a very good movie, or a convincing one, or an involving one. Nor is it even serious Sci-Fi, being at most a bland, relatively minor adolescent cosmic cowboys'n'indians. The crock of humbuggery surrounding it tho, will have it end up the highest grossing movie of all time –its (sic) doing alarmingly good business and raking in herds of money and people ..." (NZFA PP JD Box 10 2ZB Film Review 18/12/77).

164 Recordings are available at the NZFA.

projects. Others also used similar language to describe Dennis' creativity, including Elizabeth Alley who said he flew into radio "on his own personal rainbow" (Personal correspondence, E. Alley op.cit.). Gareth Watkins described with enthusiasm the cinematic manner in which Dennis managed to layer his sound work (Personal correspondence, G. Watkins op.cit.). Dennis said he was "incredibly" excited by the possibilities of radio and the challenge of making a visual media work in a sound format (Dennis in Alley et al., 2001). It was Dennis' personal creative endeavour, more so than the previous filmmaking such as *Mana Waka,* in which he as producer supported the vision of others such as Merata Mita. Now he was the creator of the material to be presented.

The *Voices on Film* series was to be Alley and Dennis' first collaboration, incorporating "half hour episodes, basically his own personal take on how cinema has progressed ... it was the first time he started interweaving different sound sources. Movie clips, interviews, music, script ..." (Personal correspondence, G. Watkins 21/11/09). In the first and second of the *Voices on Film* series, "New Zealand film from its earliest efforts" was presented using recordings of early filmmakers Rudall Hayward, John O'Shea, John Grierson and others from the archives as well as music of NZ and the wider Pacific. The third programme covered the "lean years" of the 1940s to early 1970s when only three feature films were made in New Zealand.

Using juxtaposition, quick cuts and layering, the third programme played with the notion of national identity and what it might mean as a filmmaking culture developed. The listener hears John O'Shea quoting the Minister of Arts Allan Highet – "NZ should have our own heroes ..." Immediately following this is a soundbite from *Goodbye Pork Pie* (Prod. & Dir. G. Murphy 1980), in which the dubious and possibly mentally unstable anti-hero John shouts – "We're taking this car to Invercargill, boy!" (a yellow mini minor as it turns out). Dennis then cuts to a Māori kuia (woman elder) chanting, and Anzac Wallace's lines from *Utu* (Dir. G. Murphy 1983) are heard – "It is a tale/Told by an idiot, full of sound and fury/Signifying nothing".[165] Dennis is humorously toying with the idea of what NZ's "own heroes" will sound like in this section.

The programme then cuts to the theme music for the 1983 colonial western, *Utu* (which was to become the theme music for Dennis' *The Film Show* in 1994). In this film, Director Geoff Murphy critiques the heroic tales of early colonists and challenges the idea that Māori were the "uncivilized" natives, as demonstrated by

---

165 Lines originally from Shakespeare's *Macbeth* (Act 5, Scene 5, lines 17–28).

Anzac Wallace, a Māori character quoting Shakespeare. A quick edit cuts to the voice of Bruno Lawrence in *Smash Palace* (Prod. & Dir. R. Donaldson 1981) speaking a line of dialogue. Lawrence's character is another anti-hero who at one stage in that film dons his ex-wife's negligee to drive his truck to her new home, where he attaches a chain to the door and drives away, ripping the door from its hinges.

Immediately following Lawrence we hear filmmaker Peter Wells describing his recollection of New Zealand films of the 1970s/early 80s cinema (from an interview recorded by Dennis) as he realised those films had more merit than he gave them credit for at the time – "I thought they were so rurally smalltown based – couched in realism, straightforward narratives, landscape, heterosexual, no analysis of racial situation … seemed to ignore what was going on at the time …" This is immediately followed by film producer Bridget Ikin saying – "I think we're stuck in a Frank Sargeson social realism mode … no sense of a broader tradition here that values non-realist filmmaking." Jonathan Dennis' voice then quotes the film industry statistics in relation to the low number of women and Māori involved as active participants. Merata Mita's description of the Pākehā "neurotic film industry" follows. The passage ends with the promotional voice-over for *Sleeping Dogs* from Aardvark Films, "ordinary man is pushed to the limit …", followed by the sounds of an explosion (Voices on Film Programme 3 NZFA AUD 0624).

Within the space of a few minutes through editing and montage, Dennis has incorporated many of the contradictory perspectives on what New Zealand film was and could be. In a very tight edit he has critiqued the privilege of the white heterosexual male. The sounds of explosions, music, and mysterious phrases such as, "we're taking this car to Invercargill, boy", would still create an interesting aural montage even if the listener had not seen these films him/herself. Dennis used playful juxtaposition of elements which included snippets from the films themselves, as well as passages from interviews with filmmakers he himself had recorded. The montage and juxtaposition is similar to that used in the *Te Ao Marama* exhibition catalogue (Dennis, Jonathan & Toffetti, Sergio, 1989) where competing viewpoints are placed in close proximity and the audience are able to interpret the effect of this in their own way. Highet's imprecation that we need to find our own heroes is playfully followed by the voices of some of the anti-heroes in prominent New Zealand films. Each programme in the *Voices on Film* series is equally rich with film references, musical interludes and quotations from New Zealand filmmaking and filmmakers.

Programme number four in the *Voices on Film* series is entirely focussed on Māori filmmakers and is co-produced and presented with Meredith Stevens. This is the only co-presentation in the series and reflects Dennis' commitment to working with, rather than talking about Māori people (Dennis, 1990). Programme five covered the 1980s period and then program six looked at the possibilities of experimental cinema. These were the six programmes broadcast in 1993 (NZFA Audio 1993 A0067, A0994, AO995, AO068, AO330, AO997). The series is playful and rich with material and offers a different view on the potential for the telling of New Zealand stories which might not centre on "social realism" (Ikin's view of the writer Frank Sargeson social realist paradigm) or the rugged "ordinary man" (played by Sam Neill, a Pākehā man) of *Sleeping Dogs*. A feature of the series is a sense of fun and playfulness.

When she listened to these programmes it was clear to Alley that Dennis was talented and capable of doing more on radio in a similar format. Alley realised that Dennis was "enormously original … a little irreverent … pulled no punches … was extraordinarily articulate, great vocabulary, rich use of language, and he just stood out from the crowd in every possible way" (Personal correspondence, E. Alley op.cit.). It is perhaps not surprising that Dennis was so articulate – he had always been quick-witted and clever with words since he was a teenager (Personal correspondence, T. Dennis 05/08/09).

At Concert FM in the 1990s there was a new creative potential in state broadcasting and Alley felt they were "no longer hidebound by regulations and parameters that made us sound stuffy and conservative, there was a new freedom but it was extremely hard to find people who were prepared to take a few risks" (Personal correspondence, E. Alley op.cit.). Alley was prepared to take a few risks herself; when Dennis first returned to radio in the 1990s she was forced to defend his speaking voice as managers at Radio NZ raised concerns, feeling that he was "too camp" for radio at the time and that he should have voice training. Alley protested, arguing that his voice was perfectly acceptable and that Dennis would not have tolerated such a request for a change in his tone of voice (Personal correspondence, E. Alley op.cit).

Alley's earlier reference to Dennis' "personal rainbow" was not explicitly a comment on his sexuality, but the suggestion echoes. Dennis' personal sense of marginalisation and difference as a young man growing up in a boarding school with strict rules and regulations and an underlying and secret bullying culture was reflected in a man who wanted to do things differently. He sought to expose hypocrisy and celebrate those who previously had little or no voice. Alley said that – "… he came in with the first programme and it just about blew our heads off. Because not only was he taking sound in a different direction, he had found ways of accessing the most amazing material, off videos in those days … using it in such a way that it sounded as though he was there" (Personal correspondence, E. Alley ibid.). Perhaps Dennis' non-heterosexual manner was also appealing to feminist women who were looking for less traditional radio personalities.

As Alley describes it, Dennis found ways to access material and present it in a refreshing and exciting manner which the audience responded to well. Alley encouraged Dennis to begin his own radio show, and *The Film Show* began in 1994 as a fortnightly programme on Concert FM (national state radio station). As one critic said after Dennis' death – "In developing *Film Show* … Dennis raised the standards of radio production to an art which few even attempt to equal. The programme's strength was in his ability to convey the feeling and style, the sense of what a film actually looked like, in a medium which excluded the use of film's only necessity, the pictures themselves" (O'Brien, 2002). [166],[167] This is high praise and was representative of the critiques of Dennis' radio work both before and after he died.

Gareth Watkins was one of Dennis' sound engineers. He remembered Dennis' total focus and ability to record a passage in one take. He never got angry or showed frustration and he was always patient with the technical process. This was thrilling for a young sound engineer. Watkins said Dennis was "prepared to accommodate new ideas and thoughts, so in terms of creativity and collaboration, you were able to say 'we could try this' and he was always ready to try things out even if it didn't work" (Personal correspondence, G. Watkins 21/11/09). Watkins described a generosity in Dennis who was prepared to accommodate the ideas of others. In all Dennis' creative works collaboration was key. Dennis was prepared to take good ideas from where he found them, and acknowledge the origin of that idea. This reflected a collaborative engagement which he had learned through the 1980s at the NZFA, where the partnership with Māori had borne such fruit with films as described previously. It also followed archival practice where sources of ideas are always referenced as part of the everyday role of the archivist.

Another exciting development in 1993 was the release of Derek Jarman, British filmmaker and AIDS activists' final film, *Blue*. All Jarman's films were experi-

---

166 Jeremy Ansell was frequently the sound engineer for these shows, as was Gareth Watkins (Personal correspondence, G. Watkins op.cit.).

167 *The Film Show* won Best Broadcaster or Feature Programme New Zealand Radio Awards 1996 and Best Daily or Weekly Series NZ Radio awards 1998 (NZFA PP JD Box 7 awards).

139

mental in some way, eschewing traditional narrative form or addressing taboo subject matter such as gay sex, but this film was even more radical. The film was a blue screen for the entire feature length, with an audio track including the voices of some of his favourite actors such as John Quentin, Nigel Terry and Tilda Swinton speaking to create a soundscape. They and Jarman himself recited excerpts from his diary, quotes from various poets, writers and other films, evoking a depiction of the illness which was killing many people at that time and was often called the "gay plague" (Dennis & Alley, 1995). Jarman himself was losing his sight to the illness (Wollen, 1996). The experimental approach of the film with the visual being a single colour and the content being sound based would have appealed to Dennis who greatly admired Jarman and experimental cinema (Personal correspondence, E. Alley 11/06/10). The film also had personal and political implications. Ferry Hendriks, Dennis' partner of many years was at that time nursing various friends through their final AIDS related illnesses and at least one of their friends went blind before he died (Personal correspondence, F. Hendriks 28/11/09).

Dennis also experienced what was described by interviewees as a "gay bashing" during the early 1990s in Melbourne when he was walking along the street during the day alone and was punched very hard in the face. His glasses came off, he was covered in blood and no one helped him. There is a letter in which Dennis describes the aftermath of being beaten. "One of my front teeth will not recover, as the dentist says, from 'the trauma' and I've got to have root canal surgery next week. I've always been very pleased with my teeth, once all neatly spaced, and carefully protected years ago by Mr-Monk-the-Orthodontist with shining-clean rooms looking out through venetian blinds over a leafy bit of the Avon [The Avon River in Christchurch where Dennis went to boarding school]. Some of Mr Monk's thoughtful work was swiftly and brutally redone" (Box 11 Personal Papers NZFA Dennis, 9 June 1991).

In response to the AIDS crisis, Jarman's film and perhaps Dennis' own experience of "gay bashing", in 1995 Elizabeth Alley and Jonathan Dennis produced a soundscape for World AIDS Day for Radio NZ entitled *A Day Without Art*. Within this production they interwove portions of *Blue* with local artists' descriptions of their own experience of being diagnosed, to narrate a local story of the current moment when "already in NZ over 500 people have been diagnosed with the HIV AIDS virus" (Dennis & Alley, 1995). They called this soundscape *A Day Without Art* to underscore the loss to the arts community of many of its members through the virus and in honour of the US movement of that name.[168]

The resulting work was an hour long collage/soundscape "blending text, dramatic excerpt, poetry and drama in tribute to those who have died of AIDS to mark World AIDS Day". The production won the radio section of the 1995 AIDS Media Awards, the NZ Radio Award for Best Documentary or Feature in 1996 and was a finalist in the New York Radio Festival.[169] Elizabeth Alley said the result was a "stunning programme … it was Jonathan's imaginative creative effort that shaped … [it] … far more than I did" (Personal correspondence, E. Alley op.cit.). Alley's work with Dennis was indicative of his collaborations with others such as Sharon Dell, Annie Collins and Witarina Harris who worked with him. The relationships were creative, reciprocal and supportive.

Dennis seemed to find a niche in the sound work he did, and it became his main source of income for the rest of his life (Dennis in Alley & Dennis, 2002). Crucially, Alley negotiated the bureaucracy of Radio NZ for Dennis, who was hired only for the programmes he made with her. This gave him a new kind of freedom to focus on the productions without worrying about the politics of the organisation, for after all he was not "a corporate animal" (Personal correspondence, E.Alley op.cit.). This was very different from his previous experience of directing the NZFA and constantly negotiating with a Board and government officials (Dennis in Fyfe & Dennis, 2001; Pivac & Dennis, 2000). Alley's support meant Dennis could focus on creating new sound programmes, soundscapes, books and exhibitions which seemed to offer him a satisfaction unavailable in the more bureaucratic work he had found himself increasingly engaged in at the NZFA as it grew (Dennis in Pivac & Dennis, 2000).

In Jane Hurley's *Radio Best* column in The NZ Listener on January 10th 1998, she described another of Dennis' sound works, the *Centenary of Cinema Soundscape* which was to play on National Radio, as – "… fragments of movie soundtracks, like a cinema billboard layered with forgotten posters, soundscape juxtaposes speech and music, Hollywood and New Zealand, the archival and the contemporary".[170] She likened the work to collage. He responded by saying he

---

168 The title refers to a US movement of that name started in 1989 to offer a national day of action and mourning in response to the AIDS crisis which has since been renamed *A Day With(out) Art* to ensure creative practices are supported while acknowledging the loss of those who have died (Retrieved 26/05/14 http://www.carnegiemuseums.org/cmag/bk_issue/2005/winter/feature3.html http://www.visualaids.org/).

169 Dennis' awards are collected with his personal papers at the NZFA and include the AIDS Media Award, New Zealand Aids Foundation Award for Excellence, 3rd December 1995 for *A Day Without Art*, The New York Festivals Finalist Award 1996 for *A Day Without Art* (NZFA PP JD Box 7). It also won Best Factual Spoken Programme for Concert FM in 1996. (The New Zealand Radio Awards 1978 –1997 published by the NZ Radio Industry Awards Committee p.83.)

170 Cleverly, Dennis managed to instigate two Centenary of Cinema celebrations – one in 1996 as the world anniversary of the first films played in cinemas (in France) and then in 1998 as the local anniversary (NZFA PP JD).

wanted to explore "thematically through sound … we tend to think of cinema as something we go to see … in order to celebrate moving images just as sound, it seemed the most interesting way to go, for me … It's nice for people to respond more emotionally, to follow an emotional line rather than a formal dramatic line …" (NZFA PP JD Box 10). This interest in the "emotional line" reinforces Dennis' remarks in his interview with Judith Fyfe that he felt his intellect was not his strongest suit – he worked with his heart not his head – he trusted his other instincts (Dennis in Fyfe & Dennis, 2001). Dennis also said in the Hurley article that "Soundscape seemed to me to be always from a local point of view" (NZFA PP JD Box 10). Although aware of global trends, Dennis was pursuing a "sense of place" in the creative works he produced, providing layers of sound to present cinema even without visuals, just as the *A Day Without Art* soundscape was the local take on AIDS.

Dennis' last major soundscape work was to follow the emotional rather than the formal dramatic line, represented the local, and was, like Jarman's *Blue*, painting a picture without visual support. It was broadcast at the turn of the millennium and reflected much of the playful juxtaposition, montage and also serious political and social commentary of the earlier works described. It evokes many of the themes of Dennis' work such as his collaborative style (he worked with a fellow radio producer Matthew Leonard, the programme being instigated by another collaborator, Elizabeth Alley) and use of archival materials in new and creative ways. In *Ocean of Time* (2000) he and Leonard presented a counter-narrative to the Pākehā vision of the exotic and idyllic "South Seas" by foregrounding voices of indigenous peoples describing their lives since the arrival of settlers to their homelands. The classic Oxbridge accented narrator's voice is absent, though voices of earlier white narrators are included, and so placed to sound anachronistic. Sound engineer Gareth Watkins commented that Dennis used layers to strong effect in *Ocean of Time* as he had done in works with Watkins for *The Film Show* – "Layering … to either accentuate something or subvert … it would be very rare that we would have a straight sound. But he was also very aware of the power of just a single voice … he certainly liked to have … layers of meaning going on" (Personal correspondence, G. Watkins op.cit.).

Watkins' description echoes Hurley's comments regarding layering and collage. Watkins' felt these techniques were "filmic … in terms of how things faded; fade to black, same with audio, fading out and then bringing in another sound. I think he was expressing kind of a filmic language in an audio way which is quite neat" (Personal correspondence, G. Watkins ibid.). Watkins is describing an innovative manner in which to present sound on radio differently from the traditional forms he had observed previously as a Radio NZ sound engineer. The description supports Dennis' stated desire to create "cinema for the ears". Matthew Leonard agreed that Dennis' practice had a film-like quality which used "film semantics" to create various effects including "dissolves" (Personal correspondence, M. Leonard 01/04/10). This could perhaps be described as a "hybrid" style of soundscape using visual cinematic means for aural ends.

In the radio programme *Ocean of Time*, Dennis and Leonard created a colourful multi-layered collection of archival materials representing a variety of perspectives.[171] This was the culmination of (by then) many years of creative engagement with archival materials, and as Dennis became increasingly aware of his own position as a Pākehā, he had tried to appropriately represent indigenous peoples through collaboration. Although he never named it as such, Dennis' work has something of the quality of Homi Bhabha's conception of hybridity (Bhabha, 1994). Bhabha contends that a new "hybrid identity or subject-position emerges from the interweaving of elements of the coloniser and colonised challenging the validity and authenticity of any essentialist cultural identity" (Meredith, 1998 p.3). Bhabha suggests that emerging from this is a third space, a hybrid place between cultures where there is a negotiation and translation which becomes a productive space of possibility (Bhabha, 1994).

Dennis and Leonard are both "colonists" in the sense of being from European origins and living in the Pacific. They had both previously worked with the sound recordings of the colonised. It is an interweaving of colonist and colonisers, challenging the notion of a fixed identity. In the *Ocean of Time* soundscape Dennis and Leonard attempt to appropriately present a multiplicity of Pacific voices. They engage with Turner's "remembering rather than forgetting" the colonist and settler's acts and the reactions of Pacific indigenous peoples to those acts and events (S. Turner, 1999). They also arguably attempt to listen to, rather than speak about the materials they have amassed, creating a "productive space of possibility".[172]

The programme is loosely structured around Samoan New Zealander Albert Wendt's poem *Inside us the Dead*, read by Wendt himself. There are eight sections:

---

171 The montage style of various Australian radio programme makers such as Tony Barrell also seems to have been important in Matthew Leonard's work and in the *Radio Eye* (now *360*) tradition on ABC where he worked at the time.

172 The work was inspired for both Dennis and Leonard by the documentary film *Mother Dao The Turtle Like* (Dir. Monnikendam, V. 1995) in which archival footage of Indonesia was used to create a story of colonisation in that region with songs and poems replacing any traditional narration (Personal correspondence, M. Leonard ibid.).

Prologue, South Seas, Colonisation/The New Way is the Cross, White Dreams, Traders, War in the Pacific, Sovereignty and Independence and finally *Migration*. It also included hip hop tracks and other forms of music, traditional and contemporary. Dennis' desire in his radio programmes, like all his work, was to evoke emotion in himself and in his listeners (Dennis in Alley et al., 2001). One of those emotions may well be frustration or anger. Dennis felt archiving was about resisting the act of forgetting, to ensure ideas and themes could last, like Ted Coubray's memories, "into the future". As Turner cautions – "The danger of forgetting is that history too will be zoned, plotted and fenced off ..." just like the picket fences that surround the settler's house "... a picketed history – leaving settlers with no feeling for the processes of settlement that are the foundation for the distinctiveness of their cultural setting" (S. Turner, 1999 p.32). The section titles indicate the conscious attempt by Dennis and Leonard to engage with colonisation and its effects, while also supporting an audio work which is in itself a creative endeavour – by explicitly naming "Colonisation" and the role of Christianity, "The New Way is the Cross", as well as later movements of "Sovereignty and Independence", they are insisting on the reality of indigenous people's experience.

One of the section titles, "White Dreams", also recalls another quote from Turner – "... in New Zealand, the white dream of a new country, which requires that indigenous inhabitants be forgotten or constructed in terms of the vision of a bright future, conflicts with the tenacious historical memory and insistent presence of Māori" (S. Turner, 1999 p.22). Leonard and Dennis appear to be deliberately "unforgetting" the tenacious memory of Māori as well as other indigenous peoples of the South Pacific. The juxtaposition of recordings challenges "white dreams" and counterpoints with non-white memories, which may be able to then become fruitful new ideas and creative works. Leonard said Dennis wanted this soundscape to be "dreamlike" so people could drift in and out of it – and therefore quite literally it is the dream of a white man; that man being Dennis himself (Personal correspondence, M. Leonard ibid.).

In this production Dennis and Leonard explored the liminal space of the broadcast incorporating multiple voices into a creative work which in Homi Bhabha's terms, is a hybrid. The very fact that it is "ephemeral" and has no visual accompaniment ensures that it is "liminal" even in the most basic sense of being. It is a "hybrid" because it is the voices of indigenous and non-indigenous peoples. The broadcast attempts to sit in between cultures, in between time and place, but is created from the situated perspective of two Pākehā. Like Bhabha's work, it can be criticised for being created by the privileged (Perloff, 1999). In Dennis' case he was a middle class white man with access to archival resources and knowledge of how to use them.[173] Alternately, *Ocean of Time* demonstrates the opportunities that Charles Merewether celebrates in his work, *The Archive* (Merewether, 2006) in which he and his fellow contributors consider the creative potential of the archive, but also question the meaning of the materials which it produces.

Dennis and Leonard enacted and invoked the importance of remembering and storytelling in order to confront the past, which is also the present of NZ and the wider Pacific. For as Turner says – "Admitting the forgetfulness of the settler opens up a diversity of culture and experience that is denied by a reactive cultural realism" (S. Turner, 1999 p.38). In the original pitch for *Ocean of Time*, Dennis and Leonard wrote that they wanted to allow the sounds to "speak for themselves" (AC PP Pitch *Ocean of Time*). They certainly do not literally narrate the programme, thereby on one level "letting" the sounds speak. However, in Frantz Fanon's words – "No one can mediate between the disempowered living, and the voiceless dead". Greg Dening appropriates this quote from Fanon to assert that – "All of us writing in a history so terrible as that of the Pacific ... have had to resolve that dilemma for ourselves" (Neumann, Thomas, & Ericksen, 1999 p.xiii).

Through this work, Dennis and Leonard provoke discussion of that terrible history, which cannot be erased by any romantic notion of "hybridity". Following the argument of Turner, what they appear to attempt is remembering; not of a colonial past, but a colonial present. Their message within the broadcast runs counter to the prevailing wisdom that producer Elizabeth Alley and Matthew Leonard originally discussed when thinking about the millennial celebrations and the kind of radio programmes that would be broadcast. They imagined most programmes for the millennium would present race relations as peaceful, that any past conflict was ameliorated by the settlement of Treaty of Waitangi claims, and that New Zealanders would be presented as unified and satisfied with the status quo (Personal correspondence, M. Leonard op.cit.).

Ocean of Time was also an example of archivists using the internet to create a new presentation of archival material with an accompanying website which provided detailed reference to all the sound used in the presentation. It is a relatively early

---

173 Leonard noted they were particularly privileged in making this work. They had a month of dedicated time in a recording studio in Melbourne with a sound engineer, Melissa May who was an important part of their process (Personal correspondence M. Leonard, 01/04/2010).

example of an interactive website with a live radio broadcast so that the ephemeral soundscape would have a longer life and a deeper engagement with its audience prior to the now ubiquitous use of podcasts (http://www.abc.net.au/arts/ocean/info.htm). It suggests where Dennis may have gone next in his work – towards digital storytelling platforms. Dennis was eager to use new technologies to creatively present archival materials and sought to push boundaries in order to do so (Personal correspondence E. Alley op.cit.; M. Leonard op.cit.; G. Watkins op.cit.; A. Collins op.cit.).

In *Ocean of Time*, in *The Silent Migration*, in *Mana Waka*, through the Ted Coubray documentary and the many film exhibitions and publications, Dennis' constant practice was to retrieve and represent archival materials and collect the memories of "ancestors". They were his ancestors and those of others, living and dead, creating new presentations for both Pākehā and non-Pākehā audiences alike. He treated all these materials as taonga, and through juxtaposition, layering, montage and collage made rich sound and visual works which deliberately provoked emotional responses from the audience and were creative works in their own right. As Cherchi-Usai explained, Dennis was a film archivist, a curator, but also an "agit-prop". Specifically through his work with indigenous peoples and materials he sought to find new and better ways for archivists to appropriately and ethically work with archival materials. Through working by "heart" rather than "head" Dennis felt he had satisfied his own ambitions to tell stories which he thought were "wonderful" and important (Dennis in Fyfe & Dennis 2001).

As Dennis made all these works, he sought to identify his own place to stand within NZ and the wider South Pacific by focussing on local themes and local responses. He also consciously left an archive of rich materials for others, which are, thanks to his own methodical archiving practices, available through the NZFA and the Alexander Turnbull Library. This constant vigilance about keeping records, not just of the final work but the many interviews and other recordings of which they consisted, results in Dennis' creative works being accessible. This also ensures that the raw material is available for others to interpret in various ways, which may be very different from Dennis' own. As he said of the Coubray film, he never intended to become a director but it was the most expedient way to record and present the material he gathered. In this way Dennis sought not to be an author but the conduit through which materials could be presented for interpretation by an audience. This is curation at its most creative.

Chapter 8

Concluding discussion: Archive as biography of the nation?

Dennis' works (listed as an appendix) contributed to the growing archive of New Zealand and South Pacific culture, and demonstrate how he was never the sole author of these works; he was seeking to frame, curate and be the catalyst for the presentation of the artistic productions of others. Dennis understood that the work he did was collaborative – because he did not have all the information or skills required nor the doxa or habitus, he sought to encourage the work of others and engage with them to create presentations in various fora. Dennis shaped materials for various ends, and sought to incorporate a critique of the society within which he lived and worked.

Although Dennis never described it in these terms, an archive is simultaneously a tangible institution in which materials are stored and an intangible concept, an ideology and a platform. Michel Foucault had many years before exposed the archive's connection to power (Amad, 2010 p.19) and yet he did not support the view that power itself was only repressive (Foucault, 1976/2008). Dennis understood the connection between the archive and power. Those who were able to control the representation of history controlled contemporary understandings of the nation. He worked with others to address the power imbalances he recognised had occurred through the marginalisation of particular voices and perspectives. When he felt his position was no longer tenable, he stepped down as Director of the NZFA and continued his work without the economic capital of the Director's position to support him.

There are many similarities between the discourse of the "archive" and the "biography". The archive cannot hold every record or object of a nation or it would be too cumbersome to manage. Decisions are constantly being made, both consciously and unconsciously about what will or will not remain in the archive. There are costs to each course of action in terms of resources which will come into play. Similarly, by necessity of length of the text alone, much will be omitted from any biography. Other considerations that lead to omission in the biography will be due to mistakes on the author's part, wilful manipulation of information, a desire to depict some people in a positive light for political or personal reasons, or ignorance of a particular fact or incident. Similarly, the archive is rife with omissions in the collection it presents to the public due to the same reasons listed above, but also because of a deterioration of objects, failure to obtain certain things for a collection or a desire to preserve an object by not presenting it if it may cause deterioration in its presentation. Alternately, there may be feelings of shame towards a historical artefact which now reveals an aspect of the society which in the present moment seems unacceptable. These omissions are a silence which shapes the archive; they are the discourse around the object. They are also similar to the decisions made by the biographer when analysing the materials associated with an author in which that author must inevitably disappear as a version of their narrative is reproduced, which can never be an authentic truth.

Dennis as an archivist and presenter of archive materials was both actively constructing the archive, and also a subject of it – he was impacted upon by the society in which he lived, and its changing socio-political forces. His place within his own archive of writings, artistic and archival productions and the narratives told by him and about him, have their own omissions and contradictions, their own deteriorating truths and authentic moments. Interviewees will have chosen what to share or refrain from telling just as the curator or archivist will select what to present from the collection of the archive.

The biography and the archive are both representations of the past which are likely to be understood as "authentic" because they are published or exhibited in the public sphere. Additionally, the biography and the archive are linked by the fact that they are both important conduits of memory and nostalgia for a reader/audience who are as significant as the biographer/archivist in the interpretation of a body of work. Dennis' archive and biography are both more and less significant than the sum of their parts – they create a space into which Dennis' life and work constantly disappear, but in the space they create there is the possibility of a discourse which frames a subject which can be labelled with his name. Dennis allows for the debate which must always be associated with the archive and its subject – who has the right to name or describe the subject of the biography, or the object in the archive? Who holds the incontrovertible truth to label either? Who is allowed, who is privileged at a given moment in history to say – this is the truth of Jonathan Dennis, his life and his work. Equally who holds the key to the true archive, the true meaning of the New Zealand Film Archive? Instead, the multiple perspectives present a view of the archive as constantly in flux, in a state of change and contestation, tension and debate just as Dennis' biography is a catalyst for a discussion about the work of the film archivist and its importance (or insignificance) in the contemporary moment.

As I have demonstrated, materials in the archive can be used to invoke notions of belonging. The archive can be charged with the responsibility to tell a story of anything, but quite frequently in the case of state funded national archives, the story required is one of evolving nationhood. But who is connected and who is excluded by the manner in which these materials are collected and presented? Whose is the real and authentic story of the nation? The archive offers a partial perspective which tells a story, a single frame which might be that of an individual, but more often will depict a wider group, possibly even a version of the nation itself, and that representation is in a constant dialogue and engagement with the reader/audience.

Dennis recognised the value of both retrieving and re-presenting archival materials, but also the importance of collecting new materials for the archive. He knew that archives are often the repositories for "forgotten" knowledges which wait to be unearthed in the future (Green & Hutching, 2004 p.2). Dennis understood that depending on the historical circumstances, the treatment a group receives will differ and therefore an individual or group considered unimportant at one particular time may be elevated in a different time period or context. Archivists attempt to take the long view, ignoring fashions and politics in order to preserve what they see as the voices of the past in order for them to be available, in Dennis' own words, "into the future" (Dennis in Alley et al., 2001).

However, he also learned that archivists are fallible and will not necessarily understand their own partial perspective which led them to elevate some materials over others. This will inevitably lead to a failure to archive everything that might be of interest to all parties within the nation, and as Paula Amad describes it, the researcher in the archive needs to be aware of "the fantasies of the future nestled amidst the documents in which she pursues the facts of the past" (Amad, 2010 p.1). Archivists are imperfect gatherers of material with conscious and unconscious motivations, just as biographers are imperfect in their telling of a person's life.

As the biographer telling the story of this particular person and the history of the Archive, I have demonstrated how Dennis' contradictory experiences of both acceptance within his own family and then the shock of his boarding school experience meant he had to learn to negotiate his self-presentation. In his own words he was lacking the "boysy" behaviours of the Canterbury farmers' sons at his private school (Dennis in Fyfe & Dennis, 2001). This caused him in later life to create his own performance of self, and also to consider the experiences of others who are less likely to be heard or registered in the story of the nation. He was aware of the false authenticity of the masculine ideal of the Kiwi bloke defined against women and indigenous peoples. I have remained fascinated over the six years of this study with Dennis' flamboyant, colourful, humourous and sometimes wicked personality. His tenacity, wit, sense of friendship and fun as well as his passionate defence of those he felt were marginalised is enormously appealing.

As we have seen, in many academic and popular fora since the 1980s it has been noted that masculinity is a strong national identifier in New Zealand; specifically a Pākehā masculinity. Hegemonic masculinities theory states that women define (or are forced to define) themselves against the notion of masculinity – "To sustain a given pattern of hegemony requires the policing of men as well as the exclusion or discrediting of women" (Connell & Messerschmidt, 2005 p.844). Jonathan Dennis did not accept the stereotype of the Pākehā kiwi bloke in his own life or in his work; nor did he accept that women should be excluded or discredited, just as he did not accept his own exclusion. As an out and proud gay man, Dennis resisted the mask of heterosexuality. He was well aware of the masculine stereotype and the related practices of physical activity (such as prowess with the rugby ball) which made men acceptable in this society. He had experienced homophobia in Melbourne when he was beaten and then not helped by passersby too scared to come to the aid of a flamboyant and possibly gay man at the time of the rise of the disease HIV AIDS which they knew to be transmitted by blood (Watkins, G. Personal correspondence op.cit; Young, D. Personal correspondence op.cit). Dennis knew the importance of his story and that of other gay men being told. His strong friendships with feminist women also taught him of their history of repression and oppression. He knew their stories were also often unacknowledged, unarchived and unrepresented in the story of the nation.

By the late 1970s, early 1980s period Dennis was becoming much more aware of taha Māori (the Māori dimension) (Dennis in Alley & Dennis, 2002). The parallel universe of Aotearoa New Zealand as both an example of empire and an indigenous country with many iwi practices alien to the British people who settled here, became increasingly compelling to Dennis. Through the Springbok Tour protest marches in which he partook which challenged Pākehā assumptions about race relations, Dennis became well aware of the increasingly vocalised resentments Māori felt towards himself and others like him. Through the 1980s Dennis learned how unjust his country had been to indigenous peoples, and he sought to address this through his work in a variety of ways which held a common thread – listening harder and giving a voice to marginalised communities.

How did Dennis "join the dots" between his own observations and experience of marginalisation and the experience of indigenous peoples, separately marginalised in his country? His feminist colleagues and friends such as Sharon Dell, Annie Collins, and Merata Mita sought to inform him through their own experiences of the multiple repressions experienced by women and indigenous peoples (Personal correspondence, E. Alley, op.cit.). Dennis' colleagues demonstrated how the "colonist lens" (Personal correspondence, A. Collins op.cit.) had an impact upon the constructions of the culture in which they worked. For example, Merata Mita observed that the 1970s and 1980s film industry was a "white" and "neurotic" one (Mita, 1996 p.47). Through her filmmaking she attempted to challenge this and tell other stories through an indigenous perspective.[174] Dennis recognised Mita's work as significant and sought to preserve and present it through becoming Mita's distributor for various films and then by asking her to direct *Mana Waka*. Mita, fellow filmmaker Barry Barclay, film editor Annie Collins and others told a different version of the story, a different biography of the nation than the mainstream version represented in other films of the time. Dennis supported this retelling, this different version of the narrative, this attempt to place emphasis differently.

Dennis became increasingly aware of the multiple pressures on the Archive to conform to the prevailing views of its time as he battled various bureaucrats who sought to change the Archive into an image they were comfortable with. They resisted difficult tasks such as funding the editing of archival footage of war canoes into a new film for a contemporary audience using an untested bicultural production model. Dennis experienced an often unspoken pressure to conform to the needs and views of those in powerful positions, such as the Board of the NZFA, and he fought hard against them. His understanding of his own ignorance of the Māori world was a great strength for the Director of a mainstream institution which was by the end of the 1980s, successful and well regarded nationally and internationally. It would have been easy to continue with the status

---

174 This is also not an unproblematic or uncomplicated assertion, as *Patu!* (Prod.& Dir. M.Mita 1983) was edited from footage produced by many of the first wave of Pākehā filmmakers Mita accuses of making "white neurotic" films such as Roger Donaldson, Leon Narbey and Alun Bollinger.

quo of archiving practice, but philosophically and emotionally, working with his heart and not his head, Dennis wanted to follow the traces and clues the archive provided. Particularly, he was learning to listen to the silences, the Māori voices which had previously been unheard in the archive. He also had a rare opportunity to shape the institution he led, given that the NZFA opened 50 years later than the first national film archives in other Western nations. He was able to learn both what he wanted the archive to be and also what he did not want it to be (Dennis in Fyfe & Dennis, 2001).

The passionate responses of various iwi to films about their community had demonstrated to him that Māori were valuing the films of the NZFA in a way that most Pākehā communities did not (Dennis, 1990). This passion from Māori communities was a driving force which continued to push him outside the accepted boundaries of Te Ao Pākehā/the Pākehā world, as he responded equally passionately to iwi engagement (Personal correspondence, M.Wall 01/10/10).

Dennis described a great fondness for the films he cared for; he could name all the classic features and major documentaries in the collection and was proud of them (NZFA PP JD Box 2). Through the various local and international exhibitions he curated, through his work at the Archive and after, Dennis attempted not to present the truth of the nation, but the many perspectives and the often irreconcilable elements in NZ society. These were reflected in the Archive through the films he knew and cared for personally. He pushed the boundaries of the film archive exhibition too, showing contemporary fine art works and responses to them in the exhibition catalogue along with more traditional moving image fare.[175] He expected his audience to be provoked, to respond, and to be "film literate" (Dennis in Alley & Dennis, 2002).

By doing this, Dennis was working well beyond the self-imposed mandate of many archivists who believe their only role is to catalogue and preserve the materials they collect. Through the exhibition process Dennis literally became Timothy Wisnieski's "framer of the kept" (Wisniewski, 2007). Dennis did this by presenting both the "said" and the "unsaid", the forgotten and the remembered, the popular and the unpopular from the archive. He entered the debate regarding the nature of the archive, he commented on the past and the present through the exhibition of archival materials and questioned the roles of the archivist and the audience. Dennis was presenting a biography of the nation as

---

175 For example there is a short essay in the *Te Ao Marama* ... exhibition book by artist Gilberto Zorio regarding the art work *Black Phoenix* by New Zealand artist Ralph Hotere (Dennis, Jonathan & Toffetti, Sergio, 1989 pp.56, 57).

problematic, exciting, creative and sometimes violently at odds with itself. He told the story of a nation which is still in exploration of its own borders by framing it in various ways through soundscapes, exhibitions, written texts and re-releases of sound recordings. By challenging the stereotype of New Zealanders as only Pākehā, male and physically, but not intellectually, socially or emotionally engaged, Dennis presented a version of New Zealand as Aotearoa New Zealand, a colonised land struggling to find its identity under multiple pressures and (in some quarters) resisting acknowledgment of its violent past and present, hoping to forget its history by creating a new version of the past.

In 2014 Gareth Watkins, photographer, sound engineer, archivist, and website manager was "Curator-at-Large" at the New Zealand Film Archive. His first exhibition of the year was *Pets* – archival images and sounds of pets and animals from the collection. His second was *30* – a commemoration of 30 years since the first HIV AIDS diagnosis in New Zealand. Watkins used the materials of the Archive – predominantly television broadcasts and film excerpts – to show the official news stories of the "gay plague", which was the language of the discourse of the time. At a given time all the screens would turn blue simultaneously. This acknowledgement of Derek Jarman's *Blue* is complemented by the voice of Welby Ings, a Professor of Art & Design, reciting a short poem to his lover who had died of an AIDS related illness. The AIDS quilt panels (including Ings') made in New Zealand, also hang through the exhibition, with Ings' being the cover art for the publicity materials. Watkins' work demonstrates the creativity possible using archival materials to both acknowledge and challenge the concept of a cohesive national identity at the time of a public health crisis which saw many people behave with prejudice and even hatred towards those with the new disease – many of whom were gay men. There is no easy nostalgia in this exhibition – the cumulative effect is in fact an overwhelming feeling of grief and sadness.

Dennis' influence on Watkins' exhibition is apparent. Just as Dennis had included an homage to Jarman's *Blue* in his *A Day Without Art*, so did Watkins (who acknowledged his admiration of Dennis' work) (Personal correspondence, G. Watkins op.cit.). The careful use of archival material to tell a difficult and sensitive story of the past is also a call to arms for the contemporary audience – it is as Cherchi-Usai described Dennis' work, "agit prop" or activist archivist work (Personal correspondence, P. Cherchi-Usai op.cit.). This does not suggest that the work is not Watkins' own, but it does acknowledge Barthes' death of the author argument, and also the "author function" of Foucault. Watkins' work is influenced by the network around him, by his own creative instincts, and by those who went before such as Jarman and Dennis who he acknowledges as artistic and creative ancestors. Just as Dennis' life and work were influenced by others, Watkins too is part of a discourse influenced by Dennis and in turn he will influence others through his work.

Watkins' work for the *30* exhibition evokes Lauren Berlant's gestures towards a narrative which moves away from the traditional biographical narrative via the work of "anti-capitalist, feminist and queer" stories (Berlant & Prosser, 2011 p.182). *30* is a history of gesture, of effect, of queer lives, which cumulatively represents the statistics of an epidemic. Watkin's archival presentations of the lives of many, perhaps offers a more effective account than a focus on the life of an individual who died of HIV AIDS because it avoids Berlant's sentimental contract with the individual story. Watkins' exhibition proves that the archive can be a platform from which to creatively present the stories of many through his curatorship, his authorship, his role as conduit for archival materials which present a queer view of the nation. It does not fit an easy nostalgic representation of the "Kiwi bloke". Watkins' work is his own, and yet it stands on the shoulders of Dennis and those others who went before him – Derek Jarman, Merata Mita, Witarina Harris, Barry Barclay, Annie Collins, Elizabeth Alley, Irihapeti Ramsden, Patricia Grace, Matthew Leonard, Sharon Dell, Paolo Cherchi-Usai, Sergio Toffetti – all those filmmakers, artists and archivists who wished to take images or sounds from the archive and challenge audiences to think harder.

Reflecting a view that museums and archives are always at the centre of contestations of the nation (McCarthy 2011) the NZFA became a space in which Māori and Pākehā battled and renegotiated their sense of selves in the 1980s. At the end of that time and before he resigned from the Archive, Dennis led a change in the constitution and title of the *New Zealand Film Archive* to *Ngā Kaitiaki o Ngā Taonga Whitiāhua*. By doing so he sought to name the changing purpose and intention of the Archive – he wanted it to be explicitly bicultural, and by that he meant actively partnering with the iwi of the motu [nation] to share responsibility, representation and power.

In 2014 the name of the Archive has changed again. It is now *Ngā Taonga – Sound and Vision Ngā Kaitiaki o Ngā Taonga Whitiāhua me Ngā Taonga Kōrero*.[176] This is partly an indication of its evolving contents. It now incorporates the state television archive as well as the state radio materials. In choosing to centre the name of the Archive on the heart of its contents and intentions, it acknowledges

---

176 Announced 1ˢᵗ August 2014 http://www.ngataonga.org.nz/

the living relationship audiences may have with the materials of the Archive which are taonga. In Paul Tapsell's words "time travellers" who meet their descendants "face to face" with iwi, wehi and wana (Tapsell, 2006 p.17). This significant triple renaming of the Archive in its first 30 years serves to indicate its various phases and functions and the multiple perspectives and understandings of these over time. Who knows what Dennis may have made of this renaming? Even after a six year study of his life and work, I maintain Keith Sinclair's caution against psychoanalysing the dead (Sinclair, 1985 p.33). Jonathan Dennis Spencer has served his purpose; to illustrate the tensions at a particular moment in Aotearoa New Zealand through his work with the New Zealand Film Archive, an institution which is guardian and steward of the images and sounds of the nation. He demonstrated how archivists can respond creatively to the materials within their archive by collaborating with those outside it. He showed that by learning to listen harder and release some control, new and creative possibilities can emerge.

The archive itself is not the biography of the nation. Its contents contain no memories. Only by an interaction with the living can the material of the archive come to life. The archive holds no intrinsic value; it tells no stories, sings no songs. When archivists and archive users choose a single photo, or a scrap of letter from the archive the process of storytelling begins.

Bibliography

Text, Film, Video, Sound

Agamben, G. (1989). *Remnants of Auschwitz: The witness and the archive.* Chicago, IL: University of Chicago Press.

Allen, A. (2002). The anti-subjective hypothesis and Foucault. *The Philosophical Forum, 31*(2).

Alley, E., & Dennis, J. (2002). *If I dreamed of anything I dreamed of being a film star – interview with Jonathan Dennis.* [Oral History Recording] Wellington: Radio NZ (Original recording date 6 December 2001). Collection of the NZFA.

Alley, E., Watkins, G., & Dennis, J. (2001). Full recording of Jonathan Dennis interview. [Oral History recording]. 14 Edgehill Mt. Victoria Wellington.

Amad, P. (2010). *Counter-archive: Film, the everyday, and Albert Kahn's Archives de la Planéte.* New York, NY: Columbia University Press.

Andrews, S. (Producer). Furlong, M. (Director). (1950). *Journey for three.* [Documentary]. New Zealand: National Film Unit.

ARANZ. (2004). *Nga taonga tuku iho: Treasures passed down.* Maori Archives and Records In ARANZ (Chair), *ARANZ.* Symposium conducted at the meeting of the ARANZ Twenty Eighth Annual Conference Rotorua. Retrieved from http://www.aranz.org.nz/Site/events/Conferences/2004_conference_programme.aspx

Azzopardi, T. (2010). *The song house.* London, England: Picador.

Bal, M. (2009) *Narratology: Introduction to the theory of narrative* (3rd ed.). Toronto, Canada,: University of Toronto Press.

Bamberg, M., De Fina, A., & Schiffrin, D. (Eds.). (2007). *Selves and identities in narrative and discourse* (Vol. 9). Amsterdam, The Netherlands: John Benjamins Publishing.

Bannister, M. (2005). Kiwi blokes – recontextualising white New Zealand masculinities in a global setting. *Genders, 42*(2005).

Barbedette, G. (1982). The social triumph of the sexual will: A conversation with Michel Foucault (trans. B. Lemon). *Christopher Street, 6*(4), 36–41.

Barclay, B. (1990). *Our own image.* Auckland, New Zealand: Longman Paul.

Barclay, B. (2003). Celebrating fourth cinema. *Illusions, 35.*

Barclay, B. (2005). *Mana tūturu, Māori treasures and intellectual property rights.* Auckland, New Zealand: Auckland University Press.

Barthes, R. (1967). The death of the author. *Aspen, 5,6.*

Barthes, R. (1972). *Mythologies.* New York, NY: Hill and Wang.

Barthes, R. (1977). The death of the author. In *Image, music, text.* New York, NY: Hill and Wang. (Original work published 1967)

Bell, A. (2006). Bifurcation or entanglement? Settler identity and biculturalism in Aotearoa New Zealand. *Continuum Journal of Media & Cultural Studies, 20*(2), 253–268.

Bennett, T., Frow, J., Hage, G., & Noble, G. (2013). Antipodean fields: Working with Bourdieu. *Journal of Sociology, 49,* 129–150.

Berlant, L. (1997). *The Queen of America goes to Washington City.* London, England: Duke University Press.

Berlant, L. (1998). Intimacy: A special issue. *Critical Inquiry, Winter 28.*

Berlant, L., & Prosser, J. (2011). Life writing and intimate publics; a conversation with Lauren Berlant. *Biography, 34*(1, Winter 2011).

Bernard, L. (2011). Unpacking the archive. *The Yale Review, 99*(4), 93–107.

Bhabha, H. (1994). *The location of culture.* New York, NY: Routledge.

Billsteen, B. (Executive Producer). Epstein, R. & Friedman, J. (Directors). (1995). *The Celluloid Closet.* [Documentary feature]. United States: HBO & Channel 4

Binney, J. (2009). *Encircled lands: Te Urewera 1820–1921.* Wellington, New Zealand: Bridget Williams Books.

Binney, J. (2010). *Stories without end: Essays 1975–2010.* Wellington, New Zealand: Bridget Williams Books.

Binney, J., & Chaplin, G. (1986). *Ngā Mōrehu/the survivors: The life histories of Māori women.* Auckland, New Zealand: Oxford University Press.

Bishop, R. (1996). *Collaborative research stories: Whakawhanaungatanga.* Palmerston North, New Zealand: Dunmore Press.

Blakeney, D. (Executive Producer). Maunder, P. (Director). (1979). *Sons for the Return Home.* [Feature film]. New Zealand: Pacific Films.

Bloomfield, T. (2013). Engaging indigenous participation: Towards a more diverse profession. *Museum Management and Curatorship, 28*(2), 138–152.

Bouhours, J.-M., & Horrocks, R. (Eds.). (2000). *Len Lye.* Paris, France: Editions du Centre Pompidou.

Bourdieu, P. (1984). *Distinction: A social critique of the judgement of taste.* Cambridge, MA: Harvard University Press.

Bourdieu, P. (1986). The forms of capital [Proofed online version] marxists.org/.../philosophy/works/fr/bourdieu-forms-capital.htm

Bourdieu, P., & Wacquant, L. (1992). *An invitation to reflexive sociology.* Stanford, CA: Stanford University Press.

Bowie, R. & Fowler, D. (Producers). MacDonald, H. (Director). (1970). *This is New Zealand.* [Documentary Feature]. New Zealand: National Film Unit.

Bowie, R. (Producer), Maunder, P. (Director). (1975). *Gone Up North For A While.* [Television feature]. New Zealand: National Film Unit. Archives NZ Reference W3471/6061 (16BW431E)

Bowser, E., Kuiper, John (Ed.). (1991). *A handbook for film archives – International Federation of Film Archivists (FIAF).* New York, NY: Garland Publishing Inc.

Boyatzis, R. (1998). *Transforming qualitative information; thematic analysis and code development.* Thousand Oaks, CA: Sage Publications.

Brady, A. (2006). All Blacks, eyeliner, and Queer Eye: Metrosexuality and the "crisis of homo/heterosexual definition". *New Zealand Journal of Media Studies, 9*(2).

Brady, A. (2012). The transgendered Kiwi: Homosocial desire and "New Zealand identity". *Sexualities, 15*(355), 355–372. sexualities.sagepub.com/content/15/3-4/355.short

Brickell, C. (2008). *Mates and lovers: A history of gay New Zealand*. Auckland: Godwit Publishing.

Bryman, A. (2004). *Social research methods* (2nd ed.). Oxford, England: Oxford University Press.

Burnard, P. (1991). A method of analysing interview transcripts in qualitative research. *Nurse Education Today, 11*, 461–466.

Butler, J. (2001). What is critique? An essay on Foucault's virtue. *European Institute for Progressive Cultural Policies*. Retrieved from http://eipcp.net/transversal/0806/butler/en

Byatt, A. S., & Harvey Wood, H. (Eds.). (2009). *Memory: An anthology*. London, England: Vintage Books.

Cardy, T. (2004, 23 July). The last days of a film fanatic [Feature article]. *Dominion Post*, p. 11.

Cherchi Usai, P. (2001). *The death of cinema – history, cultural memory and the digital dark age*. London, England: British Film Institute.

Cherchi Usai, P., Francis, D., Horwath, A., & Loebenstein, M. (Eds.). (2008). *Film curatorship –archives, museums, and the digital marketplace* (Vol. 9). Pordenone, Italy: Synema, Le Giornate del Cinema Muto.

Clare, J., & Hamilton, H. (2003). *Writing research – transforming data into text*. New York, NY: Churchill Livingstone.

Clifford, J. (1987). Of other peoples: Beyond the "salvage" paradigm. *Dia Art Foundation: Discussions in Contemporary Culture, 1*, 120–130, 142–150. (Original work published Seattle Bay Press).

Club,. Ngāti Pōneke Young Māori Club . (2001). Ngāti Pōneke Young Māori Club historic recording re-release. Producer Dennis, J. [Compact Disc]. On *He Puiaki Puoro Treasures in Sound*. Wellington: National Library of NZ Te Puna Maatauranga o Aotearoa Alexander Turnbull Library.

Collini, S. (2012). *What are universities for?* London, England: Penguin.

Collins, A. (Director). (1987). *Double Take*. [Documentary film]. New Zealand: Pakehas Against Racism.

Collins, A. (Producer). Dennis, J. (Director). (1998). *Mouth Wide Open*. [Documentary film]. New Zealand: Moa Films.

Connell, R. W., & Messerschmidt, J. W. (2005). Hegemonic masculinity: Re-thinking the concept. *Gender and Society, 19* (829).

Conrich, I., Murray, Stuart (Eds.). (2008). *Contemporary New Zealand cinema: From new wave to blockbuster*. London, England: I.B.Tauris.

Cormack, D., & Robson, C. (2010). *Ethnicity, national identity and "New Zealanders": Considerations for monitoring Māori health and ethnic inequalities*. Wellington, New Zealand: Ministry of Health.

Crosbie, S. (1990, March 11). Films have been his mission in life. *Dominion Sunday Star Times*.

Davies, R. (1988). *The Lyre of Orpheus*. London, England: Penguin.

Davis, J. C. (1985). *Biography in New Zealand*. In J. Phillips (Ed.). Wellington, New Zealand: Allen and Unwin.

Davy, S., & Pivac, D. (2008). With a strong sense of place: The New Zealand Film Archive/Nga Kaitiaki O Nga Taonga Whitiahua. In I. Conrich, Murray, Stuart (Eds.), *Contemporary New Zealand cinema: From new wave to blockbuster*. New York, NY: I.B.Tauris. pp.85–99.

Dell, S. (1987). Te hokinga mai ki Whanganui. Volume 16 February, *New Zealand Film Archive Newsletter:NZFA* Wellington, New Zealand.

Dell, S. (2010). *Working together, learning together: How experiences of working with iwi shape more than collection management practices*. Paper presented at the meeting of the Australasian Registrars Committee, Christchuch.

Dennis, J. *Personal Papers Box 11*. Wellington: New Zealand Film Archive.

Dennis, J. *Letters to his parents, Alexander Turnbull Manuscript Collection*. Wellington, New Zealand: Alexander Turnbull Library.

Dennis, J. (1982–1991). *NZFA reports to FIAF (International Federation of Films Archives) Congress*. Brussels:National Film and Sound Archive Australia.

Dennis, J. The New Zealand Film Archive NZFA FD9/4/71. (1985). National Film Sound Archive Australia file, New Zealand Film Archive.

Dennis, J. (1987). Taha Maori: The Maori dimension. *Hawaii International Film Festival Catalogue*.

Dennis, J. (1989). The process of change at the New Zealand Film Archive/Nga Kaitiaki o Nga Taonga Whitiahua. *AGMANZ Art Galleries and Museums Association of New Zealand, 20*(1), 10–11.

Dennis, J. (Producer). Mita, M. (Director). (1990). *Mana Waka*. [Documentary feature]. New Zealand: New Zealand Film Archive.

Dennis, J. (1990). *Uncovering and releasing the images – the case of ethnological film*. Presented at the meeting of the Documents That Move and Speak, Audiovisual Archives in the New Information Age. Proceedings of a symposium for the International Council of Archives., Ottawa, Canada.

Dennis, J. (Producer) (1993). *Girl's own stories*. [Television Episode] New Zealand: TVNZ.

Dennis, J., & Alley, E. (1995). A day without art; World Aids Day Soundscape. [Radio soundrecording] Wellington, New Zealand: Radio NZ.

Dennis, J., & Bieringa, J. (Eds.). (1996). *Film in Aotearoa New Zealand*. Wellington, New Zealand: Victoria University Press. (Original work published 1992) .

Dennis Jonathan. (1987). *He pito whakaatu a nga iwi Màori, films of the tangata whenua catalogue*. Auckland, New Zealand: Auckland City Art Gallery.

Dennis Jonathan, & Cherchi Usai, P. (Eds.). (1993). *Aotearoa and the sentimental strine – making films in Australia and New Zealand in the silent period*. Wellington, New Zealand: Moa Films.

Dennis, Jonathan, & Toffetti, Sergio (Eds.). (1989). *Te ao marama, il mondo della luce, il cinema della Nuova Zelanda*. Torino, Italy: New Zealand Film Archive and Le Nuove Muse.

Derrida, J. (1996). *Archive fever, a Freudian impression*. Chicago, IL: The University of Chicago Press.

Dhunpath, R. (2000). Life history methodology: "Narradigm" regained. *Qualitative Studies in Education, 13*(5), 543–551.

Donaldson, R. (Producer & Director). (1977). *Sleeping Dogs*. [Feature film]. New Zealand: Aardvark Films Ltd.

Donaldson, R. (Producer & Director). (1981). *Smash Palace*. [Feature film]. New Zealand: Aardvark Films Ltd.

Drent, A., & Sutherland, P. (1989, Sourced 14 March 2009). *Library treasures –New Zealand art works from the collection of the Canterbury Public Library*. Exhibited at the C.S.A Gallery Gloucester St, Christchurch. Retrieved from http://christchurchcitylibraries.com/Heritage/Publications/CanterburyPublicLibrary/Library Treasures/

Durie, M. (2005). *Ngaa tai matatuu: Tides of Maaori endurance*. Oxford, England: Oxford University Press.

Dyer, G. (2005). *The ongoing moment*. New York, NY: Pantheon Books.

Eagle, A. (2000). *Biculturalism in Aotearoa New Zealand: The public service response (Master's thesis)*. Victoria University, Wellington, New Zealand.

Edwards, S., & Martin, H. (1997). *New Zealand film 1912–1996*. Otago, New Zealand: Otago University Press.

Empson, W. (1984). *Using biography*. London, England: The Hogarth Press.

Fadyl, J. K., & Nicholls, D. A. (2012). Foucault, the subject and the research interview: A critique of methods. *Nursing Inquiry, E-pub ahead of print*, 1–7. doi:10.1111/nin.12011

Farquhar, C. (2011). *Rugby culture*. New Zealand Film Archive (Ed.). Auckland: NZFA.

FIAF, International Federation of Film Archives (2002). Retrieved 21/02/09 http://fiatifta.org/fiatifta-organisation/statutes/

Fischer, W., & Goblirsch, M. (2007). *Biographical structuring: Narrating and reconstructing the self in research and professional practice*. Amsterdam, The Netherlands: John Benjamins Publishing.

Fisher, K. (2010, 22 September). *Identities and subjectivities in cross-cultural research*. Presented at the meeting of the Manu Ao Network lecture AUT.

Foucault, M. (1969, 22/02/1969). *What is an author?* Presented at the meeting of the Societe Francaise de philosophie. Retrieved from https://wiki.brown.edu/confluence/download/attachments/74858352/FoucaultWhatIsAnAuthor.pdf?version=1&modificationDate=1296272754000 PDF

Foucault, M. (1972). *The Archaeology of knowledge and the discourse on language*. New York, NY: Pantheon Books.

Foucault, M. (1976). *History of sexuality Vol. 1*. London, England: Penguin.

Foucault, M. (1982). The subject and power. *Critical Inquiry, 8*(4), 777–795. (Original work published The University of Chicago Press).

Foucault, M. (1984). Polemics, politics and problematizations (L. Davis, Trans.). In P. Rabinow (Ed.), *Essential Works of Foucault* (Vol. 1): New York, NY. The New Press. http://foucault.info/foucault/interview.html

Foucault, M. *The order of things* (2002 ed.). Great Britain: Routledge. (Original work published 1966)

Foucault, M. (2008). *The history of sexuality* (R. Hurley, Trans., Vol. One). London, England: Penguin. (Original work published 1976).

Fowler, D. (Producer). Maunder, P. (Director). (1975). *Landfall: A film about ourselves.* [Feature film]. New Zealand: National Film Unit.

Fry, S. (1997). *Moab is my washpot.* London, England: Hutchinson.

Fyfe, J., & Dennis, J. (2001). *Interview with Jonathan Dennis.* [Video recording]. Wellington. NZFA.

Glesne, C., & Peshkin, A. (1993). *Becoming qualitative researchers.* New York, NY: Longman.

Grace, P. (1986). *Potiki.* Auckland, New Zealand: Penguin.

Grace, P., Ramsden, I., & Dennis, J. (Eds.). (2001). *The silent migration – Ngāti Pōneke Young Màori Club 1937–1948.* Wellington, New Zealand: Huia.

Grant, B. M., & Giddings, L. S. (2002). Making sense of methodologies: A paradigm framework for the novice researcher. *Contemporary Nurse, 13,* 10–28.

Gray, D. E. (2009). *Doing research in the real world.* London, England: Sage.

Green, A., & Hutching, M. (Eds.). (2004). *Remembering – writing oral history.* Auckland, New Zealand: Auckland University Press.

Green, A., & Troup, K. (Eds.). (1999). *The houses of history; a critical reader in twentieth-century history and theory.* Manchester, England: Manchester University Press.

Grishakova, M., & Ryan, M.-L. (2010). Intermediality and storytelling. *Narratologia: Contributions to Narrative Theory.* 24 New York-Berlin: De Gruyter.

Hall, K. (2010). A progressive champion: R. N. O'Reilly, MCCahon and the Canterbury Public Library Art Loan Collection. *The Journal of New Zealand Art History, 31.*

Halperin, D. M. (1995). *Saint Foucault; Towards a gay hagiography.* Oxford, England: Oxford University Press.

Hannay, D. (Producer). Williams, T. (Director). 1977. *Solo.* [Feature film]. New Zealand: Tony Williams Productions.

Haraway, D. (1988). Situated knowledges; the science question in feminism and the privilege of partial perspective. *Feminist Studies, 14*(3 Fall), 575–599.

Hato, A., & Waretini, D. (1995). *Ana Hato with Deane Waretini; historic recording re-release.* Wellington: National Library of NZ Te Puna Maatauranga o Aotearoa Alexander Turnbull Library.

Hayward, R. (Producer & Director). (1928). *The Bush Cinderella.* Ginger/Hayward. New Zealand.

Hayward, R. (Producer & Director). (1940). *Rewi's Last Stand.* New Zealand: Frontier Films Ltd.

Hayward, R. & Hayward, R. (Producers & Directors). (1972). *To Love A Maori.* New Zealand: Rudall & Ramai Hayward Film Productions.

Healy, S. (2013, 09/09/13). *Ngaapuhi speaks presentation.* Presented at the meeting of the Presentation at Auckand University of Technology Akoranga, North Shore, Auckland.

Heilbrun, C. G. (1988). *Writing a woman's life.* New York, NY: W.W.Norton.

Hodder, I. (1995). The interpretation of documents and material culture. In N. K. Denzin & Y. S. Lincoln (Eds.), *Handbook of qualitative research* .339–402. London, England: Sage.

Holroyd, M. (2010, 28 June –1st July 2010). *Plenary session on oral history interviews.* Presented at the meeting of the International Autobiographical Association, University of Sussex.

Horrocks, R. (1979). Colossal, exquisite – and lost. *The New Zealand Listener, April 7, 1979.*

Horrocks, R., Labrum, M., & Hopkins, S. (2009). *NZ Film Archive: Review of government agency funding arrangements and service delivery.* Wellington: New Zealand Government.

Howard-Malverde, R. L., 1990. (1990). *The speaking of history: "Willapaakushayki" or Quechua ways of telling the past.* London: University of London Latin American Studies.

Howe, C. (2004). Foucault, gay marriage, and gay and lesbian studies in the United States; an Interview with David Halperin. *Sexuality Research and Social Policy, Journal of National Sexuality Resource Center* Vol. 1 No.3.

Hurley, J. (1998). Radio Best. *The New Zealand Listener, January 10.*

Jackson, S., & Scott, S. (2010). *Theorizing sexuality.* Maidenhead, NY: McGraw Hill Open University Press.

Jagose, A. (1996). *Queer theory; an introduction.* New York, NY: New York University Press.

Jarman, D. (1996). *Kicking the Pricks (2nd ed.).* London, England: Vintage.

Jensen, K. (1996). *Whole men: The masculine tradition in New Zealand literature.* Auckland, New Zealand: Auckland University Press.

Jimerson, R. (2010). Archivists and the call of justice. On *Nights with Bryan Crump.* [Broadcast]. Wellington: Radio New Zealand. (30 August 2010).

Keane, B. (2012). *Ngā rōpū tautohetohe – Māori protest movements – Rugby and South Africa.* http://www.TeAra.govt.nz/en/nga-ropu-tautohetohe-maori-protest-movements/page-4

Keating, A. (Producer), & Tuckett, G. (Director). (2009). *Barry Barclay: The camera on the shore* [DigiBeta]. New Zealand: Acute Film.

Keith, H. (2007). *The Big Picture: A history of New Zealand art from 1642.* Auckland, New Zealand: Godwit.

Kelly, E., & Lavranos, E. (2011). "Sometimes I hate them": In what ways do identity and subjectivity currently influence forms of documentary expression? *Auckland University of Technology.* Symposium conducted at the meeting of the Expanding Documentary, Nga Wai o Horotiu Marae, Auckland University of Technology. Retrieved from http://www.aut.ac.nz/study-at-aut/study-areas/communications/profile/research/expanding-documentary/conference-proceedings

Kelly, E., & McCarthy, N. (2010). *Kiwis who should be famous – Jonathan Dennis.* [Podcast] New Zealand: Radio New Zealand. Retrieved from http://www.radionz.co.nz/national/programmes/summernoelle/20100104

Kelly, E. J. (2012). The greatest love story ever told. *OnFilm, January 2012.*

Kelly, J.,& E. (2011). *Interview from collection Queer stories our fathers never told us* [Oral history recording digital format] Auckland: Oral history section of National Library of New Zealand.

King, M. (1977). *Te Puea – A biography.* Auckland, New Zealand: Hodder and Stoughton.

King, M. (1985). *Being Pakeha.* Auckland, New Zealand: Hodder & Stoughton.

King, M. (1999). *Being Pàkehà Now*. Auckland, New Zealand: Penguin.

King, M. (2000). *Wrestling with the angel; a life of Janet Frame*. Auckland, New Zealand: Penguin.

Kiraly, S. C. D. a. J. (2010). *subREAL website*. Retrieved 25/08/10 http://www.plueschow.de/fellows/subreal/subreal.html

Kloot, B. (2009). Exploring the value of Bourdieu's framework in the context of institutional change. *Studies in Higher Education, 34*(4), 469–481. doi:10.1080/03075070902772034

Kuia and Kaumatua of Ngāpuhi Nui Tonu (with Healy, S. et.al), (2013, 09/09/13). *Ngaapuhi speaks presentation*. Presented at the meeting of the Presentation at Auckand University of Technology Akoranga, North Shore, Auckland

Kula, S. (2002). Mea culpa: How I abused the nitrate in my life. In R. Smither & C. A. Surowiece (Eds.), *This film is dangerous – a celebration of nitrate film*. Brussels, Belgium: Federation Internationale des Archives du Film.

Labrum, M., & Dennis, J. (1993). Talk to NFSA staff about Pordenone Silent Film Festival. [Cassette Recording] *AEK000454 Tape One of Two*: NFSA.

Laemmle, C. (Producer) Collins, L. (Director). (1929). *Under the Southern Cross/The Devil's Pit/Taranga*.[Feature film]. White Island New Zealand: Universal.

The Last Film Show; funeral of Jonathan Spencer Dennis (2002 January 29). Paramount Theatre, Wellington: Recorded by Radio NZ Engineer, Jeremy Ansell. [Video] Copyright 2003. Radio New Zealand Ltd.

Longford, R. (Director). Longford, R. & Lyell, L. (Producers). 1916. *A Maori Maid's Love*. [Feature film]. Australia: Vita Film Corporation and The Zealandia Photo Play.

Longford, R. (Director & Producer). 1916. *The Mutiny of the Bounty*. [Feature film]. *Lye*. [Video]. New Plymouth,New Zealand: Len Lye Foundation.

Main, S., & Wells, P. (1993). *Desperate remedies*. [Feature film] New Zealand: Miramax.

Martin, H., Cairns, Barbara. (1994). *Shadows on the wall – a study of seven New Zealand feature films*. Auckland, New Zealand: Longman Paul.

Matykiewicz, L., & McMurray, R., Modern Matron: a "site" for leadership. *Gender in Management: an international journal*. 28, 6. 321–337.

McCarthy, C. (2011). *Museums and Māori: Heritage professionals, indigenous collections, current practice*. Wellington, New Zealand: Te Papa Press.

McCarthy, C. (2013). The rules of (Māori) art: Bourdieu's cultural sociology and Māori visitors in New Zealand museums. *Journal of Sociology, 49*, 179–193.

McGill, R. (1975, September 19). Unknown title. *Craccum Magazine*. New Zealand: University of Auckland.

McHoul, A., & Grace, W. (1993). *A Foucault Primer; discourse, power and the subject*. Melbourne, Australia: Melbourne University Press.

McHugh, S. (2012). *Oral history and the radio documentary*. University of Wollongong, Scholarly Commons online. Retrieved from http://www.google.co.nz/url?sa=t&rct=j&q=&esrc=s&frm=1&source=web&cd=4&ved=0CD sQFjAD&url=http%3A%2F%2Fro.uow.edu.au%2Fcgi%2Fviewcontent.cgi%3Farticle%3D 1259%26 context%3Dcreartspapers&ei=1VqdUoriBMuRiQekn4GoDQ&usg=AFQjCNFOjtwQM9U UTtrAppGf9TncKH6uvQ

Melies, Gaston. (Producer & Director). 1913 *Hinemoa*. [Feature film]. Rotorua New Zealand: Melies Films.

Mellor, D., & Haebich, A. (Eds.). (2002). *Many voices; reflections on experiences of indigenous child separation*. Canberra, Australia: National Library of Australia.

Meredith, P. (1998, 7–9 July 1998). *Hybridity in the third space: Rethinking bi-cultural politics in Aotearoa/New Zealand*. Presented at the meeting of the Te Ora Rangahau Maori Research and Development Conference, Palmerston North.

Merewether, C. (Ed.). (2006). *The archive*. Cambridge, MA: MIT Press.

Millar, P. (2010). *No fretful sleeper: A life of Bill Pearson*. Auckland, New Zealand: Auckland University Press.

Ministry for Culture and Heritage website. (2011). *Rugby in 1888 – New Zealand Natives' rugby tour*. Retrieved 16 February, 2012, from http://www.nzhistory.net.nz/culture/nz-natives-rugby-tour/rugby-in-1888

Ministry of Research Science and Technology. (2005). *Vision mātauranga*. Royal Society of New Zealand website: New Zealand Government Retrieved from http://www.royalsociety.org.nz/programmes/funds/marsden/application/vision-matauranga/

Mita, M. (30/03/89). *Statement of Te Manu Aute Ki Tamaki Makaurau to the New Zealand Film Archive*. Auckland, New Zealand: Te Manu Aute. NZFA Personal Papers Jonathan Dennis Box 19.

Mita, M. & Pohlmann, G. (Producers & Directors). (1980). *Bastion Point – day 507*. [Documentary film]. New Zealand / Aotearoa.

Mita, M. (Producer & Director). (1983). *Patu!* [Documentary film]. New Zealand: Awatea Films.

Mita, M. (Producer & Director). (1988). *Mauri*. [Documentary film]. New Zealand / Aotearoa: Awatea Films/New Zealand Film Commission.

Mita, M. (1992). *The preserved image speaks out: Objectification and reification of living images In archiving and preservation, documents that move and speak "Ces documents qui bougent et qu parlent."* Presented at the meeting of the Audiovisual Archives in the New Information Age. Proceedings of a symposium for the International Council of Archives, Canada.

Mita, M. (1996). The soul and the image. In J. Dennis, Beiringa, Jan (Ed.), *Film in Aotearoa, New Zealand*. Wellington, New Zealand: Victoria University Press.

Mita, M., & Dennis, J. (1991). Plenary session – Mana Waka presentation. On *6th Film and History Conference*. La Trobe University, Melbourne, Australia: New Zealand Film Archive AUD 0075 Audio Cassette.

Moeke-Maxwell, T. (2005). Bi/multiracial Maori women's hybridity in Aotearoa/New Zealand. *Discourse: studies in the cultural politics of education, 26*(4), 497–510.

Morris, C. (2013). Kai or kiwi? Maori and 'kiwi' cookbooks, and the struggle for the field of New Zealand cuisine. *Journal of Sociology, 49*(2–3), 210–223.

Morrison, R. (1984). *Sense of place: Photographs of New Zealand*. Auckland, New Zealand: Seto.

Murphy, G. (Producer & Director). Hutchinson, N. (Producer). (1980). *Goodbye Pork Pie*. New Zealand: A.M.A.

Murphy, G. (Producer & Director). (1983). *Utu*. [Feature film]. New Zealand: Utu Productions Ltd.

Nakata, M. (2007). *Disciplining the savages, savaging the disciplines*. Canberra, Australia: Aboriginal Studies Press.

Neumann, K., Thomas, N., & Ericksen, H. (Eds.). (1999). *Quicksands; foundational histories in Australia and Aotearoa New Zealand*. Sydney, Australia: University of New South Wales.

Ngaapuhi elders. (2012). *Ngaapuhi speaks he wakaputanga o te rangatiratanga o nu tireni and Te Tiriti o Waitangi: Independent Report on Ngaapuhi Nui Tonu Claim*. Whangarei, New Zealand: Te Kawariki & Network Waitangi Whangarei.

NOHANZ. (2011). Code of Ethical and Technical Practice. In National Oral History Association of New Zealand (Ed.). Wellington: NOHANZ.

NZFA Board minutes. (1989–1992). *Minutes of the NZFA board meetings 1989–1992*. Wellington: New Zealand Film Archive.

O'Brien, T. (2002, January 31). Farewell to a critic who pulled no punches. *Dominion Post,* p.20

O'Driscoll, M., & Bishop, E. (2004). Archiving. *Archiving, 30* (1 March).

O'Reilly, M. (2009). *Ron O'Reilly: The collectors eye*. Paper presented at the meeting of the Christchurch Art Gallery Exhibition Talk, Christchurch Art Gallery:Collection of the author.

O'Reilly, R. N. (1968). Maori art. *Ascent: A Journal of the Arts in New Zealand, 1*(2).

O'Shea, J. & Mirams, R. (Producers & Directors). (1952). *Broken Barrier*. New Zealand: Pacific Films.

O'Shea, J. (Director & Producer). (1966). *Don't Let It Get You*. New Zealand: Pacific Films.

O'Shea, J. & Walters, C. (Producers). Barclay, B. (Director). (1985). *The Neglected Miracle*. [Documenary film]. New Zealand: Pacific Films.

O'Shea, J. (Producer). Barclay, B. (Director). (1987). *Ngati*. [Documentary film]. New Zealand: Pacific Films.

O'Shea, J. (Producer). Barclay, B. (Director). (1991). *Te Rua*. [Documentary film]. New Zealand: Pacific Films.

O'Shea, J. (1970, 10–13 April 1970). Programme of the Arts Conference 1970 Symposium conducted at the meeting of the Arts Conference 1970, Victoria University of Wellington.

O'Shea, J. (1996). *Centenary of cinema trailers*. [Short film] New Zealand: New Zealand Film Archive.

O'Shea, J. (1999). *Don't let it get you*. Wellington, New Zealand: Victoria University Press.

O'Sullivan, D. (2007). *Beyond biculturalism – the politics of an indigenous minority*. Wellington, New Zealand: Huia.

Orange, C. (1987). *The Treaty of Waitangi*. Wellington, New Zealand: Bridget Williams Books.

Perloff, M. (1999). Cultural liminality/aesthetic closure? The "interstitial perspective" of Homi Bhabha. *Literary Imagination, 1*(1999), 109–125.

Petraki, E., Baker, C., & Emmison, M. (2007). "Moral versions" of motherhood and daughterhood in Greek – Australian family narratives. In M. Bamberg, A. De Fina, & D. Schiffrin (Eds.), *Selves and identities in narrative and discourse* (Vol. 9). Amsterdam, The Netherlands: John Benjamins Publishing Company.

Phillips, J. (1987 first ed.). *A man's country? The image of the pakeha male, a history.* Auckland, New Zealand: Penguin.

Pivac, D. (2005). The early years interview with Ron Ritchie. *Newsreel, July 2005*(53).

Pivac, D., & Dennis, J. (2000). Interview with Jonathan Dennis [oral history recording]. Wellington (28th January) NZFA

Pivac, D., Stark, F., & McDonald, L. (Eds.). (2011). *New Zealand film; An illustrated history In association with the Film Archive.* Wellington, New Zealand: Te Papa Press.

Pohlmann, G., & Mita, M. (Producers & Directors). (1982). *The Bridge: A story of men in dispute.* [Documentary feature]. New Zealand.

Pollock, J. (2004). "We don't want your racist tour!": The 1981 Springbok tour and the anxiety of settlement in Aotearoa, New Zealand. *Graduate Journal of Asia-Pacific Studies GJAPS, 2*(1), 32–43.

Pollock, J. (2005). *From colony to culture: Historiographical discourse and historical identity in Aotearoa/New Zealand, 1883–2003.* University of Auckland.

Pope, V. (Producer). Feast, J. (Director) (2013). *Gardening with soul.* [Documentary Film] New Zealand: Pop Film.

Portelli, A. (1991). *The Death of Luigi Trastulli and other stories: Form and meaning in oral history.* New York, NY: New York State University Press.

Powick, K. (2003). *Màori research ethics: A literature review of the ethical issues and implications of kaupapa Màori research and research involving Màori for researchers, supervisors and ethics committees.* Hamilton, New Zealand: Wilf Malcolm Institute of Educational Research, School of Education, University of Waikato.

Pringle, J., Wolfgramm, R., & Henry, E. (2010). Extending cross-ethnic research partnerships: Researching with respect. In S. Katila, S. Merilainen, & J. Tienari (Eds.), *Making inclusion work: Experiences from academia around the world.* London, England: Edward Elgar Publishing Limited.

Puutaiora Writing Group. (2010). *Te ara tika; guidelines for Maaori research ethics: A framework for researchers and ethics committee members.* Auckland, New Zealand: Health Research Council.

Marriage invitation and order of ceremonies – Ramsden, Irihapeti and Paul. (1997). Wellington NZFA Personal Papers Jonathan Dennis Box 11

Ramsden, I., & Grace, P. (1995). 26/8/95 LC-6725 Oral History Collection – 10539 OHA-3647. *Ngati Pōneke author discussions.* Wellington, New Zealand: Unpublished.

Ramsden, I., Grace, P., & Dennis, J. (1995). Ngati Pōneke OHA-3646 Tape 2 Side A. On *Ngati Pōneke author discussions.* Wellington, New Zealand: Tape 2 Side A.

Ratima, M. (2008). Making space for kaupapa Màori within the academy peer commentary. *MAI Review, 1 2008.* Retrieved from http://www.review.mai.ac.nz

Reece, M. (1976). *The God Boy.* [Television film]. New Zealand: TV One.

Reynolds, H. (Director). (1922). *The Birth of New Zealand.* [Feature film]. New Zealand: Tiki Films.

Reynolds, J., Frizell, D. (2010). *In conversation*. Discussion Auckland Readers & Writers Festival. New Zealand.

Royal, T. (24/08/10). *Lecture to Manu Ao Network*. Presented at the meeting of the Manu Ao Network, Victoria University.

Ryan, P.M., (1995). The Reed Dictionary of Modern Māori. Birkenhead, New Zealand. Reed Publishing NZ Ltd.

Said, E. (1978). *Orientalism*. New York, NY: Pantheon.

Sanderson, M. & Mita, M. (Producer & Director). (1979). *Keskidee Aroha*. [Documentary feature]. New Zealand.

Scott, G. & Morton, C. (Producers). Brake, B. (Director). (1955). *Snows of Aorangi*. New Zealand: National Film Unit.

Sedgwick, E.K. (1990). *Epistemology of the Closet*. Berkeley, California. University of California Press.

Sedgwick, E. K. (1993). *Tendencies*. Durham, NC: Duke University Press.

Sekula, A. (2003). Raiding an archive; Photography between labour and capital. In L. Wells (Ed.), *The Photography Reader*. London, England: Routledge.

Sharp, A. (1997). Why be bicultural? In M. Wilson & A. Yeatman (Eds.), *Justice and Identity: Antipodean Practices*. Wellington, New Zealand: Bridget Williams Books.

Shelton, L. (2002). Obituary for Jonathan Dennis republished. *SPADA, 67*, 5. Retrieved from http://www.spada.co.nz/documents/News02-02.pdf

Shelton, L. (2005). *The selling of New Zealand movies: The inside story of the deal-making, shrewd moves and sheer luck that took New Zealand film from obscurity to the top of the world*. Wellington, New Zealand: Awa Press.

Shepard, D. (2009). *Her life's work; conversations with five New Zealand women*. Auckland, New Zealand: Auckland University Press.

Shusterman, R. (2008). Knowledge and the author: The intentional fallacy revisted and (perhaps) removed. *Cycnos, Volume 14*(2) Retrieved from http://revel.unice.fr/cycnos/document.html?id=1420

Sigley, S. (2003). *Film culture: Its development in New Zealand, 1929–1972*. University of Auckland, Auckland. PhD thesis.

Silverman, D. (1997). *Qualitative research: Theory, method and practice*. London, England: Thousand Oaks.

Simmons, D.R.,& Penfold, M. (Trans). (1994). *Te Māori; Treasures of the Māori*. Auckland: Reed.

Sinclair, K. (1985). Essay In J. Phillips (Ed.), *Biography in New Zealand* (pp. 33). Wellington, New Zealand: Allen and Unwin.

Sinclair, K. (1991). *The history of New Zealand*. Auckland, New Zealand: Penguin Books. (Original work published 1959).

Smith, J., & Abel, S. (2008). Ka whawhai tonu maatou: Indigenous television in Aotearoa New Zealand. *NZ Journal of Media Studies, 11*(1), 1–14.

Smith, T. L. (2005). On tricky ground: Researching the native in the age of uncertainty. In N. Denzin, Lincoln, Yvonna (Ed.), *The sage handbook of qualitative research* (3rd ed.). New York, NY: Thousand Oaks.

Smither, R., & Catherine, S. A. (Eds.). (2002). *This film is dangerous – a celebration of nitrate film*. Brussels, Belgium: Federation Internationale des Archives du Film.

Sontag, S. (1964). Notes on "Camp". *Partisan Review, December* (Fall), 515–530.

Sontag, S. (1969). *The aesthetics of solitude*. New York, NY: Farrar, Straus and Grouse.

Sontag, S. (1996). The decay of cinema. *New York Times*. Retrieved from *www.nytimes.com/books/00/03/12/specials/sontag-cinema.html*

Sorrenson, M. P. K. (2012). Ngata, Apirana Turupa. *Dictionary of New Zealand Biography. Te Ara -the Encyclopedia of New Zealand,* . Retrieved from http://www.TeAra.govt.nz/en/biographies/3n5/ngata-apirana-turupa

Sorsoli, L. (2007). Like pieces in a puzzle: Working with layered methods of reading personal narratives. In M. Bamberg, A. De Fina, & D. Schiffrin (Eds.), *Selves and identities in narrative and discourse* (Vol. 9). Amsterdam, The Netherlands: John Benjamins Publishing Company.

Sowry, C. (1984). *Film making in New Zealand – a brief historical survey*. Wellington, New Zealand: New Zealand Film Archive, Friends of the Film Archive.

Spivak, G. C. (1988). Can the subaltern speak? In C. Nelson & L. Grossberg (Eds.), *Marxism and the interpretation of culture*. London, England: MacMillan.

Spoonley, P. (2009). *Mata toa; The life and times of Ranginui Walker*. Auckland, New Zealand: Penguin.

Stark, F. (2006). From treasure hunters to asset managers: Delivering the digital archive. In New Zealand Film Archive (Ed.). Wellington, New Zealand: New Zealand Film Archive Internal Document.

Sweetwater, I. (2003). In memorial Dr Irihapeti Merenia Ramsden. *The Aboriginal Nurse, 18*(2), 14.

Tahiwi, T. W. (1998). The Tahiwis historic 1930 recordings by Te Whaanau Tahiwi [Recorded by J. Dennis]. On *He Puiaki Puuoro Treasures in Sound*. Wellington, New Zealand: National Library of NZ Te Puna Maatauranga o Aotearoa Alexander Turnbull Library. (1998)

Tapsell, P. (2006). *Ko tawa; Maaori treasures of New Zealand*. Auckland, New Zealand: David Bateman.

Tarr.G (Producer & Director). 1914. *Hinemoa*. New Zealand: Auckland Chamber of Commerce.

Te Ara Encyclopedia online (2004). The Treaty of Waitangi Conservation. *Te Ara Encyclopedia*. Retrieved from http://www.teara.govt.nz/en/photograph/35912/treaty-of-waitangi-before-conservation

Te Awekotuku, N., Manatu Maaori. (1991). *He tikanga whakaaro, research ethics in the Maaori community*. Wellington, New Zealand: Manatu Maaori.

Te Papa Tongarewa. (2011). *The marae*. Retrieved from http://www.tepapa.govt.nz/WhatsOn/exhibitions/Pages/TheMarae.aspx

Tebbutt, J. (2009). The object of listening. *Continuum Journal of Media & Cultural Studies, 23*(4 August), 549–559. doi:10.1080/10304310903012644

Tuhiwai Smith, L. (2012). *Decolonizing methodologies: Research and indigenous peoples* . (2nd ed.). London, England: Zed Books. (Original work published 1999).

Turner, S. (1999). Settlement as forgetting. In K. Neumann, N. Thomas, & H. Ericksen (Eds.), *Quicksands; foundation histories in Australia and Aotearoa New Zealand.* Sydney: University of New South Wales.

Turner, S. (2002). Being colonial/colonial being. *Journal of New Zealand Literature: JNZL,* 39–66.

Turner, W. B. (2000). *A genealogy of queer theory.* Philidelphia, PA: Temple University Press.

Unknown (1975, March 25) *Critic: Otago University Student Magazine.*

Waititi, K. (2008). Màori documentary film : Interiority and exteriority – Intern Research Report 6. *MAI Review, 1, 2008.*

Walker, R. (1990). *Ka whawhai tonu matou: Struggle without end.* Auckland, New Zealand: Penguin.

Walker, S., Eketone, A., & Gibbs, A. (2006). An exploration of kaupapa Maori research, its principles, processes and applications. *International Journal Social Research Methodology, 9*(4), 14. (Original work published Routledge).

Waller, G. A. (2008). The New Zealand Film Commission: Promoting an industry, forging a national identity. In I. Conrich & S. Murray (Eds.), *Contemporary New Zealand cinema from new wave to bockbuster.* London, England: I.B.Taurus.

Wanganui Chronicle, (1973) *Actors Who Perform Only New Zealand Plays.* Wednesday March 21st. New Zealand.

Ward, V. (Director). Maynard, J. (Producer). (1988). *The Navigator: A medieval odyssey.* [Feature film]. New Zealand: Arenafilm.

Watkins, G. (2012). *24 frames: The greatest love story ever told* [Broadcast]. National Radio: Radio New Zealand. Retrieved from http://www.radionz.co.nz/concert/programmes/24frames

Wells, P. (Director). (1983). *Little Queen.* [Short film]. New Zealand.

Wells, P. (1997). *Frock attack! Wig wars! Strategic camp in desperate remedies.* Auckland, New Zealand: University of Auckland.

Wells, P. (2001). *The long loop home, a memoir.* Auckland, New Zealand: Vintage.

Wells, P. *Production notes for Jonathan Dennis film Book 1* (Notes). (2001–2004).

Wells, P. (Producer & Director). (2004). *Friendship Is the harbour of joy* [Documentary film]. New Zealand: New Zealand Film Festival.

Wisniewski, T. (2007). Framers of the kept: Against the grain appraisal of ephemeral moving images. *The Moving Image, 7*(2 Fall).

Wolford, L., & Schechner, R. (Eds.). (1997). *The Grotowski sourcebook.* London, England: Routledge.

Wollen, R. c. (Ed.). (1996). *Derek Jarman; a portrait artist, film-maker, designer.* London, England: Thames and Hudson.

Woolf, V. (1967). The new biography. In *Collected Essays Volume 4.* London, England: The Hogarth Press.

Appendix I

James McDonald films catalogue

Films by James McDonald of the Tangata Whenua He Pito Whakaatu A Te Maori Na James McDonald 1919–1923 The New Zealand Film Archive catalogue with The National Museum

James McDonald (1865–1935) began working for the Dominion (now the National) Museum in 1904 and in 1907 also began filming various scenic attractions for the Tourist Department. He made several ethnographic film records for the Museum (although his filmmaking was additional to his general activities there). In 1926 he retired from his position as Assistant Director, to Tokaanu where he organanized a school of Maori arts and crafts

> Te Hui Aroha Ki Turanga – Gisborne Hui Aroha
> 1919 35mm, b&w silent, 10 mins

In 1918 James McDonald proposed an expedition to the Hui Aroha to be held in Gisborne the following year. The purpose of this, and the three subsequent Dominion Museum expeditions, was to collect and record information on the crafts, activities and tribal lore retained in the various areas.

The week long Hui Aroha, in April 1919, was organized to welcome home from France the Maori Pioneer Battalion, to honour those who did not return, and to celebrate peace. The Museum party consisted of their ethnologist, Elsdon Best, the Librarian at the Alexander Turnbull Library, Johannes C Andersen, and McDonald. The surviving film shows poi dances and string games.

> He Pito Whakaatu I Te Hui I Rotorua – Scenes at the Rotorua Hui
> 1920 35mm b& w silent 24 mins

In April 1920 the tribes gathered at the Rotorua Racecourse, to greet the Prince of Wales. The Dominion Museum party of Best, Andersen and McDonald too the opportunity to be present and McDonald recorded on film the ARawa welcome at the reception camp to the visiting tribes, together with various demonstrations of action songs, hand and string games, flute playing and skills such as fire making and stone drilling.

> He Pito Whakaatu I Te Noho A Te Maori I Te Awa O Whanganui – Scenes of Maori Life on the Whanganui River 1921, 35mm b&w silent, 48 mins

In March and April 1921 several weeks were spent by Best, Andersen and McDonald at Koriniti, Hiruharama (Jerusalem) and Pipiriki in the Whanganui River Valley. Te Rangi Hiroa (Dr Peter Buck, Director of Maori Hygiene) joined them for a few days at Koroniti. On this expedition over 300 still photographs were taken, over 50 cylinder recordings made of speeches and songs, and between 5000–6000 feet of film exposed (not all of which has survived). The scenes in the film record games such as skipping and string games, crafts such as dyeing and weaving of flax for many purposes, cultivation and fishing. The making of traps for eels and the setting of traps inh the weirs are shown in detail. Also included are scenes of divinatory rites such as niu and raurau. The niu consists of making predictions from the manner in which fern stalks, or sticks, fall when balanced or thrown. The raurau is performed publicly to determine the outcome of a battle. The tohunga causes sticks to advance towards branches of karamu (coprosma) standing in the ground. The number of leaves which fall when the branch is struck by the stick indicates the number of men who will fall in the approaching battle.

> Hi Pito Whakaatu I Te Noho A Te Maori I Te Tairawhiti – Scenes of Maori Life on the East Coast 1923, 35mm b&w silent 26 mins

Āpirana Ngata, Member of Parliament for Eastern Maori, was very keen for the Museum group to visit the East Coast to obtain records of his people, the Ngati Porou. So in March 1923, having been delayed by an outbreak of typhoid and influenza in the area, the final expedition set out for Ngata's home at Waiomatatini, which was to be their base. Best, Andersen and McDonald were again joined by Te Rangi Hiroa and they also had the help and sympathy of many leading Maori in the area who regarded the recording of their arts and crafts and tribal lore as a matter of considerable importance. From Waiomatatini visits were made to Whareponga, Kahukura, Rangitukia, Te Araroa, Ruatoria and other parts of the district. McDonald recorded in this film examples of the old-time skills retained in the area for making fishnets and traps, methods of netting and catching fish, weaving, hand games and music making. The digging and storing of the kumara and the cooking of food in a hangi are shown. Tribal lore and songs were also recorded on a phonograph during this expedition and numerous still photographs were secured.

Further expeditions planned to Taupo, the Bay of Plenty, Rotorua and the Urewera never took place.

Preservation of the McDonald Films

There is very little evidence of the films being shown at the time they were made, although some of the Whanganui film was shown – in towns with electricity – during the East Coast expedition, and a lecture given by Te Rangi Hiroa in Auckland in June 1923 was accompanied by scenes from the films. However, no prints have ever been located. When it was established in 1981, The New Zealand Film Archive received the surviving unedited nitrate negatives of the films, and their preservation has been taking place ever since. The negatives were in very poor condition and some had begun to decompose badly. First, the films had to be painstakingly repaired by hand, then carefully reprinted on to stable acetate film stock. The fragmentary scenes were then assembled into sequences, based on notes McDonald scratched on the leader to each roll of film. When deciphered, these notes gave the date, location and sometimes information on who or what was in a scene. Gradually a series of titles were prepared, based on these notes which were then translated into Maori. As the preservation work progressed screenings took place whenever and wherever possible, of successive early prints of the films. These were shown (often for the first time) in the areas where they had been shot and for people who were skilled in the activities documented. The work was completed in March 1986.

Director Jonathan Dennis
Film Repair and Editorial Restoration – Anne Manchester
Translations – Gisborne Hui – Amster Reedy
Rotorua Hui – Ruka Broughton, Sharon Dell
Whanganui River – Ruka Broughton
East Coast – Amster Reedy
Film Cataloguer – Elizabeth Street
Documentation Peter Sakey
Film Repair Wendy Osborne
Technical Officer – Colin Feldwick
Secretary Heather McLean
Accountant Bonita Roberts
Accessions Alison Whyte
Librarian Jo Seton
Composer-in-Residence Dorothy Buchanan

Research and Technical Supervision Clive Sowry
Lab NFU

During the five years spent on the restoration and preservation of these films the Archive has received the help and support of numerous people. In particular we would like to thank: Sharon Dell, Geoff Rogers, Ruka Broughton, Bill Cooper, Emily Schuster and the Maori and Pacific Weaver's Hui, Bronwyn Simes, Witarina Harris, Erenora Puketapu Hetet, Keri Kaa, Norm Hubbard, Jan Bieringa, Bill Gosden, Whanganui Historical Society, Matahiwi Marae Komiti, Juliet Hobbs, Warwick Wilson

Photographs – held in the photographic section of National Museum – album in Alexander Turnbull

Sound Recordings – the surviving cylinder recordings are held by the Archive of Maori and Pacific Music at the University of Auckland

Appendix II

Jonathan Dennis' bibliography

Non exhaustive list of publications, exhibitions, sound and film works by Jonathan Dennis arranged chronologically:

1.1981 BOOK *Tin Shed: The Origins of the National Film Unit* Clive Sowry author, NZFA (JD Editor)

2.1984 BOOK *Film making in New Zealand* Clive Sowry author, NZFA (JD Editor)

3.1987 CATALOGUE & EXHIBITION Dennis Jonathan. (1987). *He Pito Whakaatu A Nga Iwi Màori, Films of the Tangata Whenua Catalogue*. Auckland: Auckland City Art Gallery. (JD Curator, Writer, Editor).

4.1987 Dennis, J. Taha Maori: The Maori Dimension. *Hawaii International Film Festival Catalogue*. (JD Curator, Writer, Editor).

5.1989 CATALOGUE & EXHIBITION Dennis Jonathan, & Toffetti Sergio (Eds.). (1989). *Te Ao Marama, Il Mondo Ella Luce, Il Cinema Della Nuova Zelanda*. Torino: New Zealand Film Archive and Le Nuove Muse. (JD Curator, Writer, Editor).

6.1989 ARTICLE Dennis, J. The Process of Change at the New Zealand Film Archive/Nga Kaitiaki o Nga Taonga Whitiahua. *AGMANZ Art Galleries and Museums Association of New Zealand, 20*(1), 10 - 11.

7.1990 PRESENTATION & ARTICLE Dennis, J. *Uncovering and Releasing the Images - the case of Ethnological Film.* . presented at the meeting of the Documents That Move and Speak, Audiovisual Archives in the New Information Age. Proceedings of a symposium for the International Council of Archives., Ottawa, Canada.

8.1990 FILM Dennis, J. Producer *Mana Waka* (directed by Merata Mita, editor Annie Collins)

9.1992 CATALOGUE & EXHIBITION Dennis Jonathan. (1992). *Headlands: Moving Images from Aotearoa/New Zealand*. Sydney: Museum of Contemporary Art.

10.1992 & 1996 (2nd edition). BOOK Bieringa, J., & Dennis, J. Eds *Film in Aotearoa New Zealand*. Wellington: Victoria University Press.

11.1993 CATALOGUE and EXHIBITION Dennis Jonathan, & Cherchi Usai, P. (Eds.). (1993). *Aotearoa and the Sentimental Strine - Making Films in Australia and New Zealand in the Silent Period*. Wellington: Moa Films. (JD and PC-U Editors, Curators, Writers).

12.1993 TELEVISION PROGRAMME *Girls' Own Stories* for TVNZ's *Work of Art* Series (JD co-produced with Annie Collins)

13.1993 SOUND Radio Programme *Voices on Film* (JD Writer, Presenter Producer with Elizabeth Alley)

14.1993 *Heart of Fiji: Photographs by Arthur Hocart 1909–1914* National Library Gallery 20th March – 19 June co-curated with Sharon Dell

15.1994 SOUND Radio programme *The Film Show* on National Radio (originally on Concert Radio) (Writer, Presenter, Producer until his death)

16.1995 SOUND Soundscape Dennis, J., & Alley, E. (1995). A Day Without Art; World Aids Day Soundscape [Recorded by R. NZ]. Radio NZ: Radio NZ.

17.1995 Hato, A., & Waretini, D. *Ana Hato with Deane Waretini; historic recording rerelease*. [Produced by J. Dennis]. Wellington: National Library of NZ Te Puna Maatauranga o Aotearoa Atoll Ltd Alexander Turnbull Library. (

18.1996 SOUND Soundscape *Centenary of Cinema, RNZ* (JD Presenter, Writer, Producer).

19.1995/1996 ARTICLE Dennis, J. Ana Hato; The Melody is Ended but the Memory Lingers on ... *Music in New Zealand, Summer*, 46–48.

20.1995 Hato, A., & Waretini, D. *Ana Hato with Deane Waretini; historic recording rerelease*. [Produced by J. Dennis]. Wellington: National Library of NZ Te Puna Maatauranga o Aotearoa Atoll Ltd Alexander Turnbull Library.

21.1996 Lye, L. *Free Radicals, Video Editions of Films of Len Lye*. New Plymouth: Len Lye Foundation. (JD involved in production).

22.1996 O'Shea, J., & Page, G. *Centenary of Cinema Trailers*. New Zealand: New Zealand Film Archive. (JD Producer).

23.1996 BOOK *Don't Let It Get You* Memoirs of John O'Shea (JD co-editor with Jan Beiringa)

24.1998 FILM Dennis, J. Director (1998). *Mouth Wide Open - Documentary of Ted Coubray*. New Zealand: Moa Films. (Producer Annie Collins)

25.1998 Tahiwi, T. W. The Tahiwis Historic 1930 Recordings by Te Whaanau Tahiwi [Produced by J. Dennis]. On *He Puiaki Puuoro Treasures in Sound*. Wellington: National Library of NZ Te Puna Maatauranga o Aotearoa Atoll Ltd Alexander Turnbull Library. (1998)

26.2000 BOOK Contribution to Len Lye book for Pompidou, Paris exhibition (Roger Horrocks editor)

27.2000 SOUND Radio soundscape *Ocean of Time* with Matthew Leonard, Radio NZ & ABC Joint Production

28.2001 ARTICLE ONLINE Dennis, J. *Tribute to John O'Shea*. Retrieved 16/08/2010, 2010, from http://www.filmarchive.org.nz/archive_presents/pacificfilms/oshea_intro. html

29.2001 BOOK *The Silent Migration: Ngāti Pōneke Young Māori Club 1937–1948 Stories of urban migration* (JD co-editor with Patricia Grace and Irihapeti Ramsden) Huia Press

30.2001 SOUND RECORDING Ngāti Pōneke Young Māori Club Historic Recording rerelease [Produced by J. Dennis]. On *He Puiaki Puuoro Treasures in Sound*. Wellington: National Library of NZ Te Puna Maatauranga o Aotearoa Atoll Ltd Alexander Turnbull Library.

Appendix III

Constitution Kaupapa of the NZFA 1988

The NZFA/NGONTW Constitution/Kaupapa 16 November 1988

First page The Treaty of Waitangi itself written in Te Reo Maaori

Translation into English. Article the second 'Her Majesty the Queen of England confirms and guarantees to the Chiefs and Tribes of New Zealand and to the respective families and individuals thereof the full exclusive and undisturbed possession of their Lands and Estates Forests Fisheries and other properties which they may collectively or individually possess so long as it is their wish and desire to retain the same in their possession ...' *states that this translation is by Professor Hugh Kawharu*

NZFA Principles

1.1 The New Zealand Film Archive/NGONTW, its staff and Trustees will incorporate the principles embodied in the Treaty into its policies and practices

1.2 Treasured cultural possessions/taonga are specifically referred to in Article 2 of the Treaty. As a storehouse/pataka tuturu of taonga, NZFA/NGONTW sees the Treaty as having specific implications for partnership, participation and protection.

1.3 It sees the Treaty as a charter of two peoples in New Zealand and recognises Maori as Tangata Whenua. It will work to uphold the Treaty as a joint partnership between Maori and Pakeha of resources, institutions and decision making which guarantees Maori people rangatiratanga over their lands, homes and taonga while giving a legitimate place to Pakeha people. The Archive regards the Treaty as a living document with a wairua of its own.

Aims

2.1 To be a storehouse/pataka tuturu of moving image materials/taonga whitiahua in accordance with the Treaty of Waitangi/Tiriti o Waitangi principles of partnership

2.2 To be national in outlook, responsible for offering balanced and equitable services at all local, regional and tribal levels

2.3 To be specific in its focus on the moving image media and their derivatives, and archival in its commitment to the dual aims of preservation and accessibility.

Objectives

3.1 To acquire and receive all moving image materials/taonga whitiahua of permanent national and cultural significance in fulfilment of the above aims, with due regard for and reference to mana tuturu and the rights of the materials themselves, the rights of the copyright owners and the rights of the depositors

3.2 To ensure the preservation of all moving image materials/taonga whitiahua of permanent national and cultural significance without loss or degradation.

3.3 To encourage and provide public access to the moving image heritage. Access and preservation are seen as complementary concepts of equal importance. The aim of preservation is permanent accessibility but the imperatives of preservation will not be compromised in order to provide access. The Archive will cater for general as well as specialist needs, encouraging and undertaking research, and creative and entrepreneurial activity.

3.4 To represent New Zealand in its field and to contribute fully to international activity through FIAF (Federation Internationale des Archives du Film) and especially in its relationships with neighbouring countries in the South Pacific region.

3.5 To maintain a special relationship with the moving image industries, whose output and history it preserves and embodies. It shall work to merit their support and trust, and to complement, aid and stimulate their creative activity

3.6 To maintain and defend its own professional integrity, independence and judgement in its role as a publicly accountable body

Definitions

The moving image material/taonga whitiahua of New Zealand/Aotearoa embraces moving images in all their manifestations, whether as art, communication, historical record, entertainment, industry, technology, science, cultural and social phenomenon or otherwise. This heritage shall include, but not be limited to, the following:

1.1 Film, television or other productions comprising moving images created or released within New Zealand, or by New Zealand, or with reference to New Zealand, whether or not primarily intended for public release.

1.2 Objects, materials, works and intangibles relating to moving images whether seen from a technical, industrial, cultural, historical or other viewpoint; this shall include material relating to the New Zealand film, television and broadcasting industries and fields such as literature, scripts, stills, posters, advertising material, manuscript material and artefacts such as technical equipment and costumes. It also includes such concepts as the perpetuation of obsolescent skills and environments associated with the presentation of these media.

Appendix IV

List of Interviewees

1.Alley, Elizabeth 11/07/10 Recorded, to be deposited (edited by EA) at NZFA

2.Armstrong, Michael 17/01/13 Email correspondence, to be deposited with MA's permission at NZFA

3.Bartel, Susan 03/12/09 Recorded, to be deposited at NZFA

4.Beiringa, Jan 14/12/09 Unrecorded, not to be deposited, Second interview with Malcolm McKinnon 01/02/11 Recorded, to be deposited at NZFA

5.Brand, Neil see Kirsten Dennis 13/07/10

6.Burrows, Elaine with Kirsten Dennis 07/07/10 Recorded, to be deposited at NZFA

7.Cherchi-Usai, Paolo 14/05/09 Recorded, to be deposited at NZFA

8.Collins, Annie 26/11/09 Recorded, to be deposited at NZFA with 25 year embargo

9.Davey, Sarah 08/11/10 Recorded, to be deposited at NZFA

10.Dell, Sharon 10/09/10 Recorded, to be deposited at NZFA

11.Dennis, Kirsten 13/07/10 with Neil Brand Recorded (quality poor) to be deposited at NZFA

12.Dennis, Simon 06/02/09 & 2904/09 Unrecorded, notes taken, not to be deposited at NZFA, 13/07/10 Recorded, to be deposited at NZFA

13.Dennis, Timothy 05/08/09 Recorded (faulty), notes taken, to be deposited at NZFA

14.Eckhoff, Douglas (Doug) 09/06/10 Recorded, to be deposited at NZFA

15.Gosden, Bill 08/11/09 Recorded, to be deposited (edited by BG) at NZFA

16.Grover, Ray 31/01/11 Recorded, to be deposited (edited by RG) at NZFA

17.Harris, Beryl & Stuart 24/05/09 Unrecorded, notes taken, not to be deposited in NZFA.

18.Hendricks, Frederick (Ferry) 28/11/09 Recorded, to be deposited at NZFA

19.Horrocks, Roger 25/10/11 Unrecorded, notes taken, not to be deposited at NZFA

20.Ikin, Bridget 05/11/10 Unrecorded, notes taken, not to be deposited at NZFA

21.Kominik, Jane & Pat Stuart 02/02/11 Unrecorded, notes taken, not to be deposited at NZFA

22.Kramer, Edith 02/04/12 Recorded, not to be deposited at NZFA

23.Kupferberg, Audrey 26/09/10 via telephone, unrecorded, notes taken

24.Labrum, Megan 08/08/11 Recorded at NZFA Canberra, recording deposited in NZFA collection

25. Leonard, Matthew 25/05/10 Recorded by ML, notes taken by EK, not to be deposited at NZFA

26. MacGillivray, Fergus 05/07/10 Recorded, to be deposited at NZFA

27. McKinnon, Malcolm 23/11/09 & 14/07/10 Recorded, to be deposited at NZFA

28. O'Leary, Clare 10/02/09 Unrecorded, notes taken, not to be deposited at NZFA

29. O'Reilly, Matthew 30/11/09 Unrecorded, notes taken, 12/06/10 Recorded, to be deposited at NZFA

30. Paul, Jane 03/02/11 Unrecorded, notes taken, not to be deposited at NZFA

31. Pivac, Diane (Di) 26/11/09 Unrecorded, notes taken, not to be deposited at NZFA

32. Rainbow, Stephen 29/01/09 Unrecorded, notes taken, not to be deposited at NZFA

33. Sheat, Bill 31/01/11 Recorded, to be deposited at NZFA

34. Shelton, Lindsay 07/12/09 Recorded, to be deposited (edited by LS) at NZFA

35. Stark, Frank (Francis) 11/03/13 Recorded, to be deposited at NZFA

36. Stuart, Pat see Kominik, Jane

37. Tapsell, Paul 09/10/2010, unrecorded, notes taken, not to be deposited at NZFA.

38. Townsend, Sef 05/07/10 Recorded, to be deposited at NZFA

39. Wall, Mattie 01/10/10 Recorded, to be deposited at NZFA

40. Watkins, Gareth 24/11/09 Recorded, to be deposited at NZFA

41. Watson, Rachel nee O'Reilly 03/10/10 Unrecorded, notes taken, not to be deposited at NZFA

42. Wells, Peter 22/04/10 Unrecorded, notes taken, not to be deposited at NZFA

43. Young nee Maunder, Denise 03/08/11 Recorded, not to be deposited at NZFA

Index